FROM LOUIS XIV TO LOUIS ARMSTRONG

A Cultural Tapestry

From Louis XIV to Louis Armstrong: A Cultural Tapestry is based on *La Louisiane, de la colonie française à l'État américain*, an exhibition organized by The Historic New Orleans Collection at the invitation of the Mona Bismarck Foundation in Paris. *La Louisiane*, held at the Foundation from December 16, 2003, through February 28, 2004, and the French edition of the catalogue were underwritten by the Mona Bismarck Foundation. The Foundation also contributed to the underwriting of the English edition of the catalogue. The Historic New Orleans Collection wishes to thank Franck and Marian Bruno and T. Windle and Susan Kierr Dyer for their support of this publication.

Somogy éditions d'art staff:
Design: Alessandra Scarpa
Translations: John Tittensor
Production: François Combal
Managing editor: Michaëlle Liénart

The Historic New Orleans Collection publications department staff:
Lynn D. Adams, acting director
Mary C. Mees, associate editor

ISBN: 2-85056-770-1

FROM LOUIS XIV TO LOUIS ARMSTRONG

A Cultural Tapestry

New Orleans, The Historic New Orleans Collection
April 13, 2004–October 9, 2004

LA LOUISIANE

De la colonie française à l'État américain

Paris, The Mona Bismarck Foundation
December 16, 2003–February 28, 2004

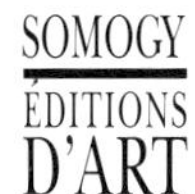

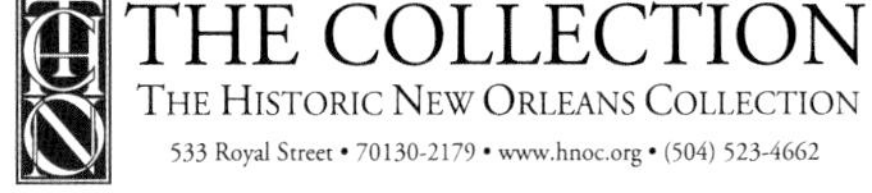

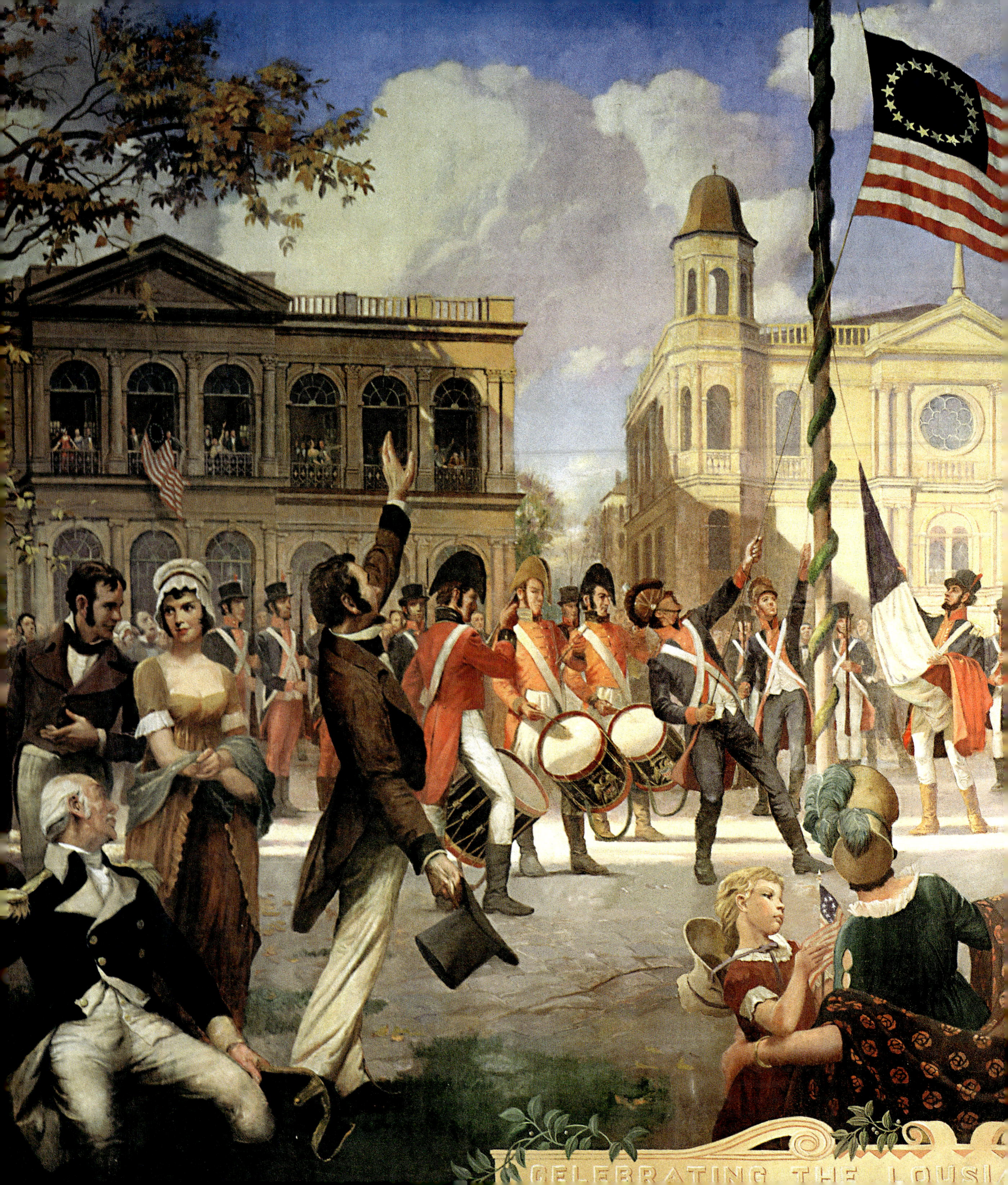
CELEBRATING THE LOUSIA

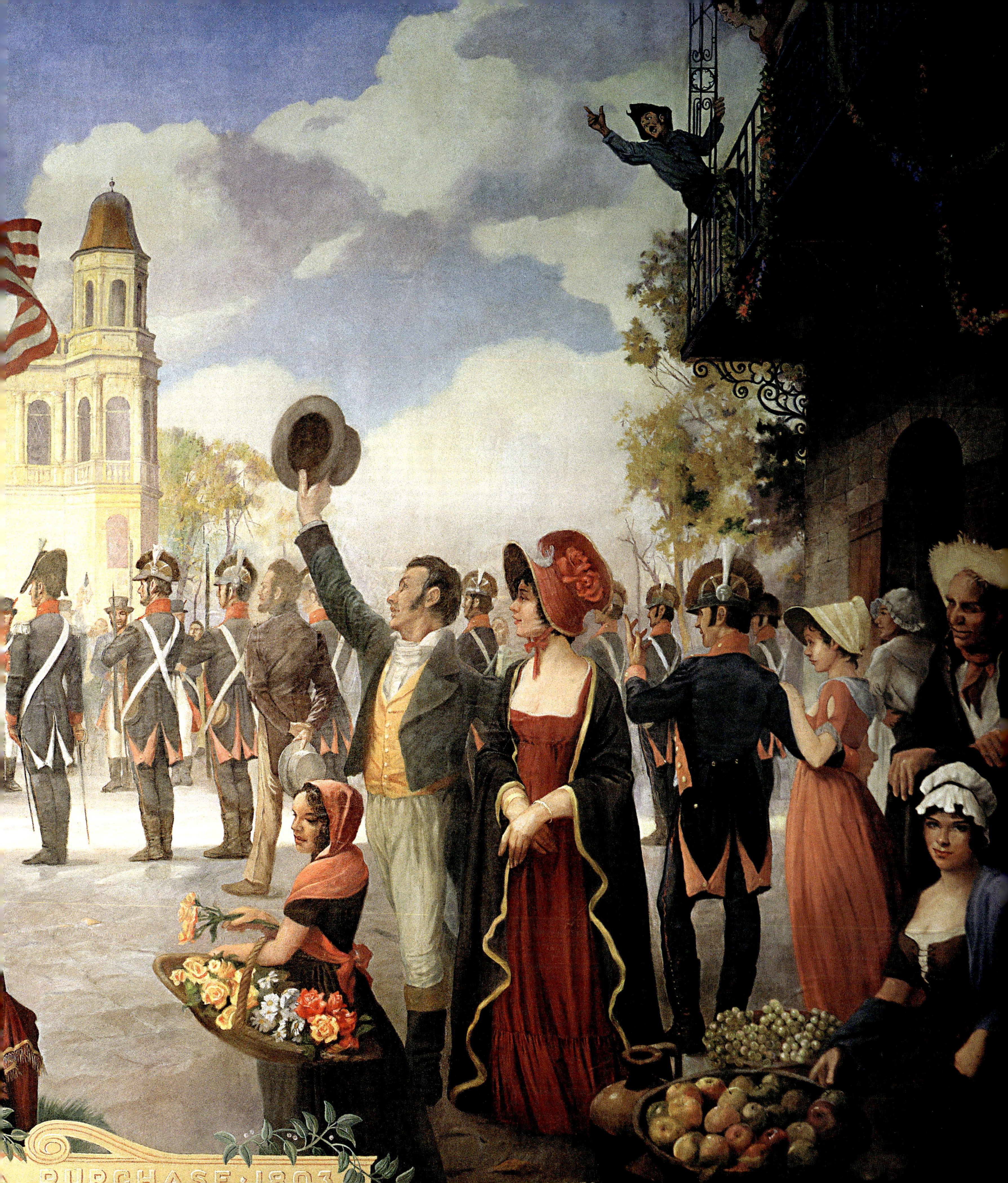
PURCHASE·1803

Preceding pages: A. Karoly and L. Szanto

Celebrating the Louisiana Purchase, 1956

oil on canvas
private collection of Kevin Kelly, New Orleans

The Louisiana Purchase affected nearly every aspect of life in Louisiana, including language, laws, religion, and land-tenure records, as well as a host of other daily activities. The artists Karoly and Szanto accurately depicted the costumes and the architecture of the Place d'Armes in 1803. However, the Presbytère—which should be to the right of the cathedral—is missing, and residences are displaced from their actual positions. The artists also spelled "Louisiana" wrong. Nonetheless, the strength of the painting is in its depiction of the strong, mixed emotions of Louisianians at the time. The mural was originally commissioned by the State of Missouri for display in the state capitol building.

Preface

Russell M. PORTER, *President of the Mona Bismarck Foundation*

One of the favorite indoor sports of the art world is that of establishing provenance. In other words, the place of origin of an art object and the reason it is on exhibition. The multi-faceted purpose of the Mona Bismarck Foundation is to promote Franco-American relations in the fields of art and history. Speaking as the individual who drafted the purpose clause of the foundation, I can say that, despite the Louisiana antecedents of some members of the board of the foundation, we initially missed the historical aspects of the Louisiana Purchase. By "we," I mean the gallant band of the board, Guy and Monica Dunham, and Tim Ramier, a graduate of Loyola University now practicing law in Paris. Through the graciousness of my former Tulane University law school classmate Frank Bruno, we came to know Mary Lou Christovich, the wife of William Christovich, another former classmate. Fortunately, she serves as chairman of the board of the Kemper and Leila Williams Foundation, which operates The Historic New Orleans Collection. When the Mona Bismarck Foundation invited The Collection to mount the exhibition *La Louisiane, de la colonie française à l'État américain*, no one anticipated a tiff between the governments of longstanding allies France and the United States. Perhaps that made the exhibition more important as it gave us moment to pause and remember the intertwined history of the two countries and in particular the French heritage of Louisiana. The critical Parisian audience appreciated our efforts and came in large numbers over a ten-week period. The press also responded enthusiastically. This said, our thanks goes to our resident Louisiana friends, particularly Priscilla Lawrence, executive director of The Collection; our academic leader, Alfred Lemmon; John Lawrence, director of museum programs; and the entire staff of The Historic New Orleans Collection, for all that they have done to make this a valid and worthwhile exhibition.

As a jurist, the real attraction to me in celebrating the bicentennial of the Purchase is the history of Louisiana law and the Louisiana Purchase itself. The law is fascinating in the sense that because Louisiana was originally a French colony, it was governed by the *coutume de Paris*, which I had the pleasure of translating for the Tulane Law School Library in 1950. In 1762, by a so-called secret treaty, Louisiana was ceded by France to Spain, but essentially explorers' rights were what was ceded. In any event, Spanish civil law was not substantially different from French, and the migration of the Acadians from Canada somewhat fortified the desire for French law with an overlay of Spanish law. All of this is to say that at the time of the Louisiana Purchase, the law for the territory was basically French and Spanish civil law.

The Purchase involved far more land than the present state of Louisiana; in fact it included the whole Mississippi Valley. For the domain of nearly one million square miles, a certain amount of haggling took place in Paris in April 1803 between Barbé-Marbois, the French representative, and Robert Livingston and James Monroe, representatives of the United States. While there was doubt about the constitutionality of the Purchase, the treaty was eventually ratified, and the territory involved would be divided into more than a dozen American states.

We are grateful to The Collection for sharing its treasures with us in France, for reminding the Mona Bismarck Foundation of its own provenance, and for assisting us in reacquainting our French audience with its former colony, La Louisiane.

The Mona Bismarck Foundation is an American foundation created by Countess Mona Bismarck for the purpose of promoting artistic, musical, literary, and educational projects, particularly those that encourage French-American friendship.

The countess, born Mona Strader, was an American citizen originally from Kentucky. During the 1920s, she married one of the greatest American businessmen of the time, Harrison Williams. After his death, she married Count Edward Bismarck, the grandson of Chancellor Bismarck. Regarded as one of the most elegant women of her generation, Countess Mona Bismarck had celebrated residences in Long Island, Paris, and Capri. Her magnificent residence in Paris is now the principal center of the varied activities of the foundation that proudly bears her name.

Preface

Mary Louise CHRISTOVICH, *Chairman of the Kemper & Leila Williams Foundation*

Two private foundations, the Mona Bismarck Foundation in Paris and the Kemper and Leila Williams Foundation in New Orleans, have linked across the Atlantic Ocean to celebrate the bicentennial of the Louisiana Purchase: 1803-2003. Thematic exhibitions with illuminating catalogues have, since 1986, placed the Mona Bismarck Foundation in the enviable position of bestowing on its Parisian audiences Franco/American history, art, and culture. Conversely, the Williams Foundation through its public face, The Historic New Orleans Collection (The Collection), has, since 1968, focused on its most specific Louisiana Territory artifacts represented in permanent and changing exhibitions and publications The Collection's exhibition at the Mona Bismarck Foundation in Paris was the culmination of a year that celebrated the Louisiana Purchase. Much of the story of the Purchase was captured by The Collection's exhibition *A Fusion of Nations, A Fusion of Cultures: Spain, France, the United States and the Louisiana Purchase*. The exhibition traced Louisiana's story from *terra incognita* to incorporation into the United States through the triple themes of exploration and discovery, diplomacy, and commercial development. A companion presentation in The Collection's Royal Street Gallery portrayed the story in a more intimate way. *Napoleon's Eyewitness: Pierre Clément Laussat in Louisiana, 1802-1804* examined the critical role of the French colonial prefect in preparing to officially receive Louisiana from Spain and, after governing for twenty days, transfer it to the United States. Augmenting these exhibitions is The Collection's publication *Charting Louisiana: Five Hundred Years of Maps*, destined to become a definitive reference. The cartographic history of Louisiana as a colony, a territory, and a modern state is portrayed in over four hundred pages including 193 maps, dozens of chapter illustrations, seven analytical essays, and a cartobibliography.

La Louisiane, de la colonie française à l'État américain at the Mona Bismarck Foundation had the distinction of being an exclusive exhibition concerning the history of a French colony from its initial claim to beyond its final peaceful transfer to the United States. Through The Collection's display, *La Louisiane* traced the transformation of a territory into the modern state of Louisiana, one of more than a dozen states created from the Louisiana Purchase territory over the course of more than a century.

The story begins in 1682. Studying the vastness of the interior lands of the United States, one can appreciate not only the great expanse, but also specifically the ambitious exploration of René Robert Cavalier, sieur de La Salle. Born in Rouen in 1643, La Salle became known as one of the most tragic (he was assassinated by his men in 1687), yet celebrated, builders of New France. On April 9, 1682, as he stood on the shifting alluvial prairie deposited by the Mississippi River at South Pass with fellow adventurer Henri de

Tonty, La Salle claimed for France "this country of Louisiana," including all lands drained by the Mississippi, Ohio, and Missouri River systems. The expedition's notary, Jacques de la Metairie, recorded the claim:

"All territory bordering on the Colbert or Mississippi River and all rivers which flow into it, from its very source, beyond the country of the Sioux or Nadouessioux, and this with their full consent and that of Otontatas, Illinois, Matsigameas, Arkansas, Natchez and Koroas, who are the most important nations or tribes living in that section of the country, with whom we have signed treaties personally or through our representatives, to the very mouth of the river in the sea or in the Gulf of Mexico and from the twenty-seventh degree of the north pole elevation to the mouth of the River of Palms upon the assurance given us by all these people that we are the first Europeans who have ascended or descended the full length of the Colbert River. And we hereby formally protest against all those who in the future would attempt or undertake to take possession of all or any of the said countries, peoples and lands afore described to the prejudice of the right which His Majesty has acquired through the consent of the aforesaid nations... "

Metairie, too, watched the narrow jaws of the serpentine Mississippi open to a wide mouth of three channels that disgorged muddy, debris-filled water sluggishly into the roily blue waters of the Gulf of Mexico. He may well have pondered the true size of the lands claimed for his king, Louis XIV, and named in his honor.

With the eighteenth-century Age of Enlightenment, exploration and aggression typified the royal agendas of European countries, often instigated by the challenge of such earlier events as the 1493 papal Bullas de Alejandro VI "that divided recently discovered lands between Spain and Portugal. Spain received the entire New World, while Portugal received Africa and India."

Though often blood relatives, European monarchs engaged in strategies to promote or discourage colonization and to extend influence throughout the world. Nouvelle-Orléans, named for the Regent Philippe, Duc d'Orléans in 1718, had maintained a Gallic flavor despite transfer to Philippe's Spanish Bourbon cousin, Carlos III, in 1762. A continuous migration of French-speaking people stretched from the French founding of Louisiana, through its administration by Spain, and well into the nineteenth century. Under Spanish governor Miró alone, seven ships, in one of the largest trans-Atlantic movements, brought four hundred Acadian families to the colony; between 1792 and 1810, ten thousand refugees from Saint-Domingue arrived in Louisiana. At the time of the Louisiana Purchase nearly a thousand French-speaking persons emigrated from Jamaica. France's temporal period of exploration and settlement covers only a brief portion of Louisiana's history; however, when one considers France's influence over more than 320 years, from La Salle's first claim to the present time, significance emerges.

At the beginning of the nineteenth century, the potential purchase of a portion of French Louisiana lingered in diplomatic channels. It suddenly gained new life with the collapse of the Peace of Amiens and the resurgence of war between France and Great Britain. Unimpaired commercial navigation of the Mississippi River, with New Orleans as an open port, motivated American president Thomas Jefferson to maintain his minister Robert R. Livingston in Paris. Livingston and, later, James Monroe were "authorized to pay ten million dollars for New Orleans, the island on which it stood, and the Floridas, thought also to be French."

French secretary of the treasury François Barbé-Marbois, wise to the American needs and keen for a bargain, raised Napoleon's price from fifty million francs to one hundred million francs but followed his emperor's suggestion to sell all of the original territory, not only the Isle of Orleans. With this sale (at a final price closer to eighty million francs, or about fifteen million dollars) Napoleon Bonaparte abandoned France's colonial ambitions and in turn provided for decades of American growth from "sea to shining sea."

The present state of Louisiana, with an area of approximately fifty thousand square miles, is about 6 percent of the Purchase's total area. In 1803, though all of the requirements for statehood had been met, Anglo-American discomfort in the nation's capital concerning the power of a French-speaking populace delayed statehood until 1812. As part of the United States, New Orleans's municipal government labored through cultural differences despite temporary unification in the city's defense against the British at the Battle of New Orleans in 1815. Separate municipalities, established in 1836 along ethnic and social lines, continued until 1852. Meanwhile, French newspapers, operas, literary groups, and language flourished well past mid-century to the time of New Orleans's fall to Union forces during the Civil War. The occupation of Union forces within the city for over sixteen years, from 1862 to 1878, has been offered as the most unifying factor for the New Orleans general public.

In the United States, the bicentennial celebrations have produced a national awareness of the importance of the Louisiana Purchase territory, once an important part of colonial France. From a burst of Internet fervor to exhibitions, published seminar papers, and books, this awareness serves to deepen exploratory inquiry for the intellectually curious, critical historians.

Following the celebratory bicentennial year, it is hoped that the same energy can be used to promote a continuum of study in France, Spain, Great Britain, and their former colonies in North America. Untouched memoirs, secret treaties and agreements, rare books, and maps in both private collections and public institutions await the scholar's inquisition.

Presently, only a veneer of French tradition and influence remains; a comparison of New Orleans and Paris seems romantic and similarities almost coincidental. The two cities, each on a major river, the Seine and the Mississippi, enjoy neighborhoods (faubourgs and arrondisements) that compete for distinctive architectural and cultural expressions and reflect political divisions.

The Seine, unlike the Mississippi, rests about thirty feet below the city streets, bordered handsomely by stone-edged quays and trees and crossed by numerous, low-level decorative bridges serving both vehicular and pedestrian traffic. The Seine enters Paris from the southeast and departs northwest as it seeks an outlet to the sea. It creates within the city a right and left bank.

The Mississippi River at New Orleans, on the other hand, rises above the city level, contained, most hopefully, by man-made spillways and levees that conceal its mighty width and swift currents from any street. Two massive bridges, solely for vehicles, connect its right and left banks, called by some the east and west banks. Always a city of ironic contrasts, the east bank actually extends north and the west bank, south. Thus, it may be said, in New Orleans east is north and west is south. The river's continuous meanderings give compass directions little meaning and force New Orleanians to give street directions as upriver or downriver, referencing the Mississippi's flow toward the Gulf of Mexico.

New Orleans, Louisiana's major city, has arrived in the twenty-first century as a historic reflection of European/African/American influences. The population is challenged, as are the populations of all major cities, with new migrations of people seeking fresh opportunities. They, too, will alter a city dominated by a river that caused its birth and continues to drain thirty-one states and two Canadian provinces. This polyglot populace may well ensure that the more things change, the more they remain the same.

Treasures of The Historic New Orleans Collection

Priscilla LAWRENCE, *Executive Director, The Historic New Orleans Collection*

The celebration of a bicentennial such as that of the Louisiana Purchase affords the opportunity to take stock of what has transpired since that point. The most productive examination results when looking at the event through different lenses. From an international perspective, we acknowledge the influence of Louisiana's French and Spanish colonial heritage on the richness of the state's present culture, especially that of the city of New Orleans. From a national standpoint, we celebrate the augmentation of the early republic with a land so vast, rich, and critical that historian Bernard DeVoto proclaimed during the 150th anniversary year (1953) that no other event in United States history, before or since, held more importance. When perceiving the event introspectively, the bicentennial permits The Collection to examine its own role in preserving and promulgating the message of Louisiana's past, so richly portrayed in this exhibition through documents, paintings, and other materials.

Louis XIV to Louis Armstrong: A Cultural Tapestry touches on major themes in Louisiana history as illuminated by The Collection's holdings: exploration and colonization, the growth of a colonial capital and later an American port city, the influence of the fine arts in shaping the identity of the region, and the importance of a unique musical form—jazz. The items that document and enliven the chronicle of Louisiana are as varied as the stories they tell. Their fundamental similarity lies in the fact that they are but exemplars of holdings that are both wide and deep. Few other institutions have the resources for the study of the heritage and culture of Louisiana and New Orleans, as does The Collection.

In the initial section of the exhibition and the catalogue, Alfred Lemmon begins the narrative of Louisiana as an eighteenth-century colony of France, later of Spain, and finally as part of the American republic. The Collection's resources for the study of this epoch date from shortly after the 1682 claim of Louisiana by René Robert Cavelier, sieur de La Salle and range from collections of letters patent issued for colonial operations to printed maps of the era and accounts of exploration and discovery. John Magill builds on this early recorded history, showing in the process the growth of New Orleans as one of the leading cities of nineteenth-century North America, due in large part to its role as a major port. John Lawrence limns the artistic legacy of interpreting New Orleans in the decades between the Civil War and World War II, identifying some of those painters and printmakers whose efforts described and defined this unique southern metropolis to the world. Finally, in an ongoing story whose ending is yet unwritten and unknown, Jason Wiese traces the early years of the development of jazz and focuses on some of its many progenitors. Together, these essays and objects offer a selective representation of the vast holdings of The Collection.

Museum collections grow in different ways. The Collection's scope was established by the mid-twentieth century, and from that core, it has continued to add materials related to new areas of study and to build on original holdings. As important as the element of display through museum exhibitions and publications is the availability of the holdings to the public at large in the Williams Research Center. Opened in 1996, this facility permits scholars and the interested general public the opportunity to consult with reference staff and to examine firsthand the images, manuscripts, and printed materials that are often eloquent witnesses to Louisiana's history. At the Williams Research Center, over seven thousand requests for information are addressed annually. Exhibitions and other educational programs have an annual attendance of many more. The activities of The Collection take place in a complex of French Quarter buildings spanning 123 years of building practice and architectural styles—from the Merieult House (1792) to the Williams Research Center (1915).

During the 1930s, The Collection's founders, Kemper and Leila Williams, began their lifelong quest to assemble materials that tell the story of Louisiana's history as a colony, territory, and modern state. It was impossible at the time for them to know what results this activity would produce. Now, in 2004, thirty-three years after Kemper Williams's death, the tangible legacy of their generosity and foresight is displayed for all to see.

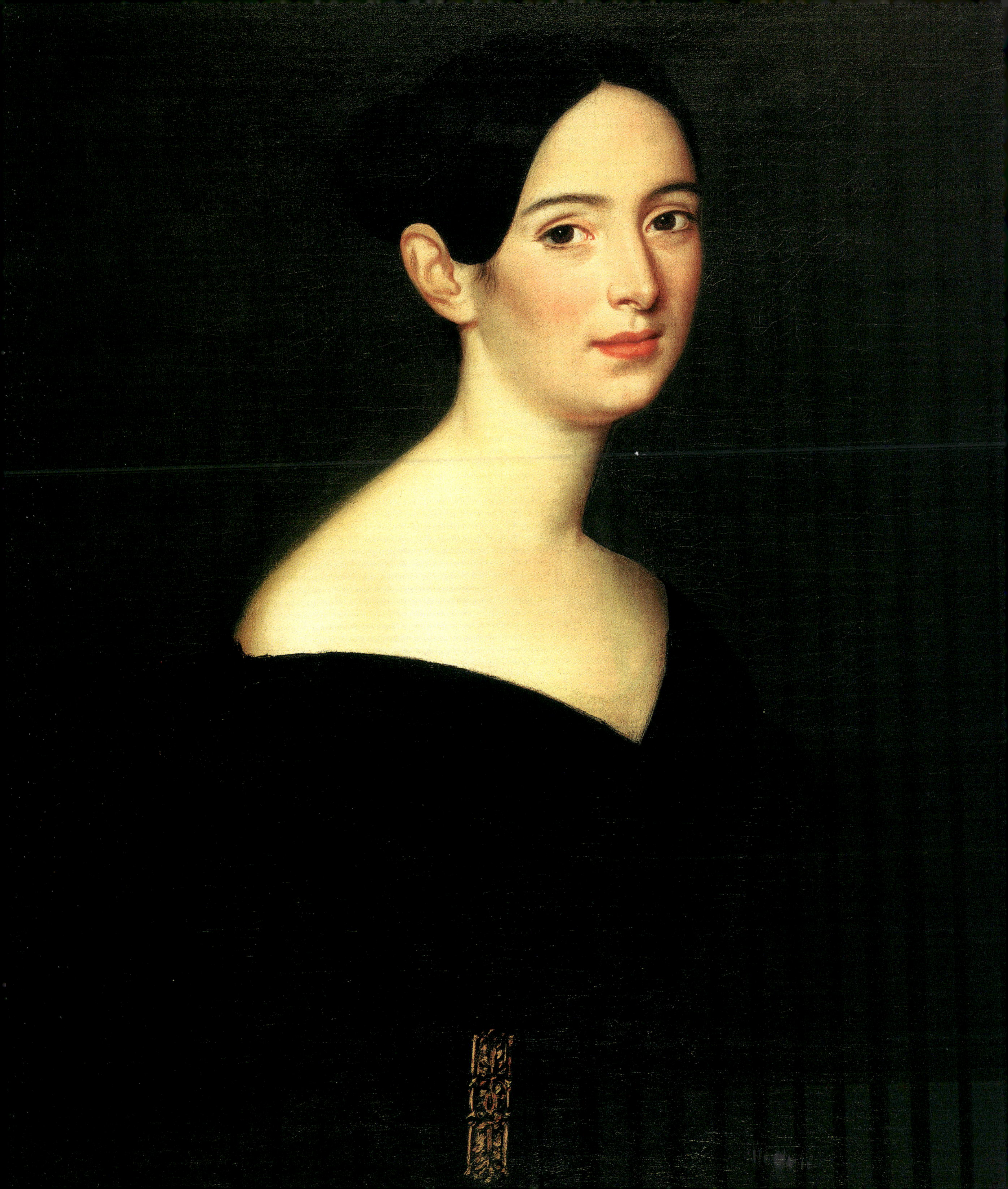

The European Quest for La Louisiane

Alfred E. LEMMON, *Director of the Williams Research Center, The Historic New Orleans Collection*

As the European search for wealth in North America intensified, Louisiana—with its rumored natural resources and strategic location—became an enviable prize for Spain, France, and England. The Spanish claim to Louisiana dated from the papal bulls of Alexander VI (1493) and the subsequent Treaty of Tordesillas (1494) that divided the New World between Spain and Portugal. With the tragic conclusion of Hernando de Soto's 1539 expedition to the present-day southeastern United States, the persistent rumors of man-eating Indians, and Louisiana's hostile terrain, Spain initially elected to focus on the readily apparent wealth of Mexico and the Andes, rather than the northern coast of the Gulf of Mexico and the Mississippi Valley.

As the maps of the period indicate, the Mississippi Valley attracted few Europeans initially. However, as the seventeenth century drew to a close, activity increased in the region. René Robert Cavelier, sieur de La Salle, a member of a wealthy family in Rouen, traveled to Canada in 1666. He quickly distinguished himself in the fur trade but soon sold his interests to devote himself to the exploration of the interior of North America. After discovering the Ohio River, La Salle continued his explorations throughout the Mississippi Valley, eventually claiming it for France's Louis XIV on April 9, 1682.

In the 1690s, the English became increasingly aggressive in the region. James Moore, an English trader from Carolina, crossed the Appalachian Mountains to establish trade with the Indians. Daniel Coxe, a London merchant, sought to create a trading company that would found a colony at the mouth of the Mississippi River. Louis Hennepin, a Belgian missionary and explorer, openly argued that England should send an expedition to the lower Mississippi River valley.

Concurrently, from 1689 to 1697, France was engaged in a bitter conflict against the British known as King William's War. While the French suffered brutal losses on the battlefield, they were relatively successful at the negotiating table. According to the terms of the Treaty of Rijswijk of 1697, France retained a visible presence in North America. Newfoundland, Hudson Bay, New France, and the vast unmapped regions of the interior of the continent extending to the Gulf of Mexico were declared French. Spain, with its enormously rich province of New Spain to the west of Louisiana, was no longer interested in pursuing a policy of colonial expansionism and preferred a French, rather than a British, presence in the region.

Adding to the political complexity of the period was the death of Charles II of Spain in 1700. As a result of his naming the grandson of Louis XIV, the duc d'Anjou, as his sole heir, there were now Bourbon monarchs on the thrones of both France and Spain. Other nations perceived a potential French/Spanish alliance as a dan-

Jacques Guillaume Lucien Amans

Madame Armand François Pitot, née Françoise Gabrielle "Rosa" Montegut, ca. 1838

oil on canvas

The Historic New Orleans Collection 1984.158
gift of Mr. and Mrs. Henry C. Pitot

Jacques Guillaume Lucien Amans (1801–1888) was born in the Netherlands and died in Paris, but he lived in Louisiana between about 1836 and 1858, working the winter months in New Orleans as a portrait painter. Amans painted portraits of many prominent New Orleanians, including this one of Madame Armand François Pitot (1807–1895). Born in New Orleans, Rosa was the granddaughter of a highly respected New Orleans physician. Her husband, whom she wed in 1828, was the son of James Pitot, the first mayor of incorporated New Orleans. The Pitots ranked among the most successful and distinguished of the large influx of refugees from Saint-Domingue following the slave uprisings there in the 1790s. The bloody uprising and Napoleon's unsuccessful attempts to recapture the island were among the factors that led him to eventually sell Louisiana to the United States in 1803.

gerous threat, and the eleven-year War of the Spanish Succession ensued. To further complicate matters, the duc d'Anjou, as Felipe V of Spain, surprisingly affirmed Spain's claim to the vast Louisiana territory in accordance with the papal bulls of Alexander VI in 1493 and the subsequent Treaty of Tordesillas of 1494. In 1713 the Treaty of Utrecht ended the War of the Spanish Succession, affirming Felipe V as king of Spain but Louisiana as a French possession. Thus Louisiana was born as part of the European search for wealth in North America against the backdrop of larger European political issues.

With the validation of the French claim to Louisiana by the 1697 Treaty of Rijswijk, the actual development of the colony was soon underway. During 1697 and 1698, Iberville prepared a prospectus detailing the colony's potential wealth and encouraging colonization. During the same period, the French built their first fort—not in New Orleans but to the east at the "baye des Bilcchy" or Biloxi Bay in present-day Mississippi. In 1700 Iberville requested that his younger brother, Jean Baptiste, sieur de Bienville, construct a fort further to the east at Mobile in present-day Alabama. By March 1702 the new town had a total population of only four families, whose inexperience in agricultural matters resulted in a shortage of food.

If simple material matters made life difficult, political affairs proved to be even more problematic. The political difficulties stemmed from dissension between the early Canadian explorers, Iberville and Bienville, and the French residents and authorities as to the amount of influence Canada—as opposed to France—should have over Louisiana. While there was dissension as to the role of Canada in the colony's development, there was strong agreement between all parties that the only way to develop Louisiana was to defend it, in particular against the British. Furthermore, the most effective way to defend the colony was to populate the vast territory and to nurture effective alliances with the Indians.

However, such efforts were impeded by France's financial difficulties. The lavish lifestyle of Louis XIV had practically exhausted the Royal Treasury, severely limiting the Crown's ability to support the colony. Seeking to develop the potential riches of La Louisiane, financier Antoine Crozat received a fifteen-year trade monopoly in the colony. Effectively the "master" of the colony, Crozat realized that he would not only have to struggle to develop the gulf-coast region of Louisiana, but he would need to develop Upper Louisiana, the region encompassing the Red River, the Arkansas River, and present-day Missouri. His purpose in Upper Louisiana was twofold—to prevent British incursions and to find wealth. After two years, the enormously wealthy Crozat, drained by financial losses in Louisiana, relinquished his control of the colony. The Crown then looked to the Scottish promoter and speculator John Law to develop Louisiana. Law contended that the colony could actually provide revenue to relieve the royal debts.

Law's company, known initially as the Company of the West and later as the Company of the Indies, strongly felt that the

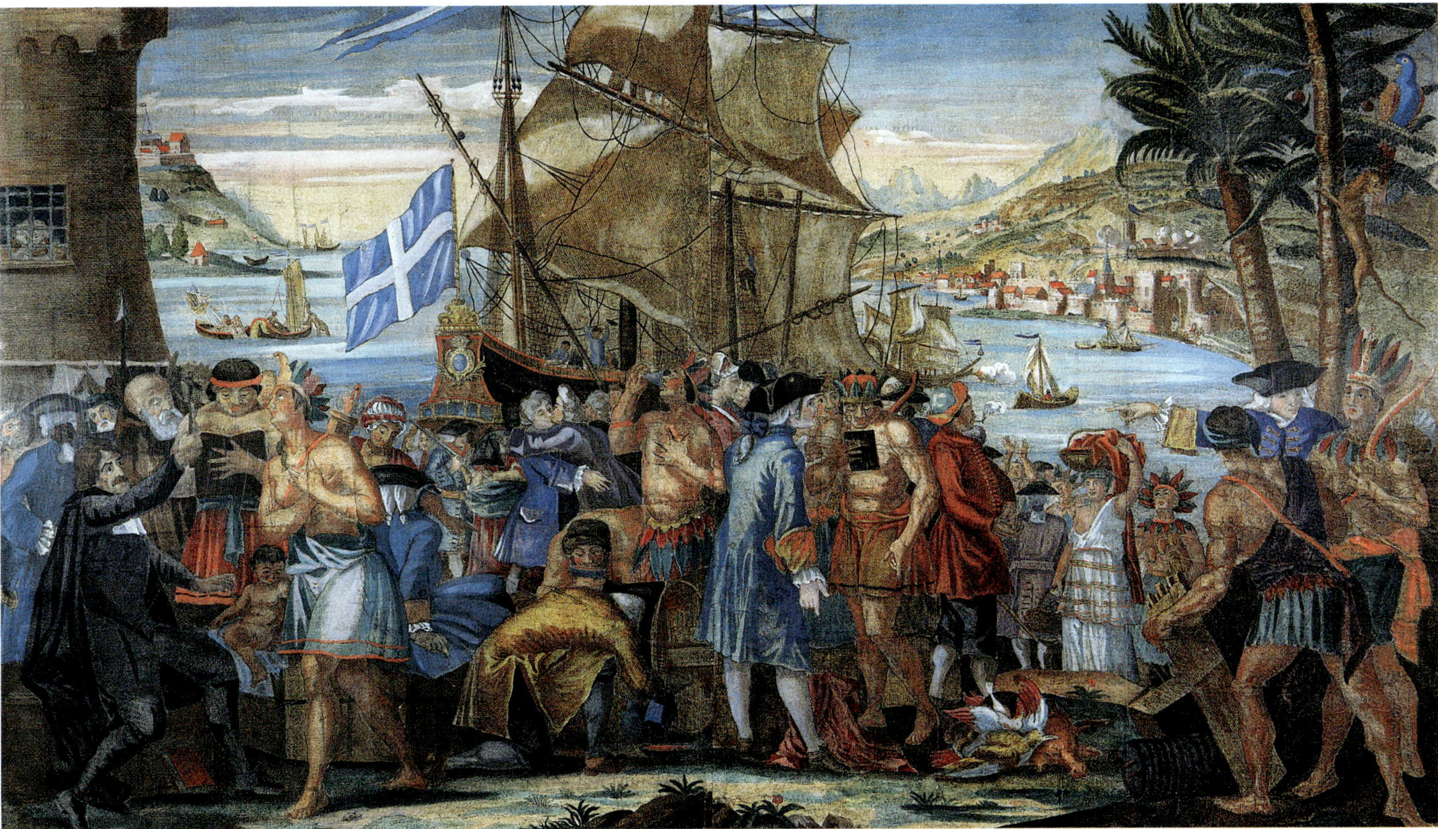

key to making Louisiana profitable was large-scale immigration. Because there were few voluntary immigrants, forced immigrants selected from correctional facilities in Paris were sent to Louisiana. Law's company also turned to the poverty stricken German principalities and sought residents willing to relocate to the promised land of Louisiana. Upon arrival, the German immigrants found themselves, for all practical purposes, stranded with no provisions to assist them in reaching the lands awaiting them in present-day Arkansas. Yet they were highly resourceful and began to cultivate the rich alluvial land on the Mississippi River north of New Orleans. While the story of these German immigrants has been greatly romanticized, their agricultural settlements, still referred to as the Côte des

François Gérard Jollain, Jr.
Le Commerce que les Indiens du Mexique Font avec les François au Port du Missisipi, ca. 1720
engraving with watercolor
The Historic New Orleans Collection 1952.3

The Company of the Indies, the financial company chartered under the infamous John Law to colonize Louisiana, distributed this poster in about 1720 to encourage immigration to the Louisiana concession. Such posters, which were made available in France and several German states, present a highly inaccurate depiction of the region being promoted. New Orleans is shown as a solidly built, fortified town, although at the time it contained only a few small houses and a warehouse. The mountainous terrain and depictions of indigenous animals are purely artistic conjecture; in reality the terrain of the area is low-lying and swampy, and parrots and monkeys, seen in the palm trees on the right-hand side of the artwork, did not exist in Louisiana. The friendliness depicted between Europeans and Native Americans is most certainly an attempt to lure settlers to an area with the idea that trade and wealth existed in abundance. With such romantic overstatement, it is little wonder that Law's company collapsed when the truth about the new colony, along with other financial problems, became known in France.

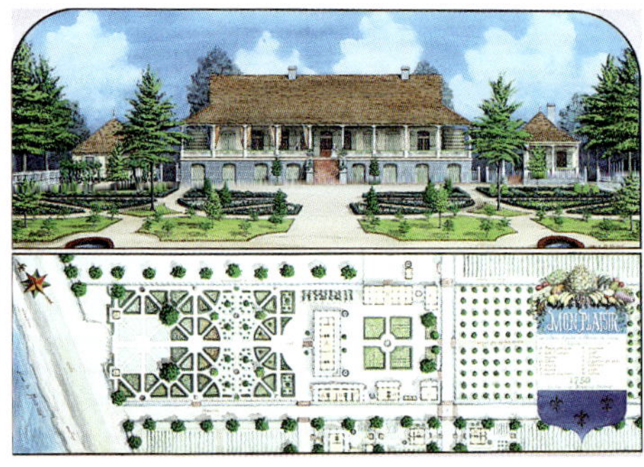

Jim Blanchard
Mon Plaisir le Château et Jardin du Chevalier de Pradel, 2001
watercolor
The Historic New Orleans Collection 2001.39.3

Louisiana artist Jim Blanchard is noted for his well researched and accurate depictions of buildings as they appeared in the past. Here Blanchard depicts Mon Plaisir, one of the finest houses in French Louisiana. Chevalier Jean Charles Pradel (1692–1764) built the home on property he purchased in 1736. Situated on the west bank of the river, Mon Plaisir was Pradel's attempt to create a genteel French environment in the New World colony. Pradel had a colorful career in Louisiana, ranging from venture trader in New Orleans to fort commandant and wealthy planter and exporter. Mon Plaisir was purchased in 1817 by John McDonogh, a man of considerable wealth who left part of his fortune for the building of public schools in New Orleans. The house eventually fell into disrepair and was inundated by the Mississippi River in about 1860.

Allemands, were critical to the development of New Orleans. John Law's company failed to produce revenues in line with royal expectations, and Louisiana reverted to its status as a Crown colony in 1731.

During the same years that witnessed the mercurial career of John Law and his German immigrants, the city of New Orleans was established. It was deemed that a Mississippi River location, where river traffic could be monitored and foreign intrusion guarded against, was preferable to the previous sites at Biloxi and Mobile. Established by Bienville in 1718, the young town remained rather primitive with no particular design until 1721. In that year, the city streets were laid out by the French engineer Adrien de Pauger. With the advent of city planning, the town began to grow rapidly. Within a few years, visitors' descriptions of New Orleans would change radically from "a savage and deserted place" to a "very pretty, well constructed and regularly built town."

During the 1720s, the Code Noir, a critical piece of legislation, was prepared at Versailles. The purpose of the Code Noir was to protect slaves from injustice and cruelty, as well as to regulate their conduct. In addition, it called for the expulsion of Jews from Louisiana and prohibited any religion other than Catholicism. While the Code Noir mandated harsh penalties for errant slaves, it granted manumitted slaves the same rights and privileges enjoyed by persons born free. The roles that the large African slave population, the free people of color, and Catholicism would play in the development of Louisiana are clearly foreshadowed in that singular document.

For nearly forty years, Bienville served as governor of the colony. His tenure was marked by any number of rivalries—Canadian/French and Jesuit/Capuchin—as well as conflicts among the Indians—the Chickasaws, the Choctaws, the Natchez, and the Alibamons. The arrival of the marquis de Vaudreuil as governor in 1743 ushered in a period of peace and prosperity. The tenure of Vaudreuil was a "golden age" for the long-suffering colony. Indeed, it was during his tenure that the sugar industry, so important to modern-day Louisiana, was established. With the departure of Vaudreuil, however, long-existing local rivalries resurfaced.

While rivalries between the religious groups and Indian tribes dominated the local scene, the competition between France and England for the Mississippi Valley was clearly evident in the French and Indian War (1757-1763). Once again the fate of Louisiana would be decided in the royal courts of Europe. With France prepared to suffer heavy losses of territory with the Treaty of Paris of 1763, Louis XV hurriedly transferred Louisiana to his Spanish cousin Carlos III in 1762. Indeed, France did lose Canada according to that treaty, but the transfer of Louisiana to Spain prevented the British from becoming entrenched in the heartland of North America.

While French rule officially came to an end in 1762, the first Spanish governor, Antonio de Ulloa, did not arrive in Louisiana until 1766. His administration was doomed upon arrival, as he had far too few soldiers to take over an unwilling colony. Indeed, Ulloa never took control of the colony. Fearing the loss of economic interests, a group of influential merchants and planters declared the colony French in October 1768 and drove Ulloa out. Thus it was in Louisiana that the first revolution against a European monarch took place on what would eventually become United States soil.

Carlos III dispatched Alejandro O'Reilly to bring the rebellious colony under control. Arriving with approximately two thousand soldiers, O'Reilly quickly sentenced some of the rebels to death and banished others. He then devoted himself to establishing Spanish rule in the former French colony during his relatively short tenure as governor, but he was careful to respect the customs of the Louisiana Creoles and, in particular, the use of the French language. His successor, Luis de Unzaga, continued to develop a policy of tolerance.

With the outbreak of the American Revolution in 1776, Spain seized the opportunity to seek revenge on its British enemy. Bernardo de Gálvez, who was governor at the time, led successful military campaigns against the British in Baton Rouge, Natchez, Mobile, and Pensacola. The victories consolidated Spanish rule in the lower Mississippi Valley. Although Spain aided the United States against England, the young republic, with designs for westward expansion, would soon come under suspicion.

The Spanish administrators were faced with the challenges of defending and populating the vast territory of Louisiana as were the French before them. Relationships with the Indian nations were nurtured and developed. The Spanish government adopted a rather pragmatic approach for the defense of the colony—to populate it. Loyal Catholics of any nationality were readily granted land. The policy accounted for the large migration of Acadian, French, German, and Irish Catholics to the colony. Spain also focused on developing the Spanish presence in the colony by encouraging the migration of Canary Islanders, known as Isleños. It was expected that they would defend the colony and increase its economic base. Later, in a similar effort, residents of Málaga were brought to present-day southwest Louisiana.

Perhaps, the most interesting immigration to Louisiana is that of the Acadians. Upon their ruthless expulsion by the British from their homes in Acadia, now Nova Scotia, these Catholic exiles were welcomed in Louisiana and given land along the banks of the Mississippi River, not far from where the German settlers brought by John Law had settled more than sixty years earlier. While they suffered many hardships, these immigrants managed to flourish in Louisiana.

Indeed, even Anglo-Americans were encouraged to immigrate, provided that they converted to Catholicism. With that goal in mind, colonial administrators recruited Irish priests studying at the University of Salamanca to serve in the colony. Finally, French refugees from the slave revolt in Saint-Domingue, seeking sanctuary in

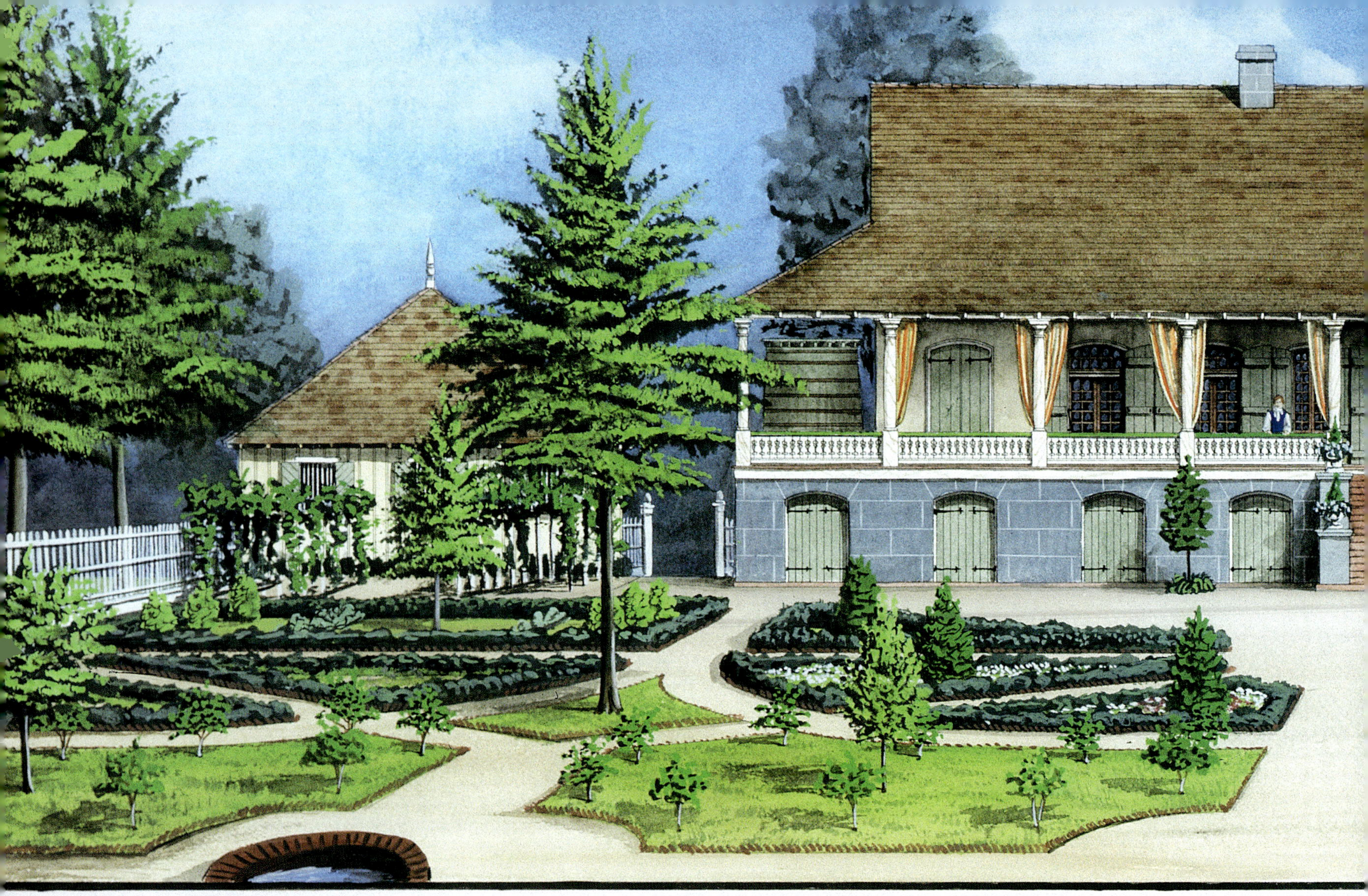

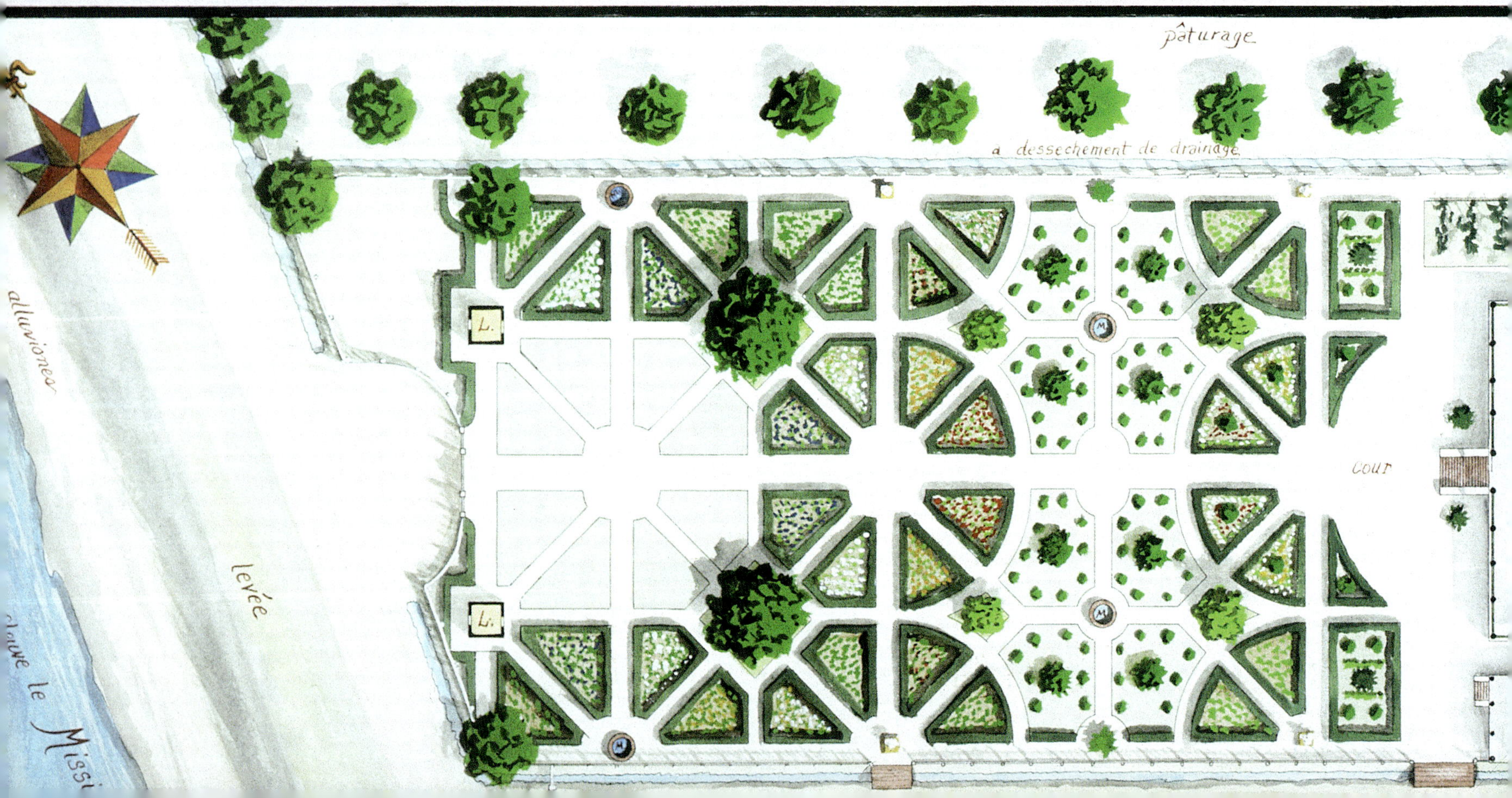

pâturage
a dessechement de drainage
alluviones
levée
cour
fleuve le Missi

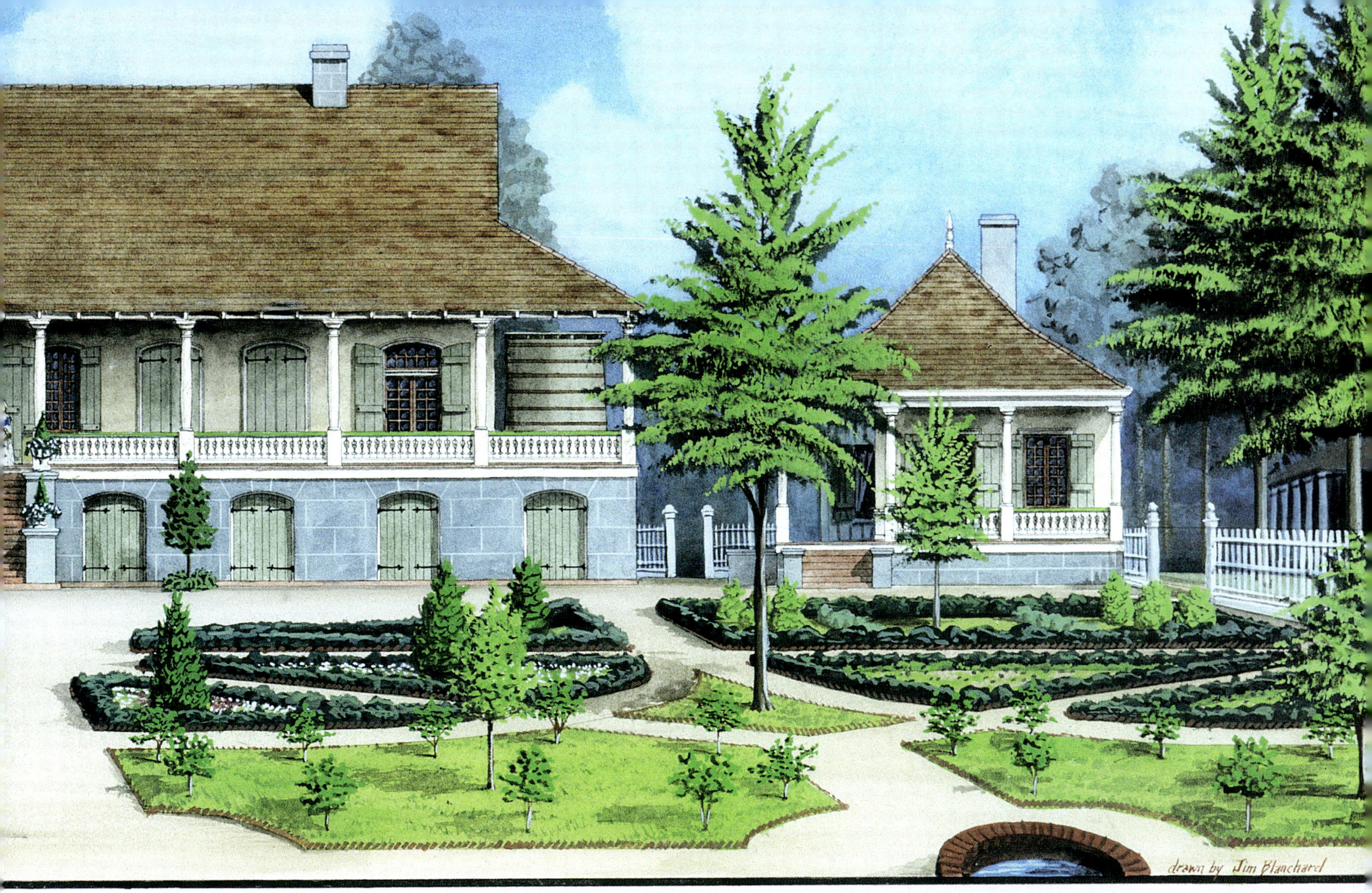

drawn by Jim Blanchard

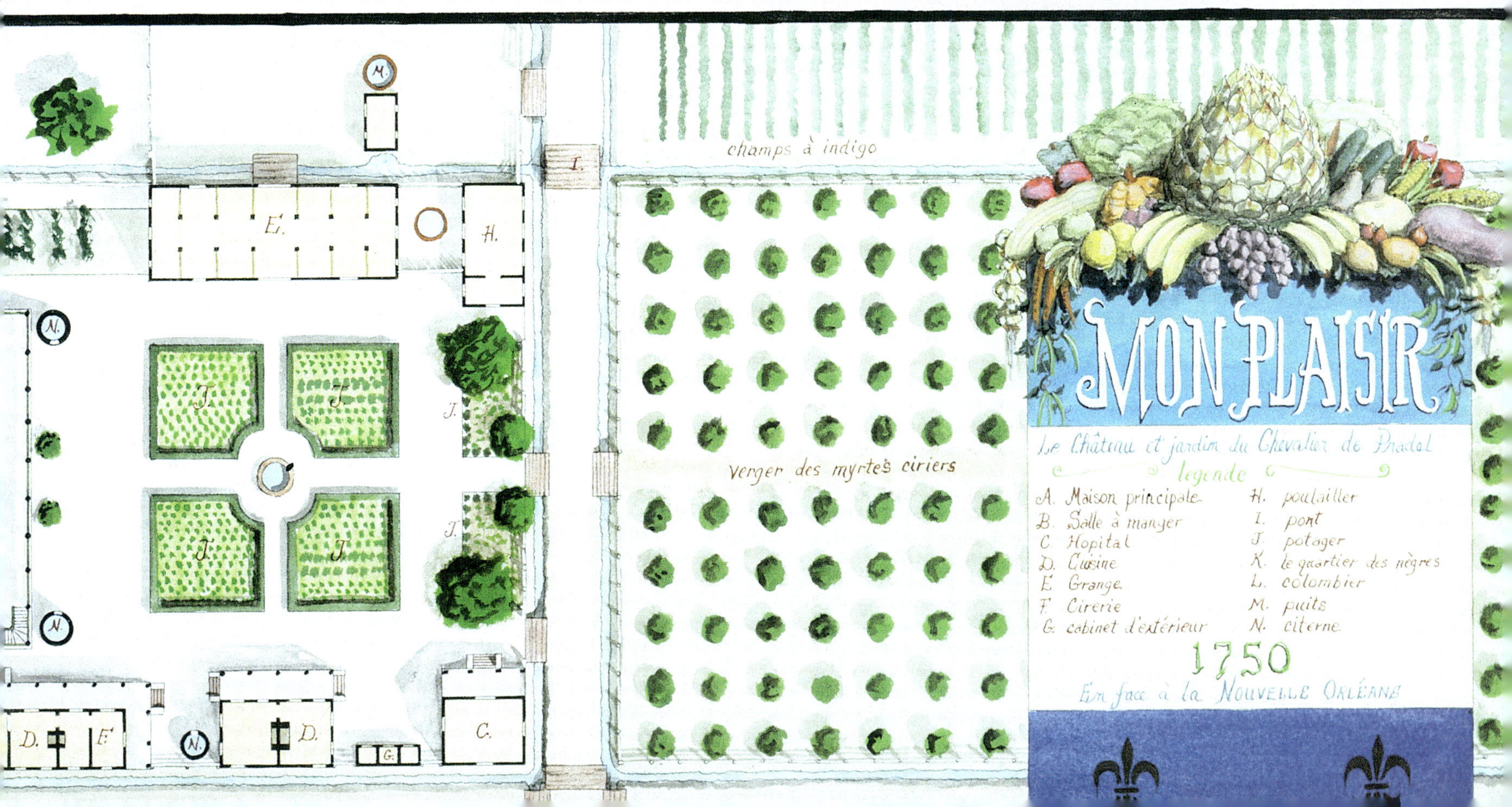

champs à indigo

verger des myrtes ciriers

MON PLAISIR

Le Château et jardin du Chevalier de Pradel

legende

A. Maison principale
B. Salle à manger
C. Hopital
D. Cuisine
E. Grange
F. Cirerie
G. cabinet d'extérieur
H. poulailler
I. pont
J. potager
K. le quartier des nègres
L. colombier
M. puits
N. citerne

1750

En face à la Nouvelle Orléans

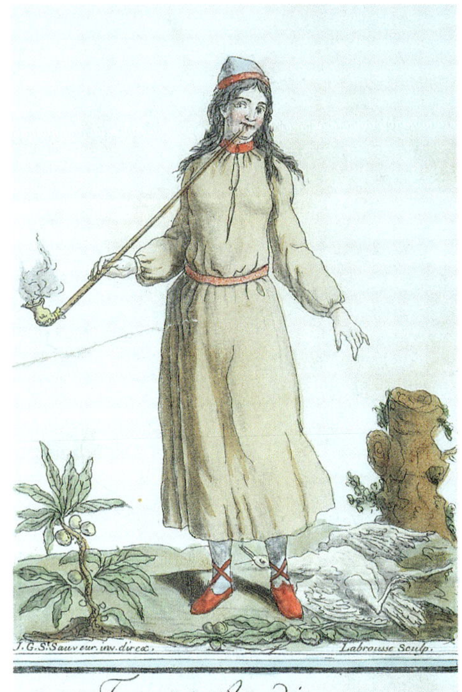

Labrousse
after J. Grusset St. Sauveur
Femme Acadienne, ca. 1800
hand-colored etching
The Historic New Orleans Collection 1985.41

French painter J. Grusset St. Sauveur and the engraver of his works, Labrousse, produced numerous illustrations depicting different peoples from around the world. This image is of a woman from Acadia in eastern Canada, now called Nova Scotia. Acadian refugees were forced from their homes when the province was taken over by the British in the early 1760s. They eventually found a new home among the swamps and marshes of Louisiana. "Cajuns," as they are now commonly called, came in several waves and settled west and south of New Orleans.

Louisiana, settled in New Orleans, significantly increasing the population. Though Spanish elements are found in the music, art, and architecture of Louisiana, the immigrants from Saint-Domingue further strengthened the French culture that had never entirely submitted to the rule of "The Most Catholic" monarchs. Indeed, under Spain, official broadsides were printed in Spanish and French, the first newspaper (*Le Moniteur de la Louisiane*) was published, and French opera was introduced into what would eventually become part of the United States.

When European rule of Louisiana ended, slaves represented approximately 55 percent of the population. The resilience and adaptive abilities of the African slaves contributed to the colony's unique culture. A substantial number of free persons of color, guaranteed certain rights by the Code Noir, provided a variety of vital services and helped to defend the colony. Furthermore, many were skilled craftsmen, such as brickmasons and ironworkers, who built much of New Orleans.

Spanish Louisiana was not immune to outside political pressures. Because of westward expansion, the United States was eager to use the Mississippi River to transport goods produced by western farmers. Finally, in 1795 the United States and Spain negotiated the Treaty of San Lorenzo, commonly referred to as Godoy's Treaty or Pinckney's Treaty in honor of the two principal negotiators. The treaty resolved boundaries between Spanish and American lands, granted navigational rights to the United States on the Mississippi River, and gave the Americans docking privileges in the port of New Orleans.

Although Louisiana advanced significantly under Spain, the colony failed as a profitable venture. Yet Spain did succeed in delaying Anglo-American control of the region for some four decades. At the end of the eighteenth century, the Spanish Empire was in a state of decline, and it became obvious that Louisiana could not be defended against a British or American attack. Spain, therefore, entered into the Treaty of San Ildefonso on October 1, 1800. According to the terms of the treaty, Louisiana was returned to France. In exchange, Napoleon Bonaparte agreed never to alienate Louisiana and to deliver the Kingdom of Etruria to Spain. The agreement was consistent with the long-standing French and Spanish strategic goal for Louisiana—namely, defense against the British. From the earliest days of the colony, the goal was to

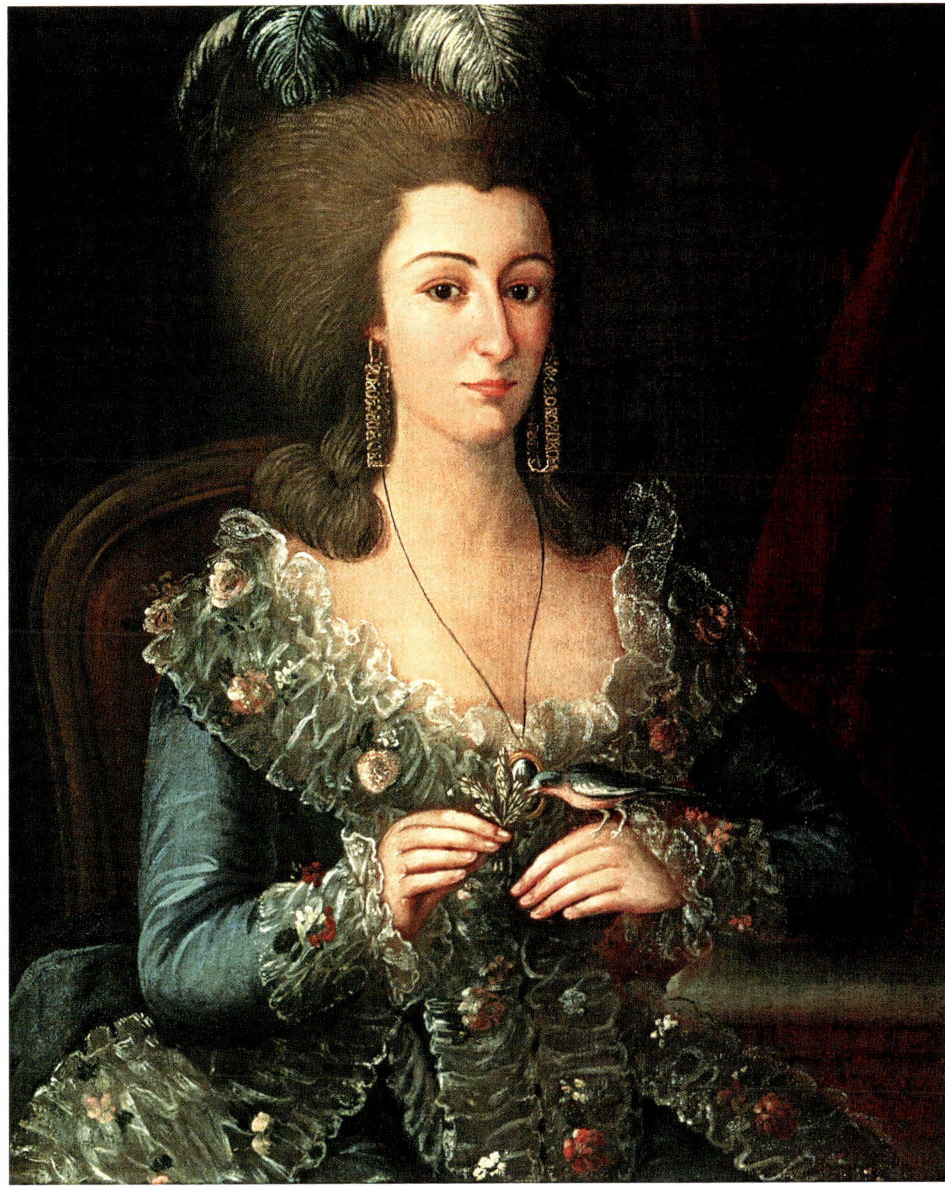

José Francisco de Salazar y Mendoza
Clara de la Motte, ca. 1795
oil on canvas
The Historic New Orleans Collection 1981.213

Portrait painter José Francisco Xavier de Salazar y Mendoza (mid 1700s–1802) came to New Orleans from Mérida, Yucatan, Mexico. Active in New Orleans from 1782 until his death, Salazar is the earliest known portraitist in the city. He painted a number of the city's most important citizens; this charming portrait of Clara de la Motte is typical of Salazar's work. Clara de la Motte came to New Orleans from Curaçao in 1787 to wed Benjamin Monsanto. They were among the earliest Jewish residents of New Orleans, but because Spanish law required that their wedding be performed in a Catholic church, they were married in the Church of St. Louis. La Motte's gown and coiffeur indicate that she was from a well-to-do family. In spite of its isolation, late eighteenth-century New Orleans already had a reputation for being a community fashionably on a par with Paris.

defend Louisiana by populating it. Neither France nor Spain found the vast sources of income that they sought so intently. When Napoleon learned in 1803 of the United States's interest in Louisiana—at the very time that his own dreams of a French empire in North America were fading—he chose to sell the colony as a means of obtaining cash to fight his own battles against the British.

But first France had to receive the colony from the Spanish, who had continued to govern it since the Treaty of San Ildefonso in 1800. On November 30, 1803, the flag of Bourbon Spain was lowered in New Orleans and the French tricolor raised over the Place d'Armes. A mere twenty days later, the process was repeated with the tricolor lowered and the American flag raised.

Thomas Jefferson, as president of the United States, had to select someone to serve as territorial governor. Many prominent individuals were recommended including Andrew

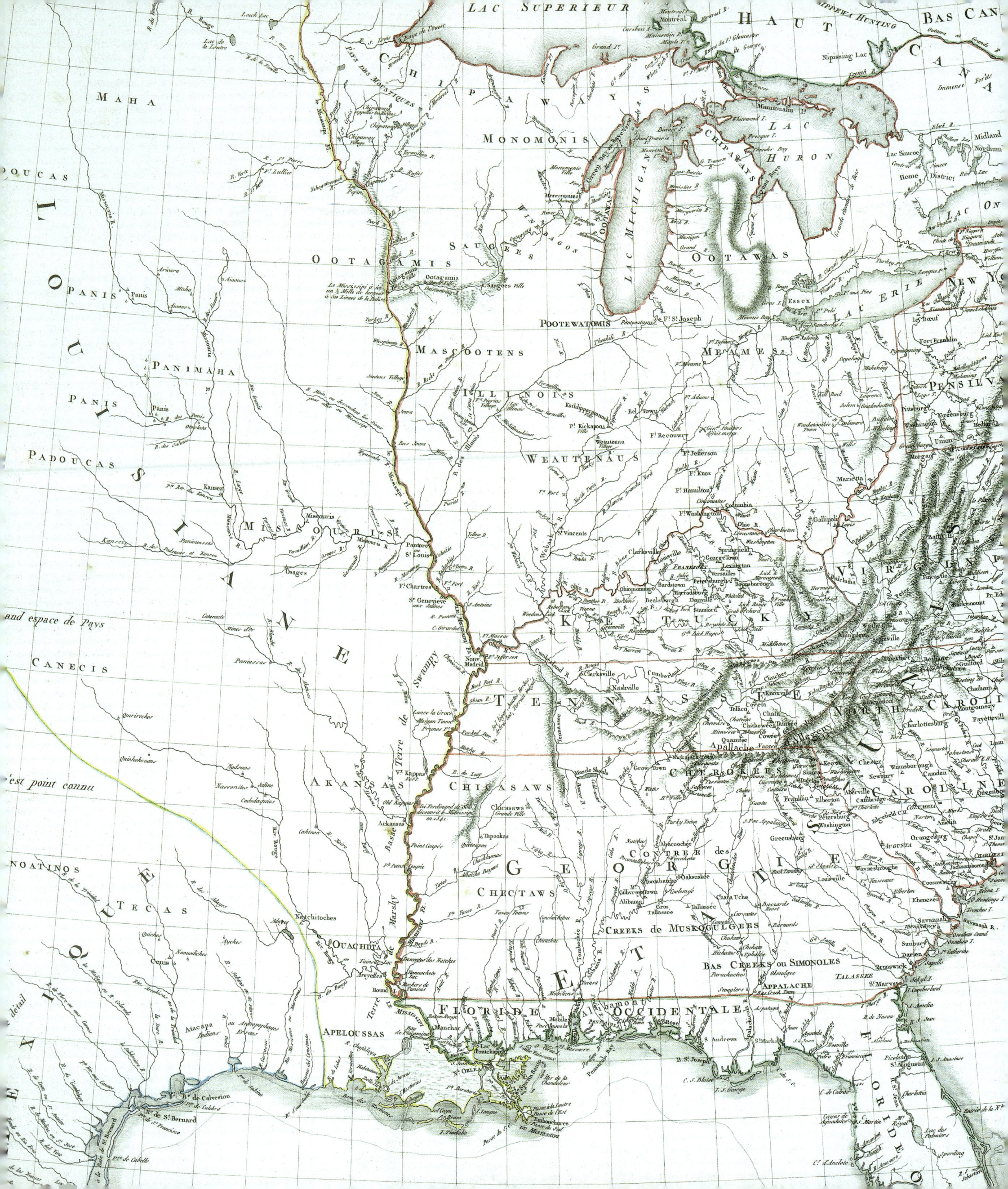

LAC SUPERIEUR
HAUT CANA
BAS CAN
LAC HURON
LAC MICHIGAN
LAC ERIE
CHIPAWAYS
MONOMONIS
WINEBAGOS
SAUGEES
OOTAGAMIS
OOTAWAS
POOTEWATOMIS
MASCOOTENS
ILLINOIS
MEAMES
WEAUTENAUS
MAHA
PADOUCAS
PANIS
PANIMAHA
MISSOURIS
LOUISIANE
CANECIS
AKANSAS
CHICASAWS
CHECTAWS
CHEROKEES
CREEKS de MUSKOGULGEES
BAS CREEKS ou SIMONOLES
TECAS
NOATINOS
OUACHITA
APELOUSSAS
KENTUKY
TENNASSEE
VIRGINIE
NORTH CAROLINE
CAROLINE
GEORGIE
PENSILVA
NEW YO
FLORIDE OCCIDENTALE
FLORIDE
St. Louis
Nashville
Pittsburg
Savannah
Charlestown
Pensacola
Mobile
Nle. Orléans
Natchitoches
Kaskaskia

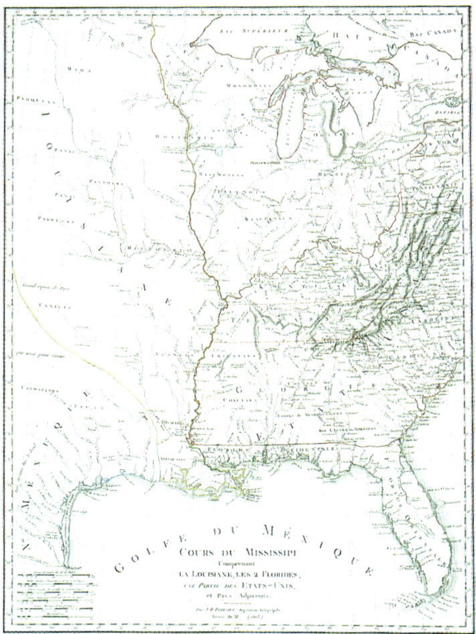

Jean-Baptiste Poirson

Cours du Mississippi Comprenant la Louisiane, Les 2 Florides, une Partie des Etats-Unis, et pays Adjacent, 1803

hand-colored engraving
The Historic New Orleans Collection 1984.3

When France's claim to the Louisiana territory was purchased by the United States, most of the vast acreage acquired was uncharted. Indeed, its full extent, populated mostly by Native Americans, could only be guessed at by Americans and Europeans. The most important part of the claim was the Mississippi River, which is the focus of this map published the year of the Purchase. Ownership of the Mississippi meant not only control of the continent, but control of the port of New Orleans. By 1803 Americans living west of the Appalachian Mountains depended on New Orleans as the port of deposit. Continued free access to Mississippi River navigation and the right to deposit goods at New Orleans were that region's economic lifeblood. This map clearly shows that there was greater knowledge about the area to the east of the river than to the west. Soon after the Louisiana Purchase, President Thomas Jefferson dispatched Meriwether Lewis and William Clark to explore the territory and determine its extent. Less than half a century after the Purchase, America's westward expansion would bring new settlers into the once unknown area.

Jackson, who would later achieve fame as the defender of New Orleans against British attack; the wealthy Irishman Daniel Clark, who had experience in New Orleans as the consul of the United States; James Monroe; and the marquis de Lafayette, an honorary American citizen who would be most acceptable to the local community. The position of territorial governor of Louisiana, however, fell to William C. C. Claiborne, one of the two commissioners who had received Louisiana from France in 1803. Claiborne had no shortage of challenges. The residents were offended when they were not given immediate statehood. The economy depended greatly on slavery, and the residents were dissatisfied with the prohibition on the importation of foreign slaves. The American legal system was totally different from French and Spanish legal tradition, and many of the immigrants who had received significant amounts of land from the Spanish felt insecure as they awaited validation of their claims by the new government. Indeed, there were questions about the permanence of American rule, and rumors were circulating that Louisiana would be returned to France or Spain. Furthermore, the Spanish officials did not hurry to leave. Eventually, in 1812, the current state of Louisiana entered the union.

Exactly one month after statehood, President James Madison claimed that a state

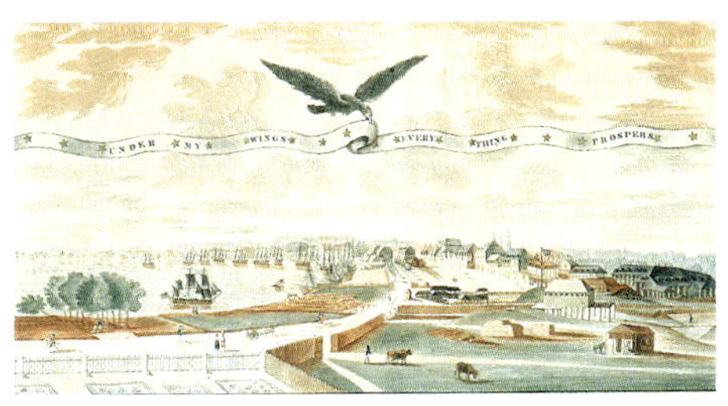

John L. Boqueta de Woiseri

A View of New Orleans Taken from the Plantation of Marigny, November 5, 1803

aquatint with etching and watercolor
The Historic New Orleans Collection 1958.42

Produced in 1803 by John L. Boqueta de Woiseri, this is the first known view of New Orleans as a soon-to-be American city. Although most Creoles living in New Orleans were not necessarily delighted with the prospect of becoming Americans, Boqueta de Woiseri thought differently. As the banner depicted above the city proclaims, de Woiseri believed United States possession of Louisiana would bring prosperity to New Orleans. This was indeed true. Already one of the most important ports in North America in 1803, the city boomed over the next half-century. The scene looks across a formal garden from the gallery of Bernard de Marigny's plantation house, where French colonial prefect Pierre Clément Laussat resided while in New Orleans. Laussat's assignment from Napoleon was to accept the colony for France from Spain on November 30, 1803, and then twenty days later, on December 20, 1803, transfer it to the United States.

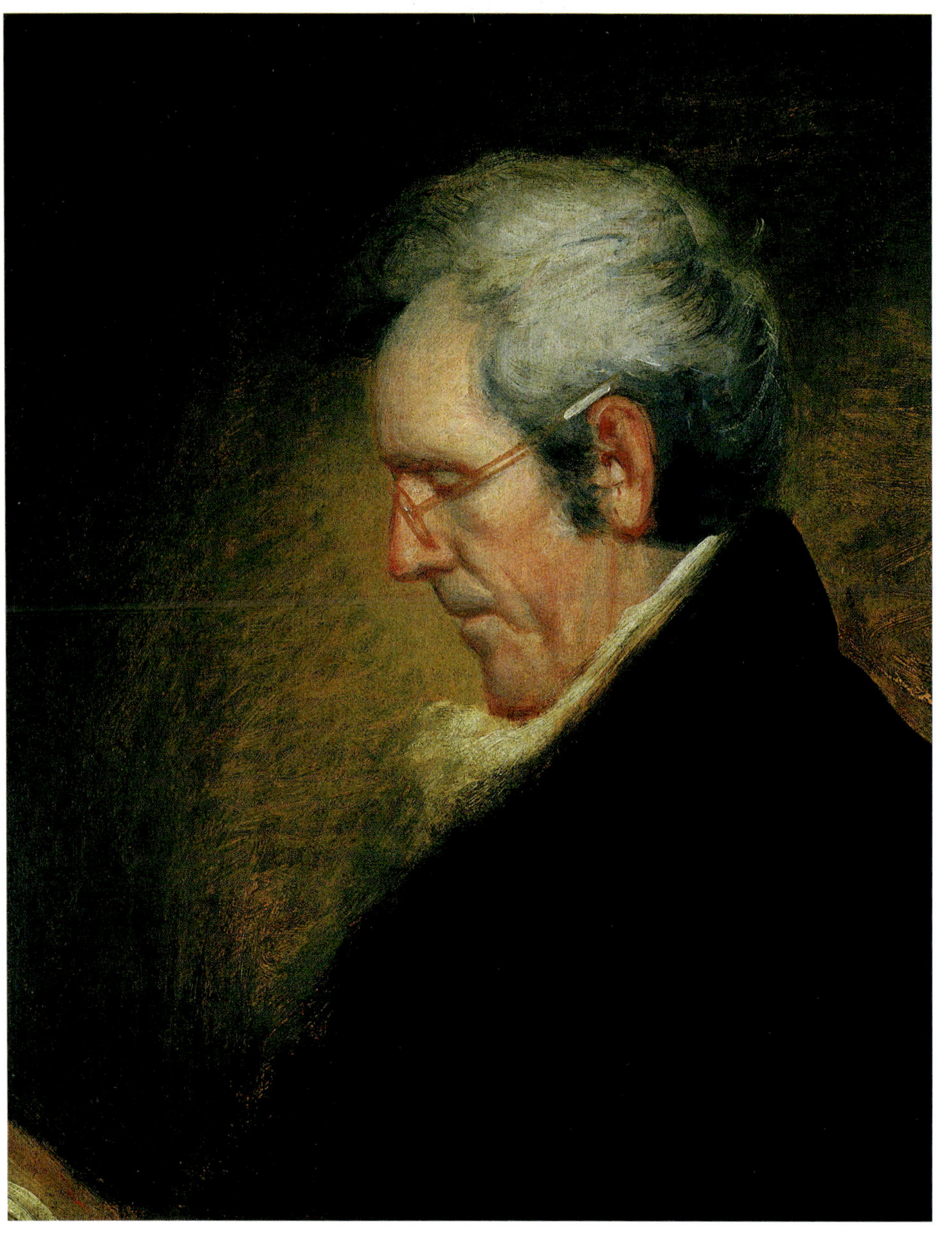

John Wesley Jarvis
Andrew Jackson, 1822

oil on panel
The Historic New Orleans Collection 1974.78

John Wesley Jarvis (1780–1840), a native of England, was brought to the United States as a young boy. Considered one of the outstanding American portrait painters of the early nineteenth century, Jarvis worked in New Orleans for several winters between 1821 and 1834. The quality of his work is evident in this portrait of Andrew Jackson (1767–1845), probably painted in New York.

of war existed: The British were interfering with U.S. seagoing vessels and were inciting the Indians on the frontier against the United States. Initially, Louisiana remained removed from the War of 1812. While there were rumors of a British invasion of the city, a blockade of the Mississippi River, and British-inspired Indian attacks, Louisiana did not respond until the British were approaching the city.

General Andrew Jackson arrived in New Orleans to command the U.S. forces on December 2, 1814. The British forces were already at sea, headed for New Orleans. Jackson assembled an army that represented the diverse population of the colonial period—Indians, free people of color, and soldiers from the nearby states of Tennessee, Kentucky, and Mississippi. Twelve days after Jackson's arrival, a British naval fleet overpowered American forces on nearby Lake Borgne. When the American forces quickly fell to the British in that battle, the community united against the British. Jackson's engineer, Arsène Lacarrière Latour, wrote in his memoirs that with the victory of the British on Lake Borgne, the entire community "breathed defiance to the British enemy." Martial airs, both French and American, could be heard throughout New Orleans, and citizens joined the Ursuline nuns in prayers that the British would fail in their attempt to capture the city.

The British forces, led by Sir Edward Pakenham, were poised to attack New Orleans on January 8, 1815. What neither side knew was that two weeks earlier negotiators had reached an agreement to end the War of 1812 with the Treaty of Ghent. Once again, Louisiana's fate had been decided in Europe. With the order given for the British to strike, a variety of circumstances, including the merciless current of the Mississippi River, doomed the attack. Only a few miles from New Orleans, the British troops were greeted with destructive fire by Jackson's ragtag forces. Among the first combatants to fall was the British commander, Pakenham. With the capture of New Orleans an utter failure, the British continued to attack Fort St. Philip on the Mississippi River. Finally, on January 19, the British realized that they could not take the fort, and their ships departed. More than a century after the French determined that a fort was necessary to defend the Mississippi River against British intruders, such a fort withstood British invasion.

During the eighteenth century, both France and Spain sought to populate Louisiana in order to defend the colony against the British. But it was with Americans and as Americans that descendents of the early French and Spanish colonists defeated the British. The vast country of Louisiana was now unequivocally American.

Dennis Malone Carter

The Battle of New Orleans, 1856

oil on canvas

The Historic New Orleans Collection 1960.22

This mid-nineteenth-century painting presents a romanticized version of the Battle of New Orleans. General Jackson, mounted on a white horse, confers with an officer as his men fire at British soldiers storming the American lines a few feet away. On January 8, 1815, Jackson's ragtag American army soundly defeated the veteran British army led by General Edward Pakenham on the Chalmette plain, about eight miles downriver from New Orleans. This surprising American victory permanently ended British designs on Louisiana and made Jackson the "hero of New Orleans."

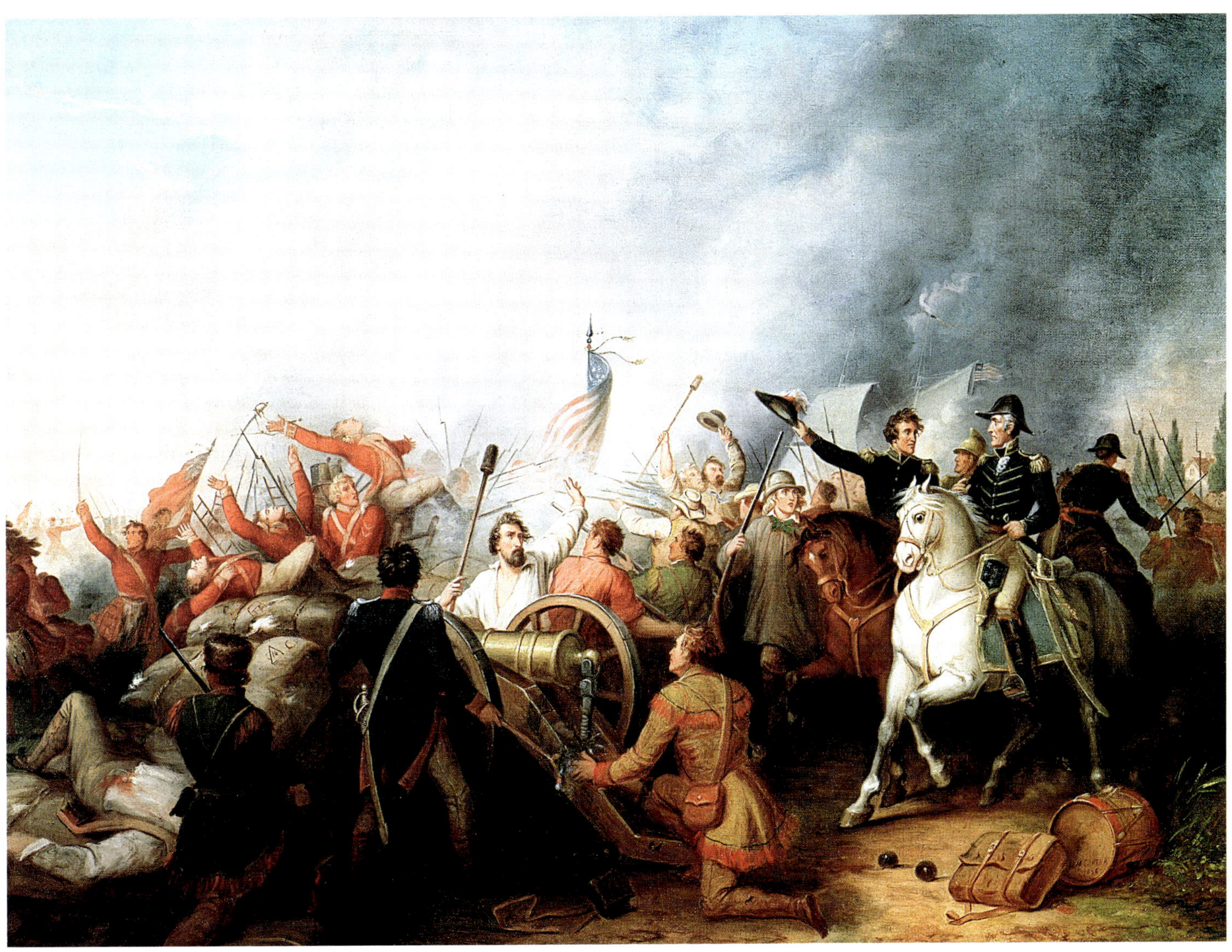

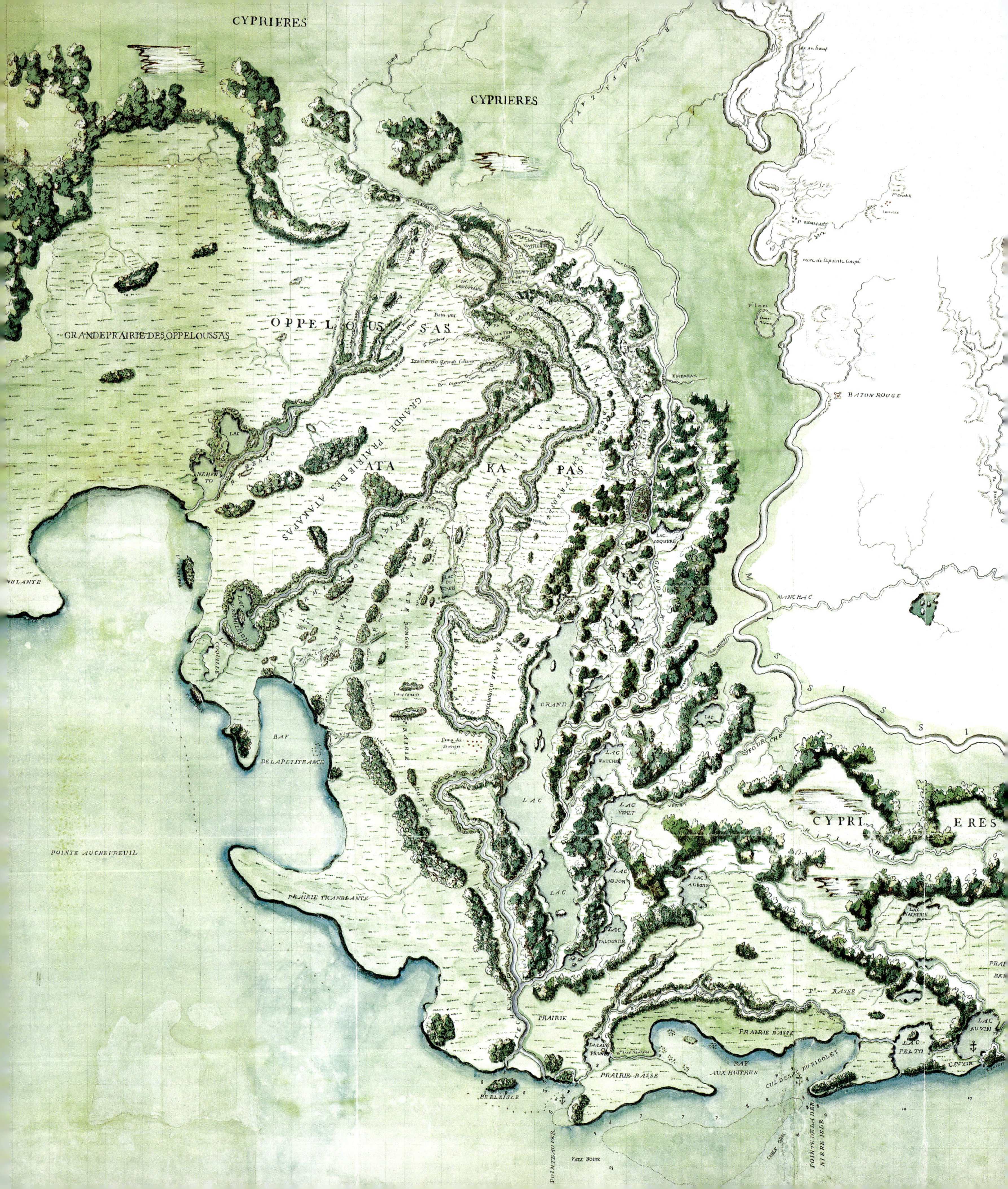

CYPRIERES
CYPRIERES
GRANDE PRAIRIE DES OPPELOUSSAS
OPPELOUSSAS
GRANDE PRAIRIE DES ATAKAPAS
ATAKAPAS
BATON ROUGE
EMBARAS
LAC COQUILLE
LAC VERRET
LAC PALOURDE
LAC AUBOIS
LAC NATCHEZ
LAC
GRAND LAC
BAY DE LA PETITE ANCE
POINTE AU CHEVREUIL
PRAIRIE TRANBLANTE
PRAIRIE
PRAIRIE BASSE
BAY AUX HUITRES
CUL DE SAC DU RIGOLET
LAC PELTO
LAC AUVIN
BELE ISLE
VASE NOIRE
CYPRI ERES
MISSISSIPI

1796: The American Saga of General Victor Collot

Gilles-Antoine LANGLOIS, *Ph.D. History, Ph.D. Town Planning, lecturer at the University of Paris XII*

Georges Henri Victor Collot, son of Jean-François Collot, a high-ranking army administrator and man of letters, and Marie-Françoise Sergent, was born at Châlons-sur-Marne, northeastern France, in 1750. He died a brigadier general and Knight of St. Louis in Paris in 1805, after devoting his life to a military career. In 1765 he joined the Chamborant hussars as a volunteer, going on to become second lieutenant (1768), lieutenant (1776), captain of the Berchény hussars (1778), aide- de-camp, and then deputy quartermaster general in Rochambeau's army for the American campaign (1780).

After the defeat of the English at Yorktown in 1781, Collot became a staff officer with the rank of lieutenant colonel. The promotions kept on coming: regimental adjutant (1787), adjutant general with the rank of colonel, then brigadier general (1791), and ultimately governor of Guadeloupe—after his rejection of the governorship of Santo Domingo. When the English landed in Guadeloupe in 1794, Collot, with no means of defense, had no choice but to surrender. Taken prisoner and paroled into the care of the Americans he traveled to Philadelphia, where he was obliged to remain despite the protests of French ambassador Pierre-Auguste Adet. Living as an exile, the general decided to make the most of his lot in the midst of the fascinating, if confused, political situation following the American and French Revolutions.

At this strange time, relations between France and America were somewhat strained. Louisiana was partly American—the east bank of the Mississippi, taken from the English—and partly Spanish—the west bank of the river and the area around New Orleans. Meanwhile the Spanish and the French were discreetly negotiating, among

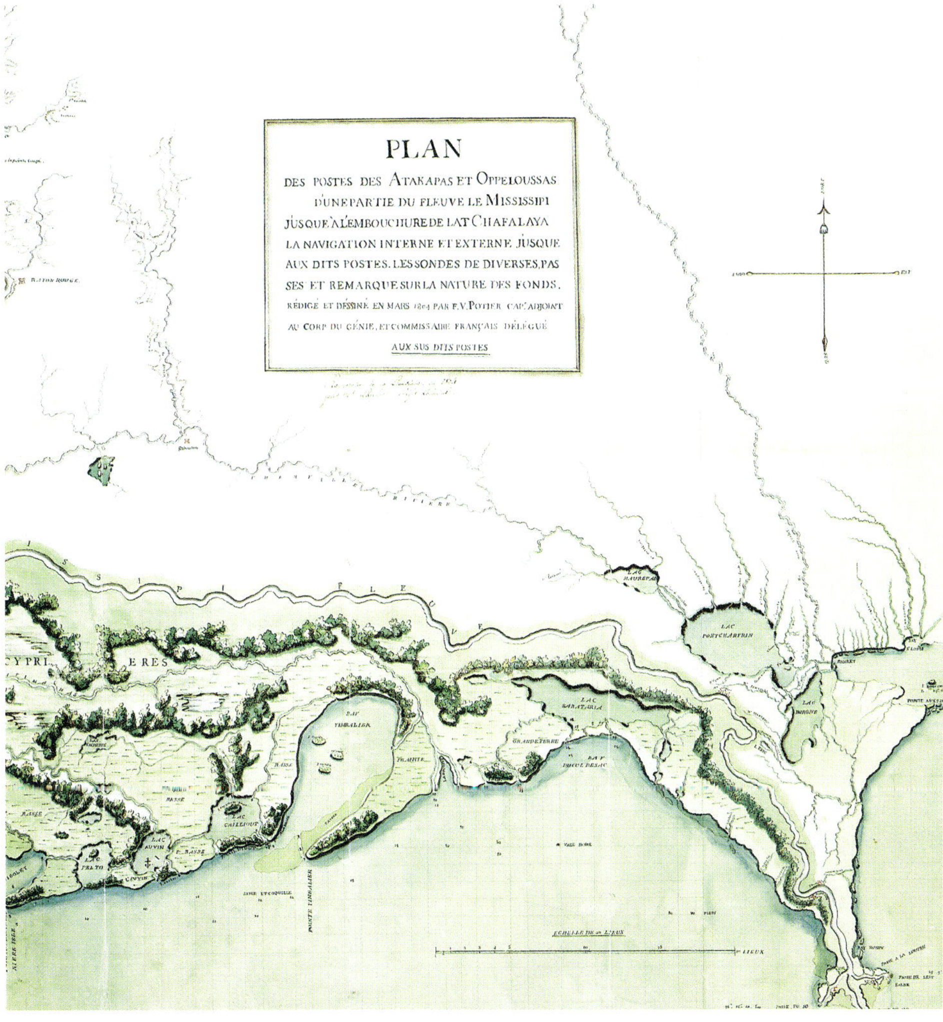

Right: Ferdinand Potier

Hand-drawn map of the Attakapas and Opelousas area, lower Mississippi basin, 1804

Service Historique de la Marine, Fort de Vincennes, France, recueil 66, pièce 7

On December 3, 1803, Colonial Prefect Laussat appointed Potier commander of the Opelousas military post, which was to be handed over to him by the Spanish. After the Louisiana Purchase, the inhabitants of the Attakapas and Opelousas area, where colonization by Acadian refugees had begun in 1770, wrote to Laussat of the sensitivity and loyalty Potier had shown in the carrying out of his duties. Meticulously drawn by the commander, this map was bought by Laussat for 300 francs, which explains how it came to be in France.

Facing page: detail

other things, the retrocession of Spanish Louisiana to France. At the same time, the Jay Treaty of 1794 (ratified 1795) between Great Britain and the United States granted the British navigation rights on the American portions of the Mississippi, shortly before the Americans reached a similar agreement with the Spanish under the terms of the Pinckney Treaty of 1796.

The Jay Treaty was badly received by the French, who saw it as a breach of the principles underpinning the Treaty of Friendship of 1778 between France and the United States. However, the latter contained a mutual guarantee of the "rights of neutral nations"—in other words, of freedom of trade for the country at peace, even when the other was at war. In 1796 the French navy was in a critical condition, reduced to a tenth of its pre-Revolution size and further weakened by regular attacks by the English. America's apparent favoritism towards the latter had a markedly adverse effect on relations between the two countries, as is clear in the diplomatic correspondence between French ambassador Pierre-Auguste Adet and American secretary of state Timothy Pickering.

Anonymous

Carte manuscrite du cours du Mississippi avec vignettes

hand-drawn map of the Mississippi prepared from the sketches by Joseph Warin for the published account of General Collot's journey 1797-1805

Service Historique de la Marine, Fort de Vincennes, France, recueil 66, pièce 7

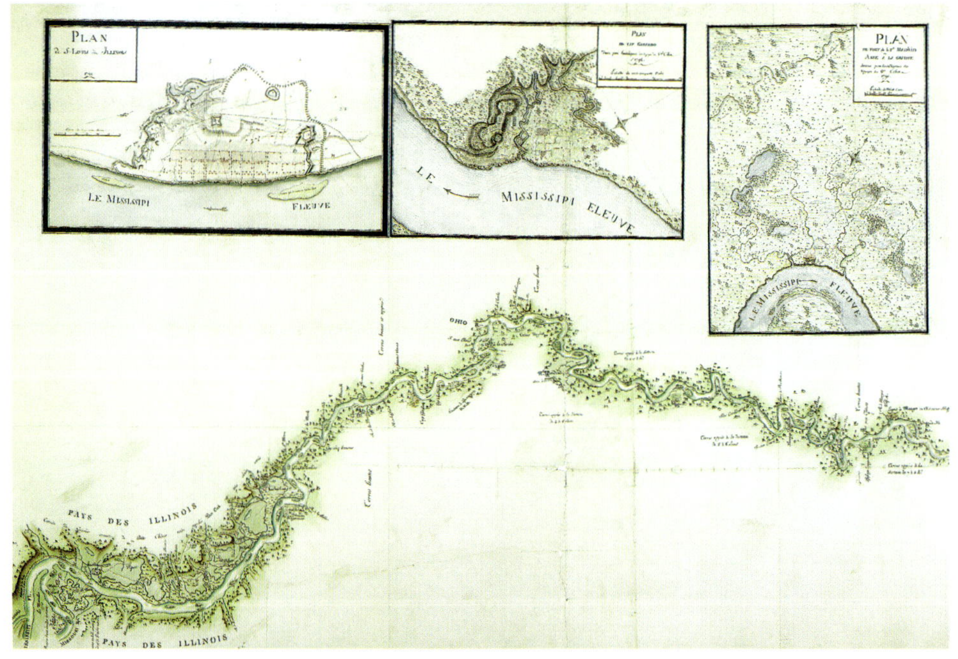

This major crisis came close to open war when, on July 7, 1798, the American president John Adams published a bill suspending all trade relations between the two countries. Faced with French protests and a period of conflict between the two countries' navies, Adams sent three commissioners to Paris to negotiate. A satisfactory solution to the crisis was found and an agreement signed in 1800, the credit going more to the commission of the French Tribunate and its secretary Adet than to the equivocal stance of foreign minister Talleyrand. The agreement annulled the treaties of 1778 and replaced them with new ones, notably involving the renunciation of all claims and indemnities—an issue that was nonetheless raised again shortly afterwards, at the time of the Louisiana Purchase.

It was in this unsettled climate, with tensions running high between Americans, English, French, and Spanish, that on March 21, 1796, Victor Collot set off down the Ohio and the Mississippi on a journey to an undisclosed destination. Was he following orders—and if so, whose? Had he even taken the trouble to ask for the necessary authorizations? Whatever the case, Collot and his faithful adjutant Joseph Warin—already at his side when he was governor of Guadeloupe—surveyed and mapped in great detail the courses of the Ohio and the Mississippi, together with the military posts and the concessions along their banks. They also took hundreds of pages of notes for a planned report on the state of the former French province.

Their journey came to an end seven months later with the general's arrest in New Orleans and his departure under heavy escort for the port of Philadelphia—Carondelet, the Spanish governor of Louisiana, considered Collot purely and simply a spy. Later, in 1804, after Louisiana had been sold to the United States, Collot made an unsuccessful attempt to publish a book retracing the course of this hazardous expedition. It was not until 1826 that his *Journey in North America* appeared in French and English versions in Paris, complete with an atlas of maps and diagrams in English, after Warin's drawings. In all, a generous dose of factual information as well as fantasy for an excursion that lasted only a few months!

In the introduction to his book Collot quotes from a letter from Adet: "I want you to know that I am retaining you in your capacity as brigadier general for the duration of the mission which I am entrusting to you." There is, however, no indication of the nature of this, supposedly secret, mission, as Governor Carondelet would observe. Nonetheless, a close reading of the *Journey* throws light on the aims of the two travelers. Before heading for Pittsburgh, formerly France's Fort Duquesne, Collot and Warin made a detour via the Alleghenies, the reason given being the need to reconnoiter the Monongahela River, a possible source of the highly strategic Ohio. They noted in passing that "for all troops other than infantry, the Alleghenies can only be crossed by forcing a passage through these narrow passes." Also included in their report were minutely detailed recommendations as to the kind of ships that should be built for the river journey to New Orleans.

Clearly this was a military intelligence mission, but one that had a political intent as well—the task being to locate people and settlements loyal to France and to draw up a political map. Collot and Warin took pleasure in liberally correcting the work of Hutchins, a geographer then regarded as an authority, but it is evident that their main concerns were political. Thus they include tables proving that a boat leaving New Orleans would take thirty-five days less to get to Knoxville by the "great liquid road" than if it left from Baltimore or Philadelphia. In other words, the Americans had everything to gain by trading with Louisiana rather than with the former English colonies. Collot was so convinced of this that, once back in France, before the publication of the *Journey*, he discussed the matter with Fulton, demonstrating to him the interest in using steamboats on the Mississippi.

The travelers' first challenge came at Cincinnati, where General Waine threatened to put the pair under arrest. At Fort Massac—short for "Massacre"—Commander Pike turned words into deeds, arresting Collot on the grounds that "he spent all his time reconnoitering the Ohio." Collot, however, showed him his notes and papers and was finally allowed to go on his way under the supervision of Captain Taylor.

Back on the road again, the soldier-explorer was quick to appreciate the siting of Fort Girardot, a Spanish military post under the command of a Frenchman named Lorimier, and of Fort St. Charles, established forty years earlier. Unique in the region in that it was built of cut stone, Fort St. Charles was now deserted. Collot was particularly struck by St. Louis, which sent him into geo-patriotic rhapsodies: "The French group worked together to form villages and towns, whereas the others are absorbed into the local population as a whole, as is the case all over the United States." He saw St. Louis as a potential command post for the entire region, in both military and economic terms.

His problems were not over, however. Letters arrived from New Orleans calling for his arrest. As Collot has it, the Spanish ambassador Jaudenés reneged on his own letters of recommendation and asked Governor Carondelet to take him into custody. Similar orders came from Philadelphia, in the form of a letter from Secretary of State Pickering. At the same time Collot learned that the English were threatening to have him murdered by hired Indian assassins. Finding himself in something of a predicament, the general acknowledged that "his journey had already created a stir and could be interpreted in a variety of ways." This led him to decline a further recommendation—this time from the ingenuous Zénon Trudeau, governor of Illinois—and to embark on the rest of his voyage more discreetly. He also took the precaution of keeping "a second journal, taking care to fill it with praise for Baron de Carondelet's administration and leaving it around for all to see, while the real journal was most carefully hidden." This precaution, as we shall see, turned out to be futile.

At Kaskaskia, Collot found himself at loggerheads with the American judge Saint-Clair. Nonetheless, he succeeded in getting the judge to sign a paper to the effect that he had had nothing to do with Collot's arrest at the hands of Captain Zebulon Pike and that he, Saint-Clair, had told Pike that Collot's only concern was the surveying of the Ohio River. Returning to Fort Girardot, he claims to have been warned by Lorimier that the English were preparing to invade Louisiana with the support of a number of Indian tribes. Collot urged the commander to warn Trudeau, while he himself informed Governor Carondelet, invoking the old French-Spanish alliance. When his letter eventually reached Carondelet, the latter was not especially troubled. The Spanish, after all, had just signed a treaty with the United States. Even so, Collot, now in Natchez and learning that a certain Chisholm had set the operation in motion from Tennessee, aiming at the area between St. Louis and Baton Rouge, warned local commander Manuel Gayoso of the English plan. Gayoso's reaction was one of—probably hypocritical—surprise.

In Collot's judgement the Spanish colony was now in an impossible position, given its lack of an adequate defense network and the size of the local population—not so much the Indians, who had been decimated, as the Americans: "The left bank of the river being already heavily populated and the right bank deserted, any military post set up by the Spanish on the right bank, for any reason other than to indicate the boundaries, will be absolutely useless as long as the political situation with regard to the United States remains unchanged."

And then tragedy struck, Joseph Warin was wounded by the two Chickasaw Indians Collot had seen stalking them since Illinois. On October 27, Collot and his wounded companion were arrested at dawn at the home of Etienne Boré. After being escorted through the crowd near the Place d'Armes in New Orleans, the two were locked up in Fort St. Charles, which became the target for sarcastic observations by Collot: "There can be no denying that these miniature forts are nicely painted and well maintained, but with their size and ridiculous layout they are more like children's playthings than military establishments. There is not one that could not be attacked, and that five hundred determined men with swords could not overrun."

Things were now moving fast. Collot presented Carondelet with the papers he claimed provided the authorization for his journey; Warin died during the night. Carondelet lent Collot a house in the town and demanded that he hand over his papers and maps, which were then copied, at Carondelet's orders, by Gilbert Guillemard, an engineer and lieutenant colonel in the Spanish service. After protesting Carondelet's refusal to return

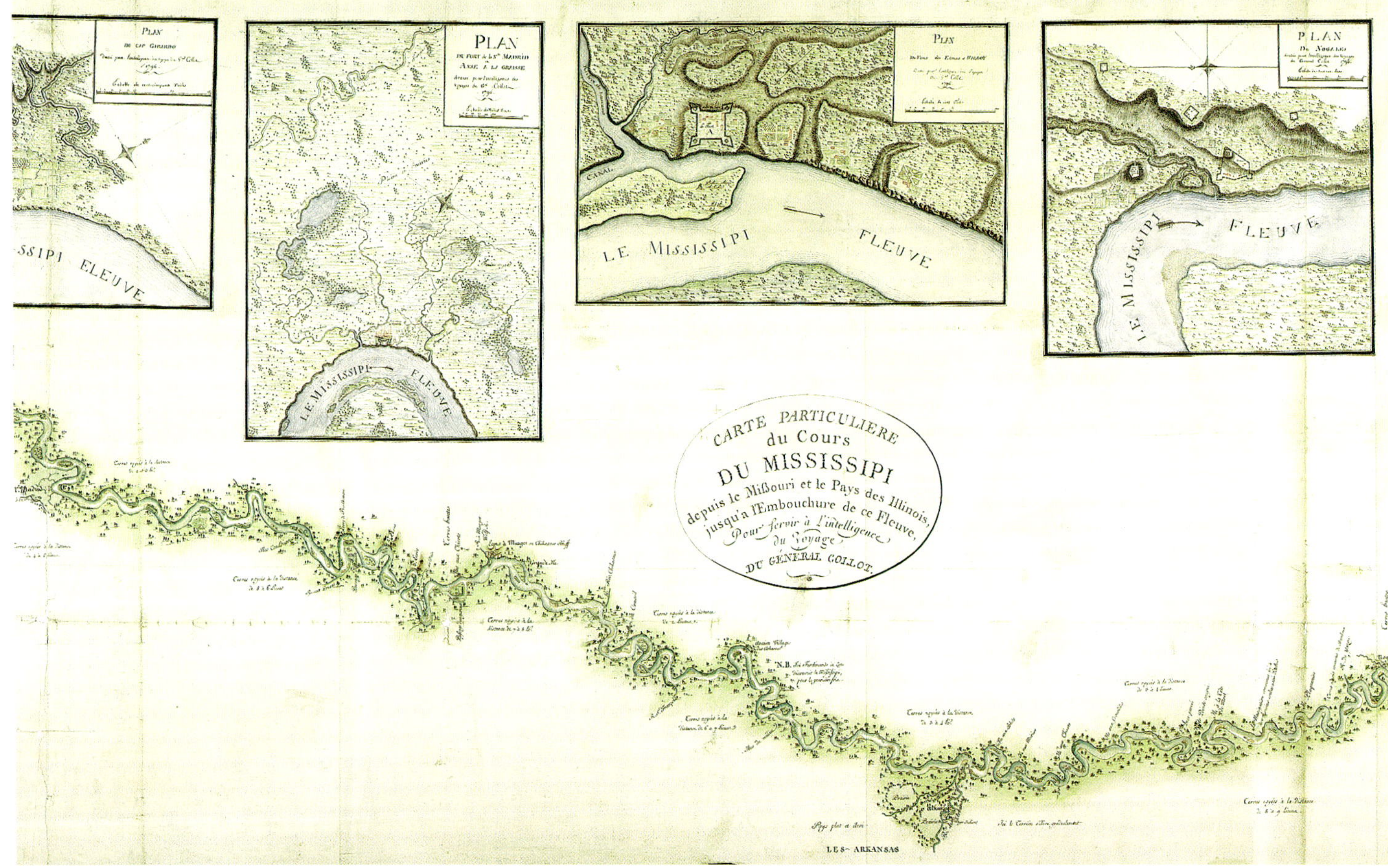

some of the documents, Collot took ship at La Balise on December 1. Arriving in Philadelphia, he at once wrote to the king of Spain, suggesting—most likely as a way of putting himself in the clear—how His Highness might best react to the anticipated English attack. Thus his notion of defense—France and Spain united against England—was nothing if not anachronistic.

The general was not to achieve recognition in his own country. On his return to France he was chosen by Napoleon Bonaparte, in February 1801, as captain general in charge of the French expedition that would receive Louisiana from the Spanish. Shortly afterwards, however, the minister for the navy informed Bonaparte that the Americans were already privy to this supposedly secret mission, and Bonaparte decided to entrust it to Bernadotte, whom he wanted out of France. Once again America's spies demonstrated their efficiency. Less than a month later, in February 1802, news of the Bernadotte expedition was out, and ultimately the last act in the history of French Louisiana was played out under General Collot and Prefect Laussat.

To the very end Collot was dogged by bad luck. Bonaparte sold Louisiana, and America was now the least of his concerns. Yet there remain those splendid large-scale maps of the courses of the Ohio, the Missouri, the Mobile, and the Mississippi, hand drawn by Warin and Collot, as testimony to a military vision of the American South: Spain and France against England and America on the majestic watercourse running from St. Louis to New Orleans. Elegant, incomparably precise and scrupulously prepared for the publication of Collot's book, the maps are ornamented with views and details that are nothing short of enchanting. Yet they seem today mere enigmatic vestiges of some vast geopolitical plan. What was this strange dance the former governor of Guadeloupe was led on by four opposing powers? Or, more exactly, did not the general's adventures only highlight the unrelenting nature of a conflict, masked by meaningless treaties, involving three European powers and a young federal state in search of independence?

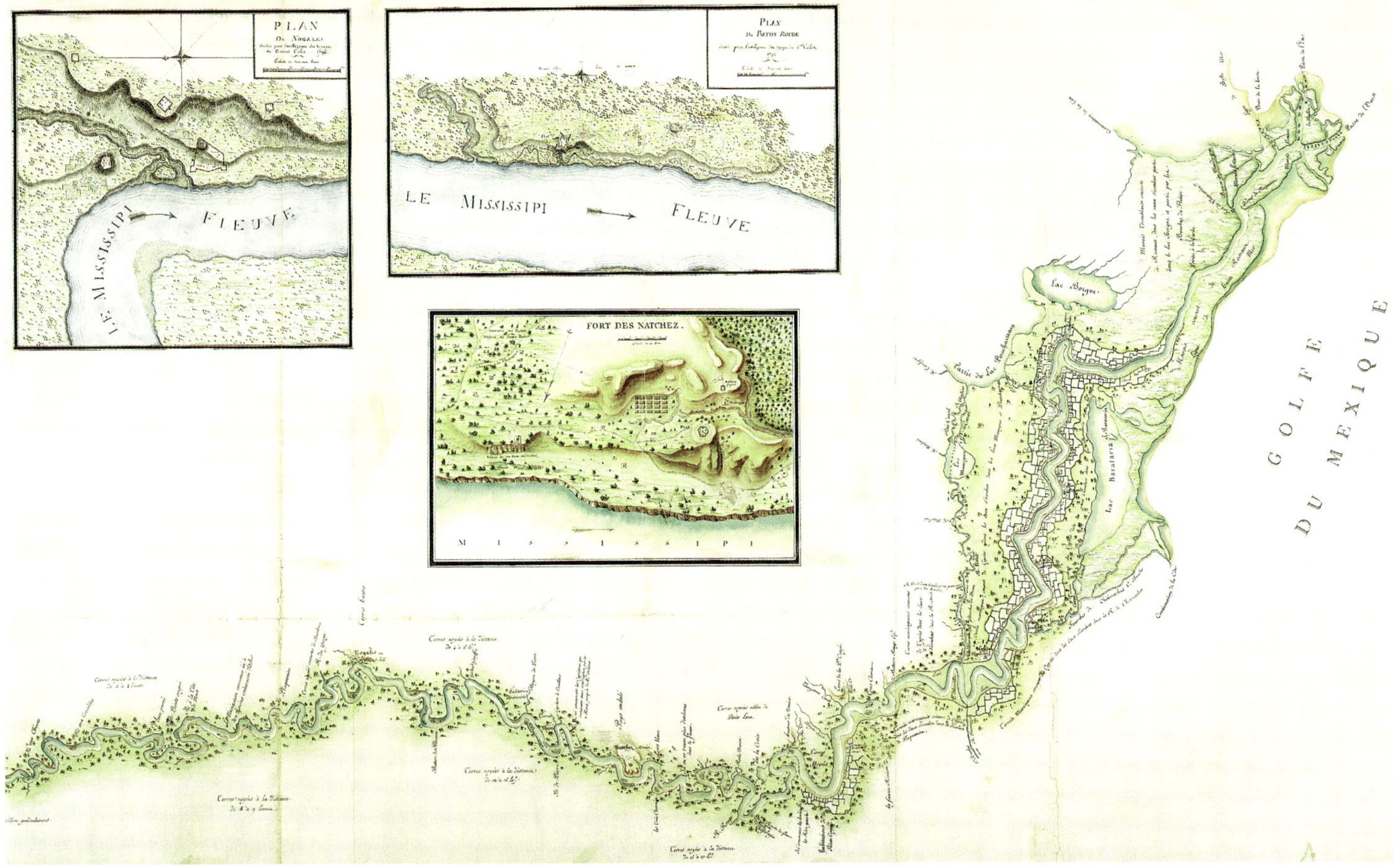

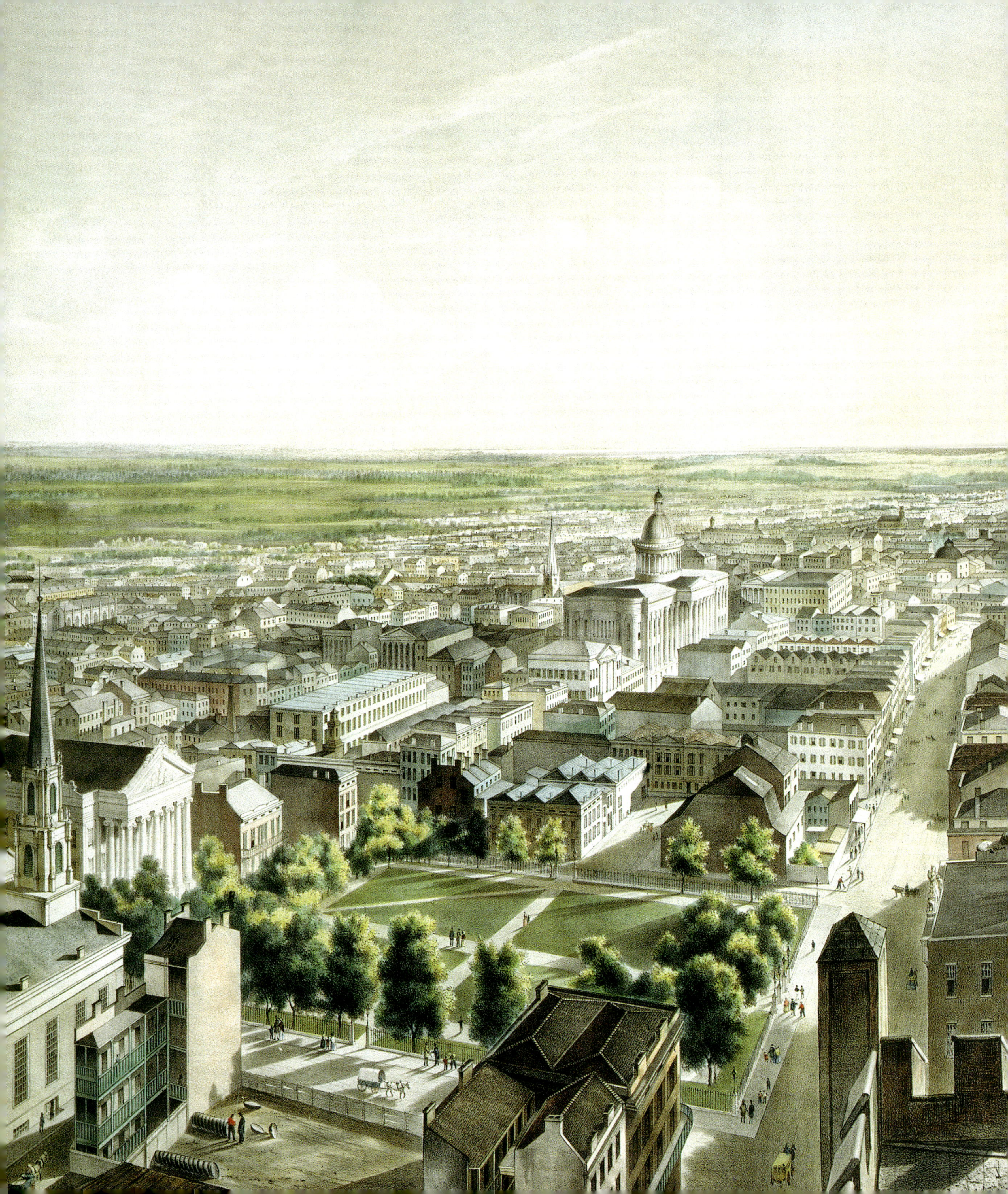

History of New Orleans

John T. MAGILL, *Curator/Head of Research Services, The Historic New Orleans Collection*

New Orleans, with its colorful history, its legends of pirates, duels at dawn, and voodoo rites at midnight, is undoubtedly one of the most romantic cities in America. The character of this enthralling city has been built by the interaction among the various peoples who settled there and by the city's location on the flat, marshy delta of the Mississippi River. Today New Orleans is an agglomeration of 1.4 million people and one of the most instantly recognizable places on earth. The city's life is enlivened by jazz, a singular cuisine, its own particular architecture, and a relaxed attitude toward life that separates it from much of the rest of the United States. New Orleans is also one of the greatest ports in the world, serving as gateway to the Mississippi River valley. It is a city whose reason for being is the Mississippi and whose wealth and position have been dictated by that mighty waterway.

In 1718, Jean Baptiste Le Moyne, sieur de Bienville founded New Orleans on the banks of the Mississippi River. The city's site, considered a folly by many people, presented a multitude of problems. The low lying, swampy area was difficult to drain, while spring floods from the Mississippi River, wind-driven water from shallow Lake Pontchartrain, and drenching subtropical rains often caused flooding. Before the introduction of massive drainage pumps in the early twentieth century, New Orleans clung to the relatively high riverfront—about ten feet above sea level—and some adjoining ridges that also protrude a few feet above their surroundings.

In spite of the drawbacks, the location was not chosen by accident. The city's site at the head of a sweeping curve in the river—from which New Orleans's nickname, the Crescent City, was later de-

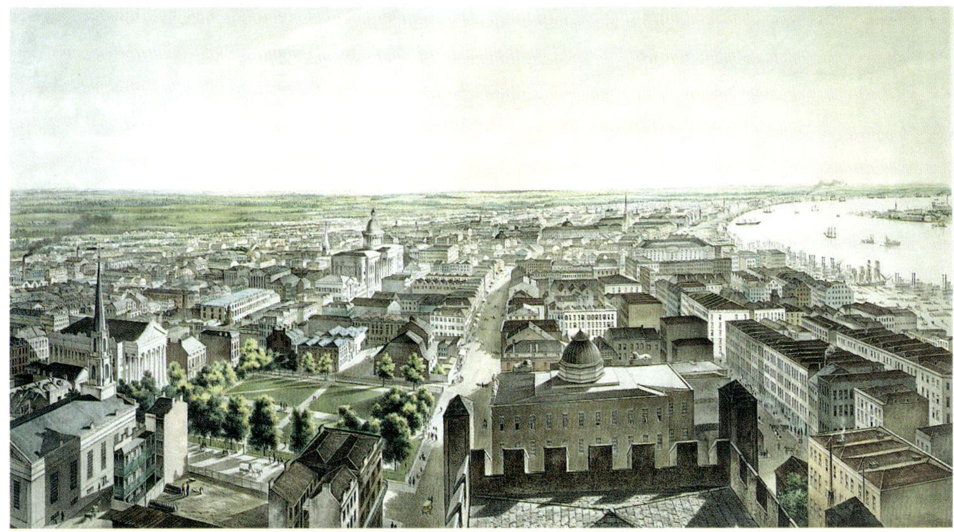

John William Hill
and Benjamin Franklin Smith, Jr.
New Orleans from St. Patrick's Church, 1852
lithograph with watercolor
The Historic New Orleans Collection 1954.3

In the mid-nineteenth century, bird's-eye views of cities were very popular. Some of the finest views of American cities came from the firm of John William Hill (1812-1879) and Benjamin F. Smith (1830-1927) in New York. When Hill and Smith produced this splendid view of New Orleans in 1852, the city, with a population of about 150,000, was by far the largest in the South and among the largest in the United States. The park to the left is Lafayette Square, named for a visit to the city by the marquis de Lafayette in 1825.
The Greek Revival building to the left of the park is City Hall, which still stands but is now called Gallier Hall for its architect, since it no longer serves as City Hall. Greek Revival architecture was extremely popular in New Orleans at the time. The domed building in the middle distance is the grand St. Charles Hotel. Built in 1836, the hotel burned down before this view was made and was rebuilt without a dome. Evident in this view is the proximity of open country, accurately showing the city concentrated on the relatively high and less flood-prone ground along the river.

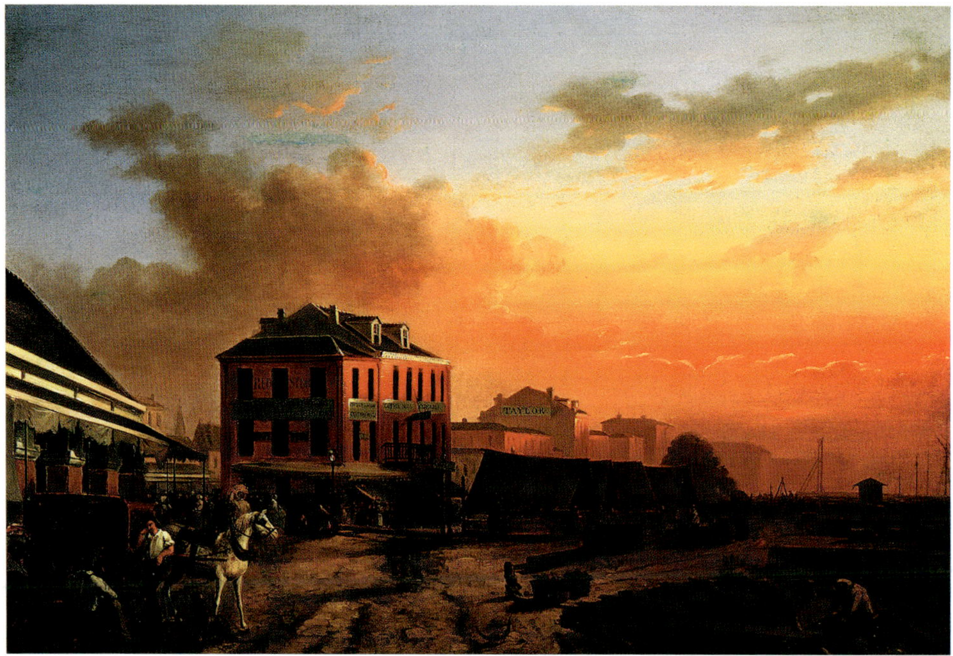

Louis Dominique Grandjean Develle
French Market and Red Store
between 1840 and 1850

oil on canvas
The Historic New Orleans Collection 1948.1

Louis Dominique Grandjean Develle (1799-1868) was born in Paris; by 1829 he had immigrated to New Orleans where he worked as a scene painter. This eye-catching painting by Develle shows part of the Mississippi riverfront at the French Quarter and a portion of the French Market. The market was actually established by Spanish authorities in the 1760s and in the 1790s was moved to a site near where it stands today. Over a period of about seventy years, the market was steadily expanded to cover about six city blocks. The no-longer extant Red Stores were privately built about 1840; replicas built in the 1970s now stand close to the site of the original buildings. In the late 1930s the entire French Market, now a popular tourist attraction, was essentially rebuilt. Develle also shows a bit of the harbor as it looked before a long, wide-plank wharf was built parallel to the river. In Develle's painting one sees the bare earthen levee with wooden piers jutting out over the water, which was typical at that time.

rived—permitted surveillance of long stretches of the river in order to provide protection from other colonial powers that might attempt to wrest control of the river from France. Other powers were well aware that whoever controlled the Mississippi River could control much of North America.

The Native Americans of the region had long understood its waterways and land links. One of their trade routes was along a three-mile portage connecting the tip of Bayou St. John and the Mississippi River. This route influenced the placement of New Orleans, not only because of the estab-

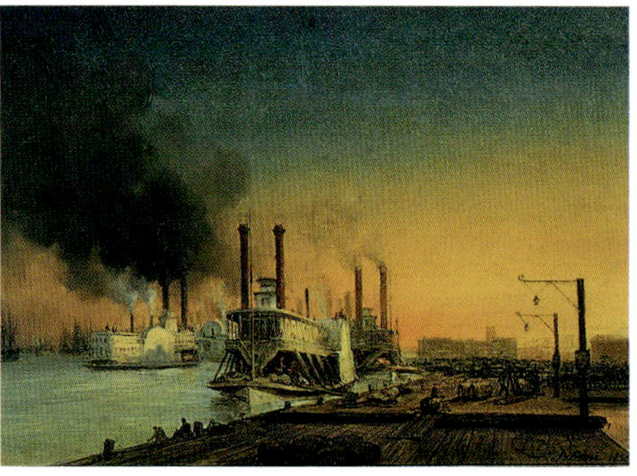

Hyppolite Victor Valentin Sebron
Bateaux à Vapeur Géants, 1850

oil on canvas
The Historic New Orleans Collection 1958.14

This oil sketch, which was the basis for a larger and more detailed painting, provides a splendid impression of the port of New Orleans during the height of the city's golden days of prosperity. Here the artist shows the profusion of steamboats that called at New Orleans after plying the Mississippi River system with goods and passengers. The plank wharves and piers lined the riverfront for miles; different types of vessels, such as riverboats, sailing ships, barges, and keelboats, were docked in assigned sections of the port. Hyppolite Sebron (1801-1879), a native of France, worked in the United States only between 1849 and 1855. While in the United States, he spent most of his time in New York City and New Orleans. Sebron was most famous for his spectacularly colored and specially illuminated dioramas, which were exhibited extensively in the United States and Europe. His view of riverboats at New Orleans clearly reveals his talent for conveying light and color.

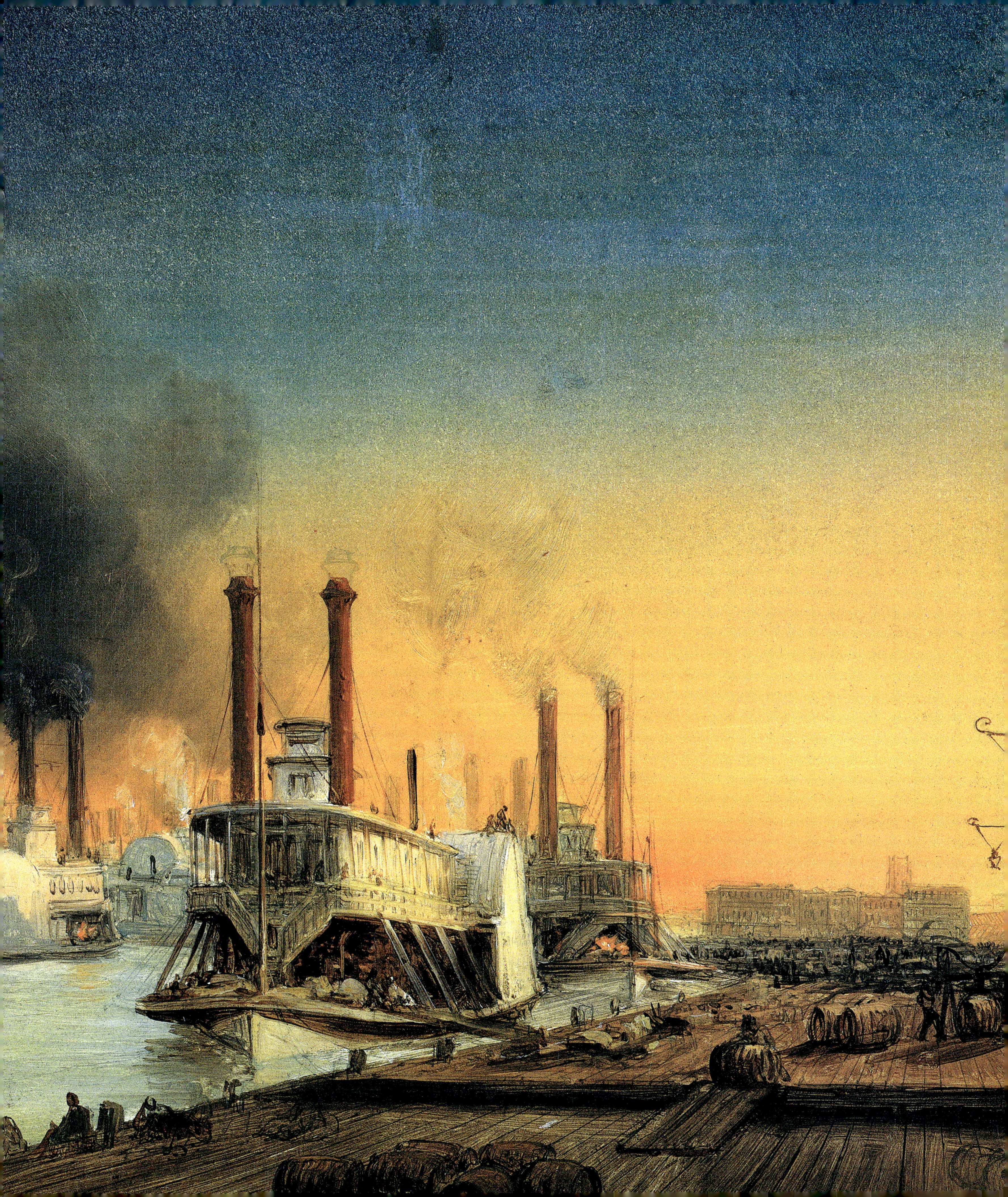

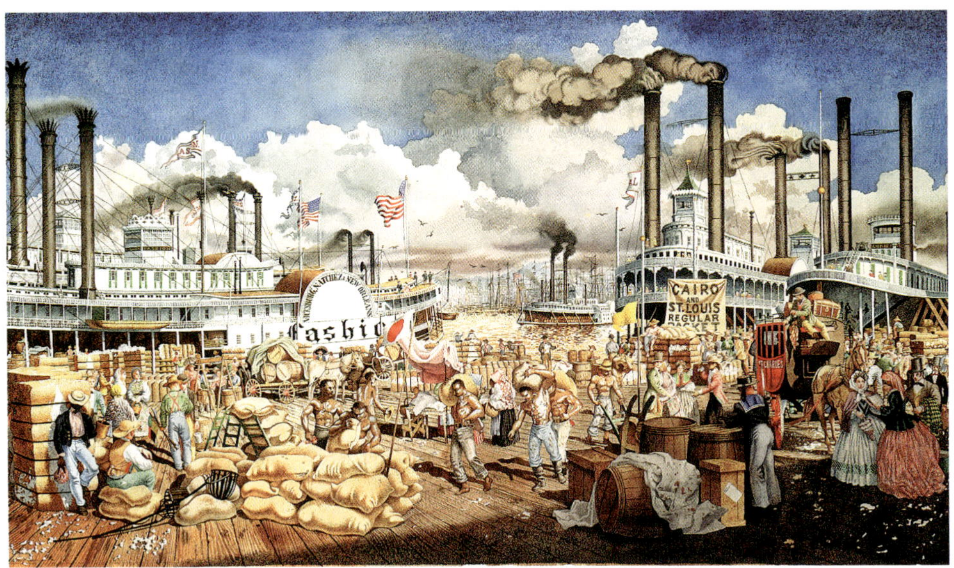

Boyd Cruise

The Levee at New Orleans ca. 1859, 1959

watercolor on paper

The Historic New Orleans Collection 1992.94
gift of Mr. and Mrs. Raymond H. Kierr in memory of Robert M. Kierr

Boyd Cruise (1909-1988), the first director of The Historic New Orleans Collection, is noted for his paintings depicting, with extraordinary detail, the streets and buildings of New Orleans as they appeared prior to the Civil War. In this painting Cruise shows the wharves of the city as they would have appeared in 1859. At that time, the wharves swarmed with sailing vessels, oceangoing steamboats, and, most impressively, tall-stacked riverboats, of which four thousand arrived at New Orleans in that year alone. Cruise shows the hustle and bustle of business in the city; its wealth is evident in the merchandise piled on the wharf. By 1859, the wide-plank wharf shown here paralleled the river for miles. It was not simply a place for laborers; here one could meet businessmen, tourists, and fashionable promenaders.

lished trade position, but because the portage and Bayou St. John allowed direct access to Lake Pontchartrain and the Gulf of Mexico, allowing ships to bypass the longer, more treacherous Mississippi River route to the gulf.

In 1721, military engineer Adrien de Pauger implemented a town plan based upon the design of his superior, Le Blond de la Tour. De Pauger laid out the city in a grid pattern, still recognizable today, with streets meeting at right angles and focusing on the Place d'Armes (present-day Jackson Square). The Church of St. Louis (now the St. Louis Cathedral) was located at the back of the square, facing the river. The old town is now generally called the French Quarter or the Vieux Carré, although in the past it was referred to by such names as French Town and the Italian Quarters, the latter reflecting the many Italian immigrants who inhabited the neighborhood around 1900.

Although New Orleans's economy struggled at first, its port grew to become one of the most important international shipping centers in the world. Nearby, agriculture flourished on plantations where initially indigo, and later rice and sugar were grown. Originally grants from the French Crown, plantations lined the Mississippi River, the bayous, and a few high land ridges, such as Bayou Road, the portage that connected the city and Bayou St. John. These tracts, generally long and narrow, stretched back from relatively high, arable land into the swamps and fronted on either a waterway or trade route.

Louisiana became a Spanish possession in 1762. By the end of the eighteenth century, the port of New Orleans had emerged as one of the most important trade centers for the fledgling United States, since it was the most accessible port of deposit for the rapidly growing agricultural region west of the Appalachian Mountains. When Spanish authorities threatened to revoke the American right of deposit at New Orleans in 1802, President Thomas Jefferson sought to purchase New Orleans and its nearby area—then commonly called the Isle d'Orléans—from France. France had regained ownership of the territory from Spain in 1800. Control of New Orleans and unencumbered docking rights there were of such importance to the United States that in 1803 when Napoleon offered to sell France's entire Louisiana claim, the United States agreed to purchase the huge, mostly uncharted territory.

With its port in American hands, New Orleans underwent a period of dramatic growth. In the 1820s and 1830s, it became

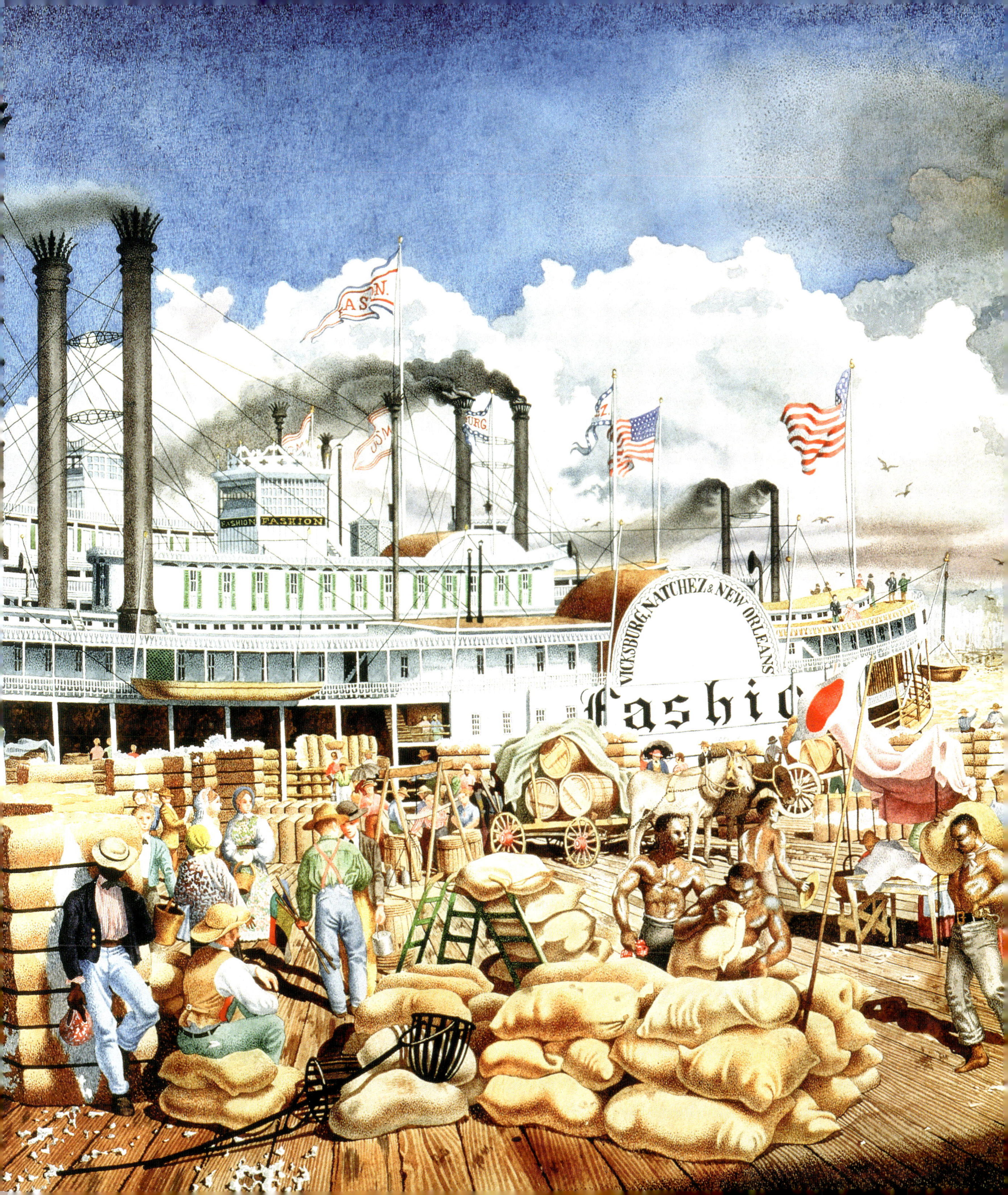
FASHION FASHION
VICKSBURG, NATCHEZ & NEW ORLEANS

one of the fastest growing cities in America. The days of booming prosperity saw the population swell from about 8,000 in 1800 to 102,000 in 1840. The city became not only the fourth largest in the young nation, but one of the wealthiest. The golden days lasted until the mid-nineteenth century, which brought the turmoil of the Civil War and postwar Reconstruction. The city's worldly importance has long been proclaimed along its wharves. Indeed, at one time a sizable portion of the city's business took place there—traders, stevedores, draymen, and laborers haggled and maneuvered around cotton bales, sugar barrels, and other products destined for all corners of the world. Initially, sailing ships simply docked directly at the city's earthen levee, but by the mid-nineteenth century a wide-plank wharf extended for miles along the riverfront. The port was so densely lined with ships that it was said that a person could walk from deck to deck without wetting his feet.

In 1812 the first steam-powered riverboat, aptly named the *New Orleans*, descended the river to New Orleans from Pittsburgh. Within a few years, these vessels, which ranged from utilitarian produce carriers to stately floating palaces, successfully tied together trade throughout the Mississippi Valley. In the last half of the nineteenth century, when "King Cotton" fueled the economy of the South, tall riverboats lined the New Orleans riverfront. Now long gone as a mode of transportation, the romantic image of the Mississippi riverboat still symbolizes nineteenth-century life and travel along the mighty river and its tributaries.

E. R.

Ursuline Convent on the Mississippi River, 1895

oil on canvas

The Historic New Orleans Collection 1960.28

An unidentified painter who signed this work only with initials provided a charming impression of the riverfront along the downriver outskirts of New Orleans in 1895. At that time the area, about three miles from the French Quarter, was only sparsely developed with a scattering of old plantation buildings, a few newer houses, and some small manufacturing businesses. The atmosphere was that of a small village. Dominating this painting are the roof and clock of the 1824 Ursuline Convent, which served the Ursulines after they moved from their convent in the French Quarter. In 1912 the Ursulines moved to yet another location, and the riverfront convent was demolished for the construction of a canal connecting the Mississippi River and Lake Pontchartrain that opened in 1923.

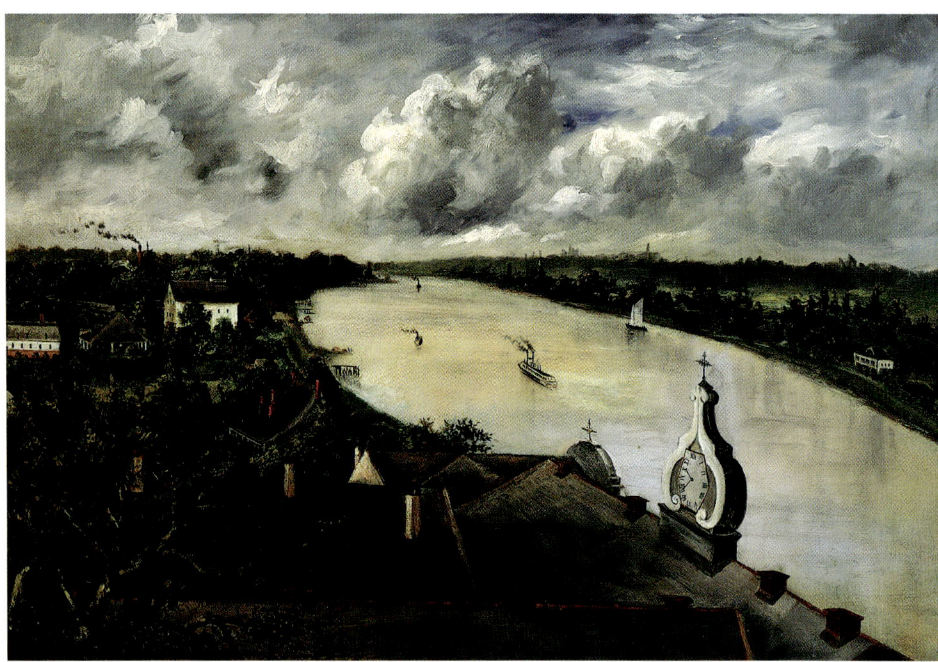

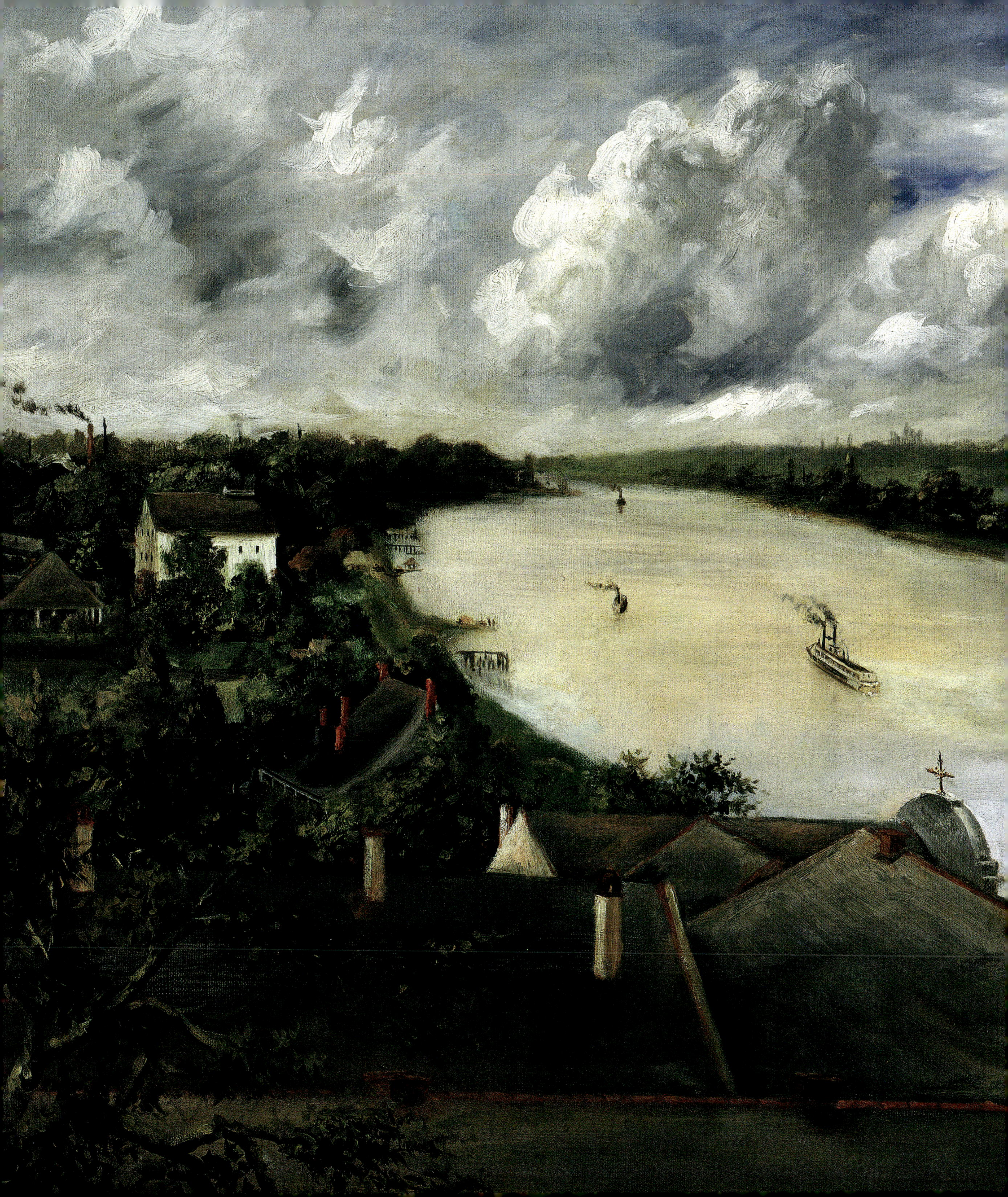

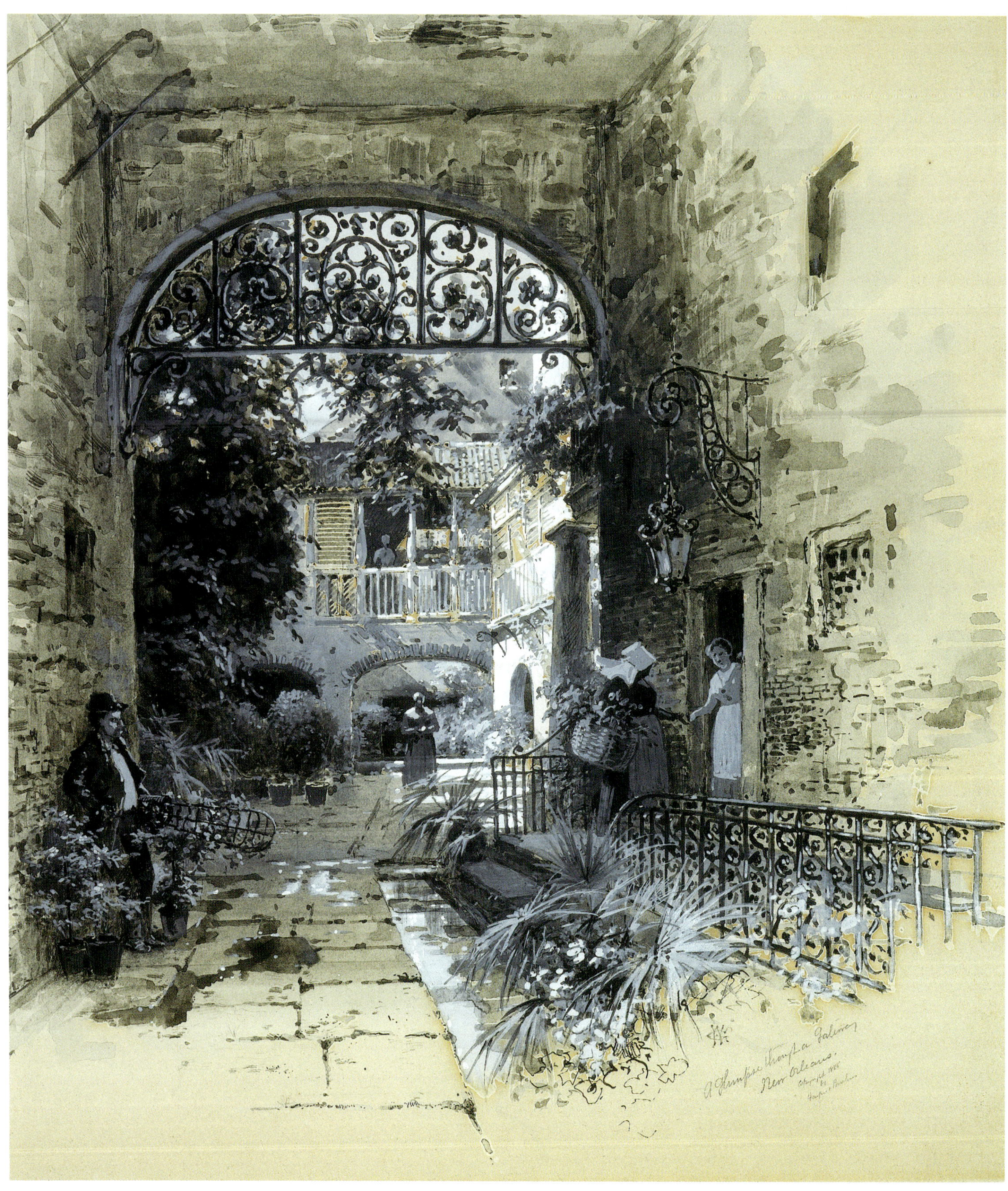
New Orleans.

The growth of the Crescent City during the late eighteenth and nineteenth centuries is revealed in many of its buildings, especially houses, which became larger and more elaborate as time passed. Today, only one building remains in the city from the French period. The former Ursuline Convent in the French Quarter, the oldest structure in the Mississippi Valley, was begun in 1745. It has not served as a convent since 1824 when the Ursuline nuns moved downriver to another location, which has since been demolished. The French Quarter convent now houses the archives of the Archdiocese of New Orleans.

Because early building materials and techniques were not well suited to New Orleans's climate and terrain, the earliest structures quickly crumbled. Two disastrous fires in 1788 and 1794 consumed much of the city. Following the fires, Spanish authorities enacted more stringent regulations requiring the use of plaster over brick-and-timber construction, as well as fireproof roofing materials such as tile or slate. Houses were built up to the sidewalk, rather than set back, to further retard the spread of fires. As buildings increased in number, new walls created courtyards which would become common throughout the old French Quarter. Beginning in the 1790s, expensive wrought iron began to grace government buildings and mansions. Less expensive, mass-produced cast iron did not appear in quantity until the late 1830s, when it took the entire city—even the American sector—by storm. When ironwork fell from fashion around 1900, it was removed from many of the city's buildings, but this was not the case in the French Quarter. Because the neighborhood had

William Hamilton Gibson

A Glimpse through a Gateway New Orleans, ca. 1888

ink and watercolor on board
The Historic New Orleans Collection 1960.65

Artists and illustrators have long been interested in the picturesque qualities of New Orleans. This was especially true in the 1880s when the city's exotic charms were often depicted in books and magazines. One such artist of the period was William Hamilton Gibson (1850-1896) who came to New Orleans on assignment for Harper and Brothers. At a time when people were beginning to perceive a visual uniformity in most cities, the unique character of New Orleans was highly appealing, especially in the French Quarter where there were French, Spanish, and American styles. Gibson shows the courtyard and ironwork, hallmarks of the French Quarter, in this inviting space in the midst of the crowded city. The courtyard depicted is particularly elegant; at the time many were utilitarian areas where the family wash was hung out to dry and farm animals roamed.

P. Langlumé
after Félix Achille de Beaupoil,
marquis de Saint-Aulaire

Vue d'une Rue du Faubourg Ste. Marie, Nelle. Orléans, ca. 1821

lithograph with watercolor
The Historic New Orleans Collection 1937.2.3

In 1820 Félix Achille de Beaupoil, marquis de Saint-Aulaire (b. 1801) visited New Orleans and made several drawings of the city that were printed by Paris lithographer P. Langlumé in 1821. One of the views was of Faubourg St. Mary. Established in 1788 as the first suburb of New Orleans, Faubourg St. Mary became popular with Americans as they moved into the city. Slavery was an integral part of the New Orleans economy at the time. Saint-Aulaire's view includes several African American slaves cleaning gutters and a female slave wearing a metal restraining collar. At the time of Saint-Aulaire's visit, Faubourg St. Mary was still a sparsely settled residential neighborhood marked by spacious houses set in large yards surrounded by wooden fences; woods and swamps were nearby. The countrified environment did not last long; within a decade, Faubourg St. Mary would become the city's central business district.

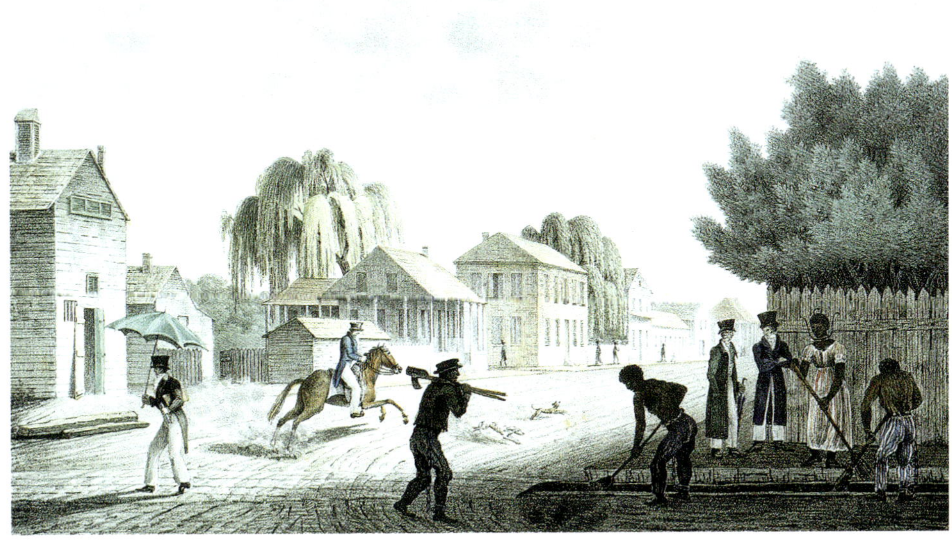

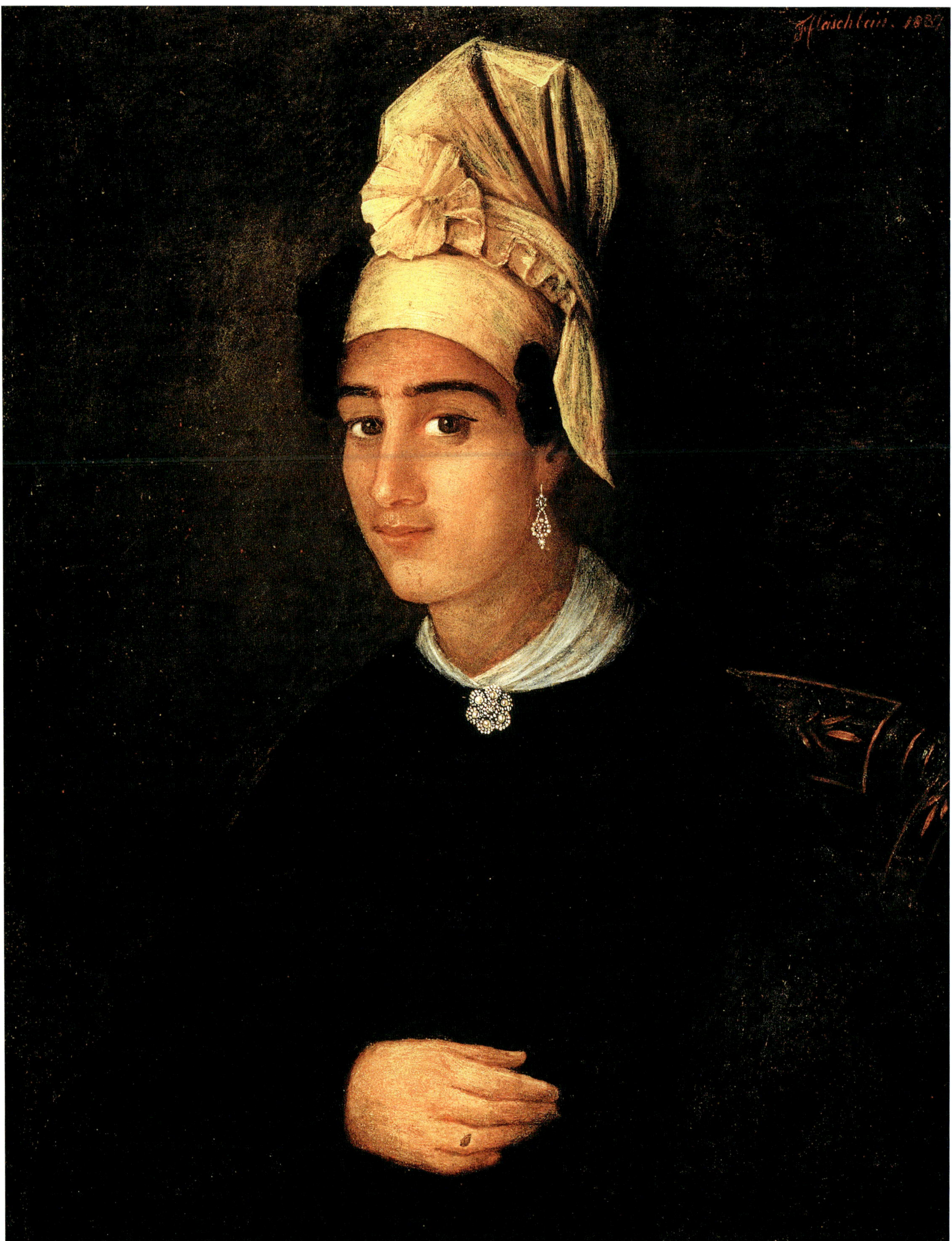

become poor and ramshackle by then, ironwork remained intact, mainly due to neglect. Today ironwork is a hallmark of French Quarter architecture.

The typical residential building type of late eighteenth- and early nineteenth-century New Orleans was the one-story Creole cottage. Built of plastered brick and timber, only a few examples remain, although they once served as the standard working-class dwelling in the city. Many Creole cottages were demolished in the latter part of the nineteenth century and replaced by long, narrow, wooden "shotguns"—houses only one room wide with doors arranged one directly behind the other. It has been said that a bullet shot through the front door will exit through the back door. Shotgun houses were the standard working-class residence in New Orleans during the late nineteenth and early twentieth centuries. They were built throughout the city, and large numbers are still standing.

As the population of early nineteenth-century New Orleans mushroomed, the city steadily expanded beyond the limits of the town arranged by its French founders. Plantations lining the river above and below New Orleans were subdivided by their owners, one after the other, to capitalize on the expanding need for housing. The first suburb, located just upriver from the city, was called Faubourg St. Mary. Dating from 1788, the section became popular with Americans and other European immigrants. As late as about 1830 the French Quarter still housed the city's main banks and retail establishments, but Faubourg St. Mary was beginning to attract business away from the original city. By the Civil War,

François Fleischbein

Portrait of a Free Woman of Color, 1837

oil on canvas

The Historic New Orleans Collection 1985.212

Free people of color made up an important segment of the population of New Orleans before the Civil War. Often of mixed ancestry, free people of color usually had French names, French manners, and were practicing Roman Catholics. Bavarian-born Franz (Gallicized in New Orleans to François) Joseph Fleischbein (1801-1868) painted this portrait of a free woman of color who may have been his family servant, Betsy. She wears a tignon, a Caribbean-style headdress, signifying her free status. Free people of color were often artisans and business owners; some amassed considerable wealth, owned substantial amounts of property, and even owned slaves.

Anonymous

Slave Auction, ca. 1832

ink and watercolor

The Historic New Orleans Collection 1941.3

This primitive watercolor by an anonymous artist shows the sale of a young African slave in the early 1830s. New Orleans had a number of auction companies and holding pens that specialized in the sale of slaves. Often held under the elegant rotundas of the city's grandest hotels—the St. Louis in the French Quarter and the St. Charles in the American sector—auctions offered everything from art and furniture to slaves at any given sale. Although New Orleans was one of the largest slave markets in America, the city itself did not have a very large slave population, since the maintenance of slaves in an urban area was prohibitively expensive for all but the rich. In the remainder of Louisiana about 50 percent of the population was African American, and virtually all were enslaved as plantation labor.

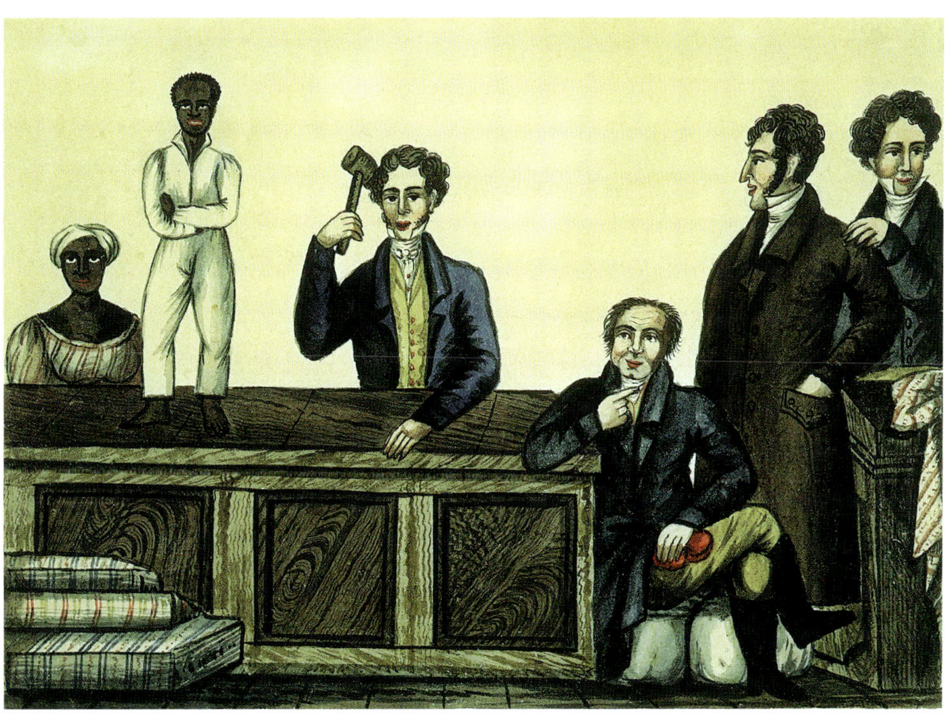

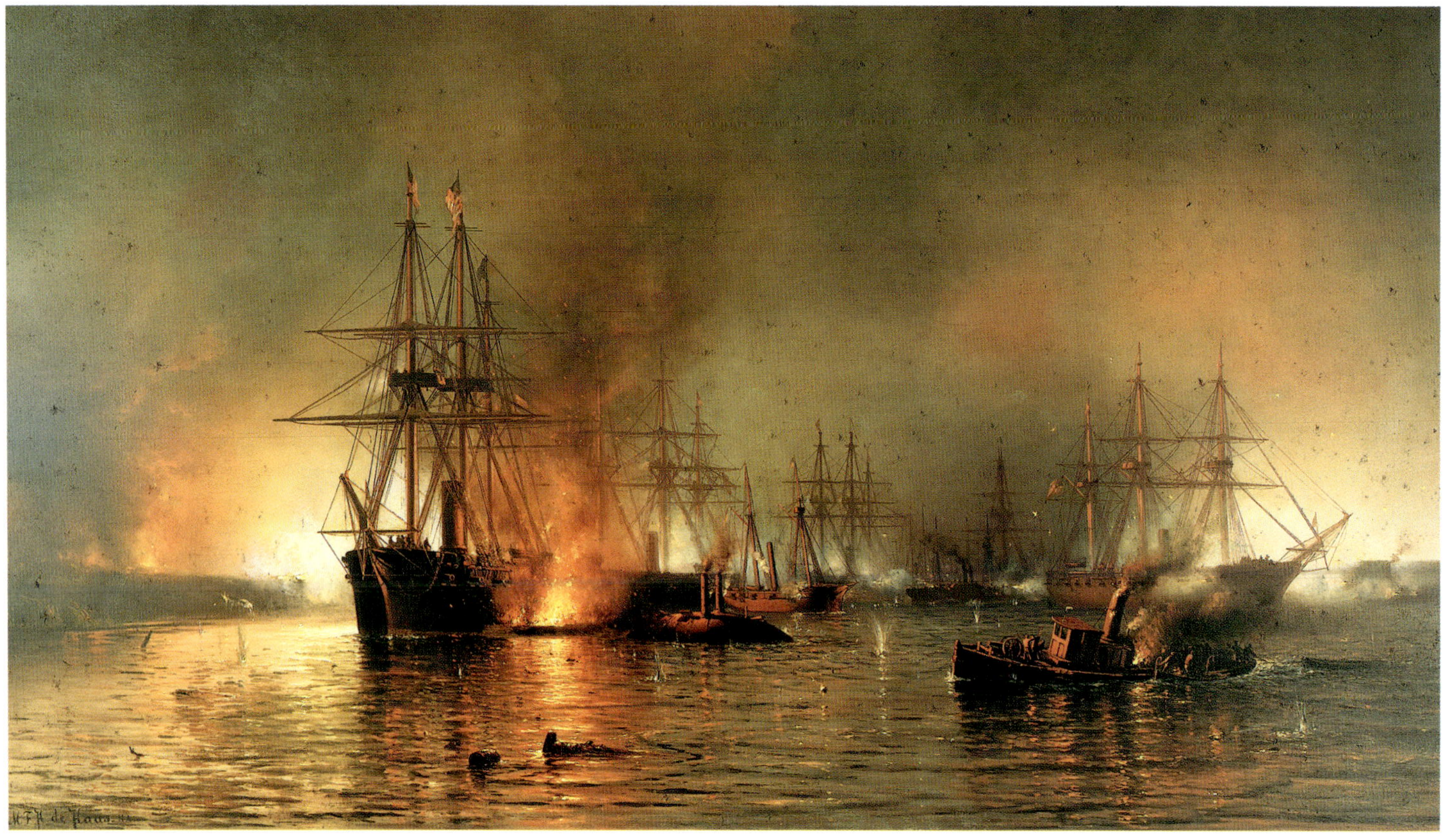

Mauritz Frederik Hendrik de Haas

Farragut's Fleet Passing the Forts below New Orleans, between 1863 and 1867

oil on canvas

The Historic New Orleans Collection 1974.80

This impressive painting depicts the Civil War bombardment of Forts St. Philip and Jackson by a United States naval fleet under Flag Officer (later Admiral) David Glasgow Farragut in April 1862. The forts were placed opposite each other in order to protect New Orleans from invasion; but after a heated battle the federal fleet was able to sail between the forts, over a chain connecting them, and capture New Orleans. A major turning point in the war, the capture of New Orleans not only damaged Southern morale, but brought about the destruction of the Confederate navy and prompted France and Great Britain to decide against supporting the Confederacy. Dutch-born painter Mauritz de Haas (1832-1895) did not witness the battle, but based his work primarily on Farragut's description of the event. De Haas painted several other naval scenes for Farragut in which the admiral played a role. Prior to coming to the United States in 1859, de Haas was a member of the Dutch navy and one of its official painters.

Faubourg St. Mary had become the city's central business district, a position it still holds. In the French Quarter, once-proud buildings were converted into rooming houses and warehouses, or torn down. In recent years preservation efforts have helped save one of the most important stocks of historic buildings in the United States and have made the French Quarter a center of the local tourist industry.

Canal Street—named for a canal that was never built—separates the French Quarter and the American section. By the 1850s this wide thoroughfare had become not only the city's main street, but the heart of its retail trade. Here residents gathered for Christmas Eve and festivals like Mardi Gras, as well as for public demonstrations. It has been said that Canal Street was the one

M. H. Kimball

Rebecca, Charley and Rosa, Slave Children from New Orleans, 1863

albumen photoprint mounted on board
The Historic New Orleans Collection 1992.68.4

Abraham Lincoln's Emancipation Proclamation of 1862 freed slaves in many sections of the South. Some abolitionists in the North were quick to use former slaves as propaganda for their efforts to further improve the lives of African Americans. Freed slave children were taken to northern cities for publicity purposes. Some of the youngsters, such as these, were photographed; the proceeds from the sale of the pictures were used to assist former slaves. Even in the 1860s, when children's rights were hardly considered, there were individuals who questioned this type of child exploitation.

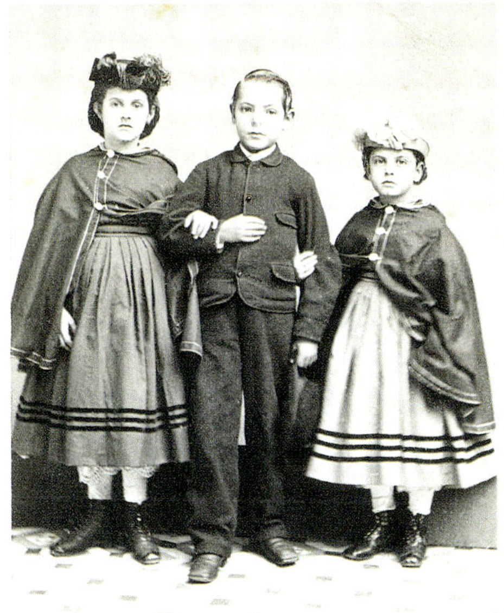

This trio from New Orleans was especially startling to many Northerners, since they expected slaves to be of darker complexion. In New Orleans fair-skinned African Americans were not unusual; many people of color were of mixed African and European ancestry, and some could easily pass for white.

point where Creoles and Americans met. Consequently, its median came to be called the "neutral ground," a term still used to indicate all street medians in New Orleans.

While Americans were attracted to the area upriver from the old city, Creoles migrated downriver to Faubourg Marigny, established in 1806, and Faubourg Treme, established in 1810, both behind the French Quarter. Animosity between Creoles and Americans became so strong in the early nineteenth century that in 1836 the city was divided into three separate municipalities under one mayor. One municipality was American, while the other two were Creole; Canal Street served as the dividing line. The city was reunited in 1852, by which time Americans and newly arrived immigrants were dominant.

The earliest ethnic group to populate the region was indigenous Native American

François Bernard

Louisiana Indian Encampment, ca. 1860

oil on board
The Historic New Orleans Collection 1992.129.5

French-born painter François Bernard (b. probably 1814) was active in New Orleans between 1856 and 1875. In this painting Bernard depicts an idyllic scene of an Indian encampment probably on the north shore of Lake Pontchartrain. When the French arrived after 1700, several Indian tribes were well established as hunters and gatherers in the region around New Orleans and Lake Pontchartrain. Jean Baptiste Le Moyne, sieur de Bienville—founder of New Orleans and periodic governor of the colony—began moving tribes around to ensure continued trade patterns. In the early years of the colony, before African slaves were brought over, Native Americans were used as slaves. As the city grew and plantations took up available land, Indians moved away from their traditional tribal lands. They did, however, come regularly into the city to sell goods such as baskets and herbs at the markets.

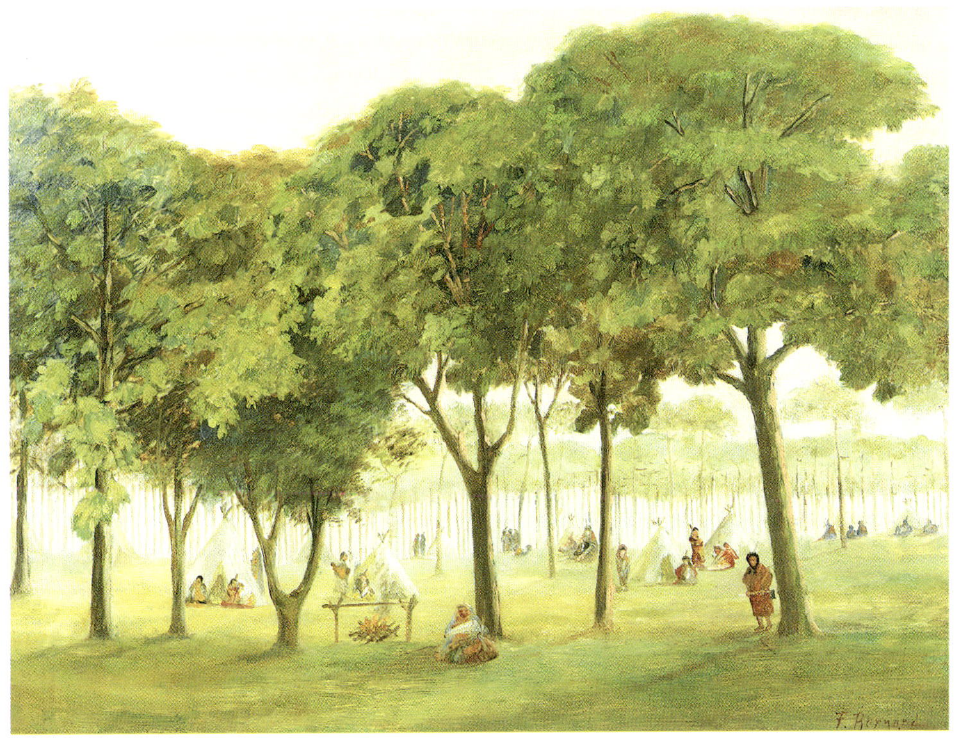

tribes. In addition to the French who began arriving in the early eighteenth century, there were Germans who began settling the region in the 1720s. Native Americans were initially taken as slaves, but were soon replaced by Africans from Senegambia and elsewhere along Africa's west coast.

The first African slaves came to New Orleans in 1719. They arrived in such large numbers that by the late 1720s African slaves made up more than 55 percent of the population, a standing they would maintain until the 1830s when waves of European immigrants began to arrive and greatly diluted the African majority. Today, although the suburbs are heavily populated by people of European origin, African Americans have regained a sizable majority of the nearly half-million population within the city limits. Thus, from the city's very beginnings, people with ancestry rooted in Africa have influenced every aspect of its culture. African American builders and artisans produced some of the fine wrought iron found in the French Quarter. Many served as household and restaurant cooks, adding their own ingredients to help create New Orleans's remarkable cuisine. Caribbean Africans brought in their brand of religion which, when blended with aspects of Catholicism, gave the city voodoo. And of course, New Orleans, with its European and African roots, gave the world jazz.

New Orleans had a sizable population of free people of color. Not only did Spanish and French authorities allow slaves to buy their freedom and to be granted liberty, but a substantial number of free people of color fled to New Orleans along with whites to escape the violent slave uprisings in Saint-Domingue in the 1790s and early 1800s. On the eve of the Civil War when the city's population of 168,000 was about 14 percent black, about half of that population was free. Free people of color made up an important segment of the city's economic com-

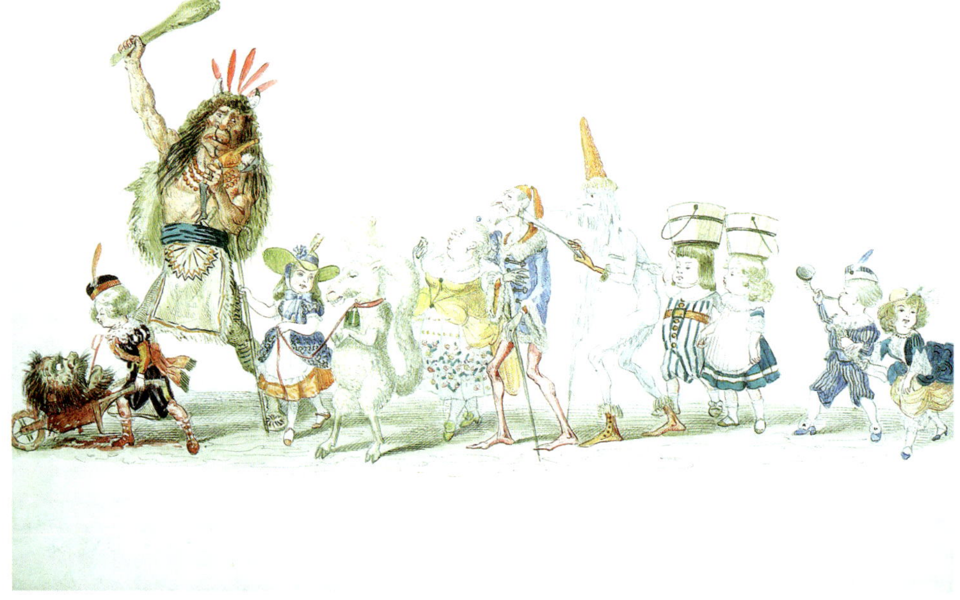

Charles Briton
Twelfth Night Revelers Pageant Design – Mother Goose's Tea Party
created for parade on January 6, 1871
ink and watercolor on bristol board
The Historic New Orleans Collection 1975.117.2

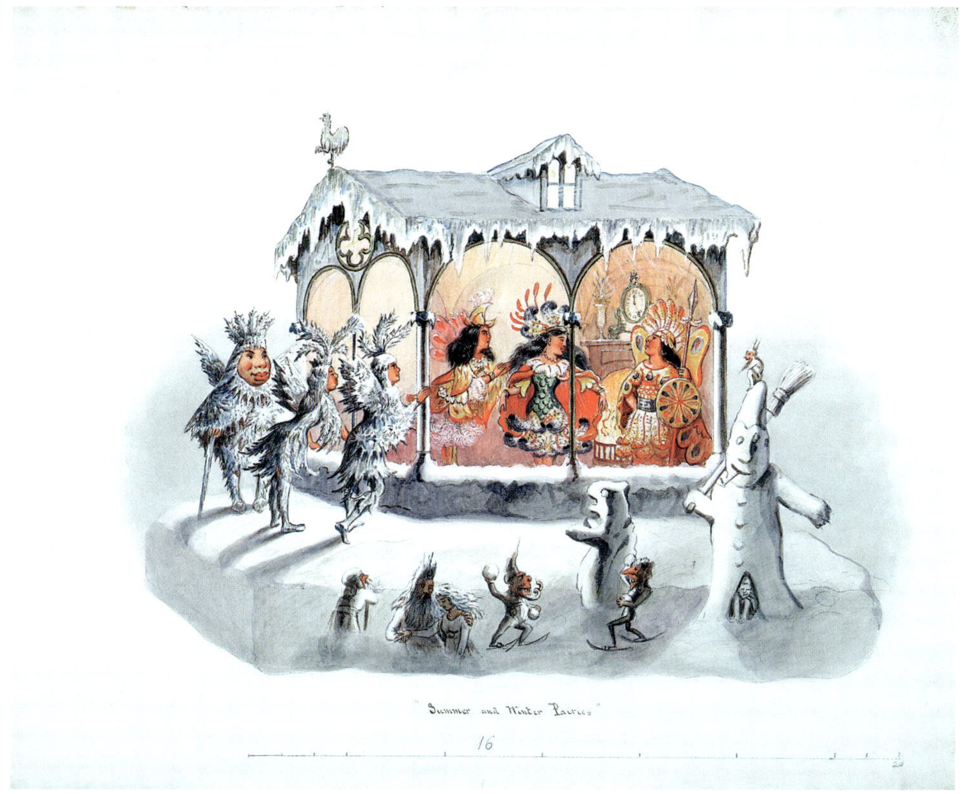

Charles Briton

Knights of Momus Mardi Gras Float Design – Summer and Winter Fairies
created for parade on February 28, 1878

watercolor on board
The Historic New Orleans Collection 1958.11.15

From its earliest days, New Orleans has celebrated Mardi Gras, although organized Carnival in the modern sense with street parades did not begin until 1857. Prior to 1857, the season was marked by elegant private balls and considerable street rowdyism. To eliminate the rough aspect of Carnival, a group organized a parade called the Mistick Krewe of Comus. Its immediate popularity brought an element of fantasy to Mardi Gras that would permeate the social life of New Orleans; in just a few years glittering tableau balls and colorful street pageants would become a part of life in the city. Two of the earliest Carnival organizations, or krewes, are the Twelfth Night Revelers and the Knights of Momus. Both krewes, which date from the 1870s, once staged parades and balls, but now only stage balls. Costumes and masks were originally imported from France, as were those shown in the drawings for the Twelfth Night Revelers parade of 1871. By 1873 costumes and masks were being made locally. Both the pageant and the float designs are by Charles Briton (1840–1884), the earliest known designer of Carnival floats, tableau balls, and costumes. Briton came to New Orleans from his native Sweden in 1864. From these simple beginnings, one of the largest businesses in New Orleans emerged; Carnival design is now a year-round enterprise, employing many people.

munity. They owned businesses and property. There were some who amassed substantial wealth, and some who even owned slaves. As a symbol of their freedom, free women of color wore colorful and sometimes elaborate cloth headdresses of Caribbean origin called tignons. New Orleans has many people of mixed African and European ancestry, and the term Creole, which once meant French or Spanish people born in the colonies, has also come to mean people of mixed ancestry. It is common in New Orleans to find fair-skinned African Americans with French surnames who are Roman Catholics.

Although France relinquished control of New Orleans to Spain in 1762, and then to the United States in 1803, many French Creole residents—both white and black—tenaciously held onto their French heritage. Indeed, there were those who continued to speak French almost exclusively as late as the 1920s and even had their children educated in that language. The city's earliest roots continue to be reflected in its longstanding ties to the Catholic Church, and even for non-Catholics, one of the city's beloved symbols is St. Louis Cathedral.

In spite of the Crescent City's long surviving emotional ties to France, during the nineteenth century it grew into one of the most ethnically diverse cities in the United States as waves of immigrants entered the community. In the eighteenth century there were those from Spain and then the Caribbean. The nineteenth century brought Irish and Germans before the Civil War, and Italians afterwards. More recent immigrants have included Eastern European Jews, Latin Americans, and Southeast Asians.

Such ethnic diversity was especially unusual in the South where populations tended to be of British or African origin and were Protestant. For most Americans, New Orleans was seen as an exotic place where ethnic variations and traditions appeared decidedly alien when compared to their own communities. Early visitors repeatedly mention the city's many racial types, quaint architecture, and its crowded markets—even open on Sundays, in a nation that was mostly shuttered on that day. New Orleans was indeed a city of public markets, with over thirty serving the community into the early twentieth century. Of especial interest was the French Market, the oldest, where people could see almost all of the various races from most parts of Europe and Africa, as well as mixtures of those races. Visitors to the markets were fascinated by Native American vendors who came daily to sell herbs, baskets, and pottery. Native Americans were an important fixture in the French Market until the World War I era.

By the 1840s New Orleans was one of the great cultural centers of America. The French brought with them a fondness for music, opera, the theater, and balls. The city's first theater opened in 1792, followed by a second in 1808. These buildings were small compared to the larger, more elegant ones that opened a few years later. As the name of the elegant Théâtre d'Orléans signifies, the language of the early New Orleans stage was French. Not until 1820 were the first English-language plays performed in the city, and soon after grandiose theaters such as the American and St. Charles appeared in the American district.

The opera, perhaps more beloved by the people of New Orleans than any other type of theater, was introduced to the city as early as the 1790s. During the nineteenth century groups of singers and musicians were almost annually brought to New Orleans, and the city sent its own troupes to perform in northeastern cities. For many years operas were performed at the Théâtre d'Orléans; then in 1859 a new opera house, which came to be called the French Opera House, opened in the heart of the French Quarter. Although it was destroyed by fire in 1919, many people in New Orleans have retained a fondness for the building which was the venue for opera and ballet, as well as countless Carnival balls.

In addition to theater and music, New Orleanians developed a fondness for dancing, gambling, horse racing, fashion, and festive gatherings. New Orleans was a high-spirited city, and its winter social season attracted rich planters and their families on a regular basis.

Perhaps the greatest urban festival in the United States is the New Orleans Carnival season. Mardi Gras, introduced to New Orleans by the French, was first observed in Louisiana in 1699. The first modern, organized parade in the city was not held until 1857. Following the traditional European observance from Twelfth Night to Mardi Gras, the Carnival season is marked by private tableau balls at which debutantes are presented, public parades, and street gatherings. Balls and parades are privately financed by social organizations, some of which are called Carnival krewes. Some organizations, such as the Mistick Krewe of Comus (the oldest), the Twelfth Night Revelers, the Knights of Momus, and the Caliphs of Cairo, only stage balls. Others, such as Rex, Zulu, Proteus, and the Knights of Babylon, stage both balls and parades. Among the street festivities is the appearance of the Mardi Gras Indians, groups of African Americans who belong to "tribes" and dress in elaborate feather-and-bead creations which often take an entire year to make. Indeed, most of the elaborate sets, floats, and costumes of the Carnival season require much time, effort, and money to design and build.

New Orleans has provided inspiration to writers and artists for much of its history. Walt Whitman, Lafcadio Hearn, Somerset Maugham, Sherwood Anderson, and William Faulkner are only a few of the renowned writers who have passed through the city and commented on its charms. Tennessee Williams, one of the most notable writers to adopt New Orleans, arrived in 1938 and was so captivated by the city that it not only influenced much of his work but served as the setting for several of his plays, including one of the theatrical masterpieces of the twentieth century, *A Streetcar Named Desire*. Williams's plays have left an indelible impression of the city on the rest of the world, especially since he provided a somewhat different interpretation of its image. Williams's New Orleans is less charming and picturesque, a bit more decadent and seamy than the New Orleans presented by nineteenth-century writers.

Steeped in history, yet full of life, New Orleans offers an endless stream of sensations and delights. Wandering its streets, one can fully appreciate why people like Sherwood Anderson and Tennessee Williams have been so inspired by the constant echoes of the city with its Gallic, Hispanic, Caribbean, and African past that has helped make such a captivating present.

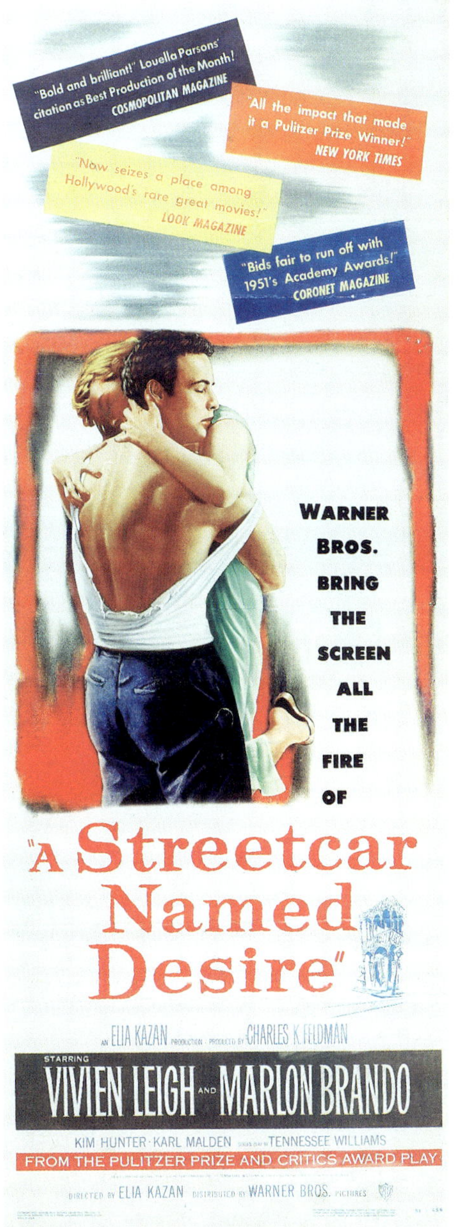

A Streetcar Named Desire

Warner Brothers Pictures, 1951

motion picture poster

The Historic New Orleans Collection 2001-10-L
The Fred W. Todd Tennessee Williams Collection

Playwright Tennessee Williams (1911–1986) certainly helped make the Desire streetcar line in New Orleans one of the most famous transit lines in the world. The route of the line, established in 1920 to serve a new residential area beyond the French Quarter, went through the Quarter to Canal Street. Williams could hear the rumbling of the streetcar on Royal Street from his home in the French Quarter, which prompted him to entitle his play *A Streetcar Named Desire*. *Streetcar* premiered in 1947, ironically about the time that the streetcars on the Desire line were replaced with buses. Tennessee Williams first came to New Orleans in late 1938, remained a short while, but later returned on a more permanent basis for the remainder of this life.

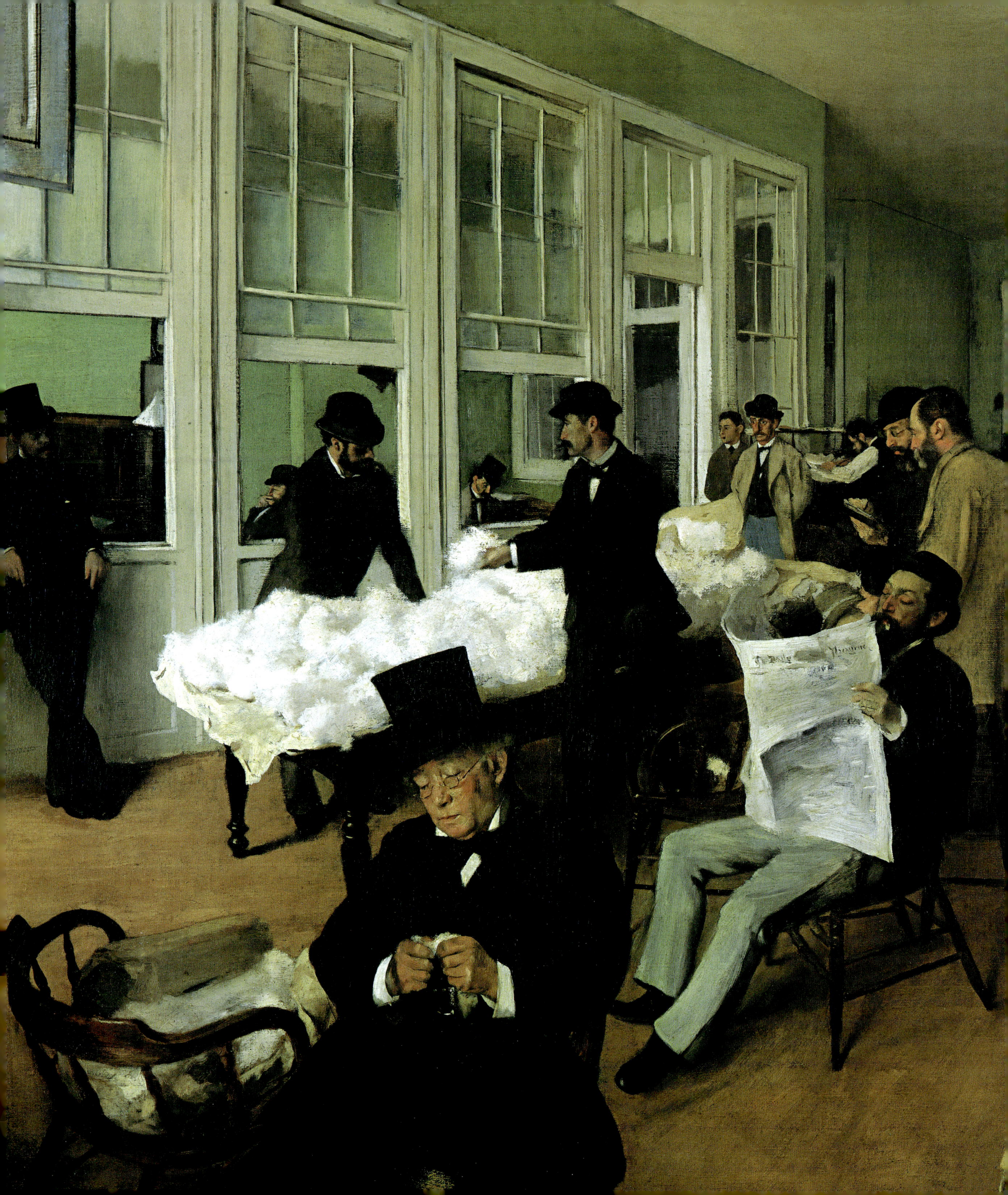

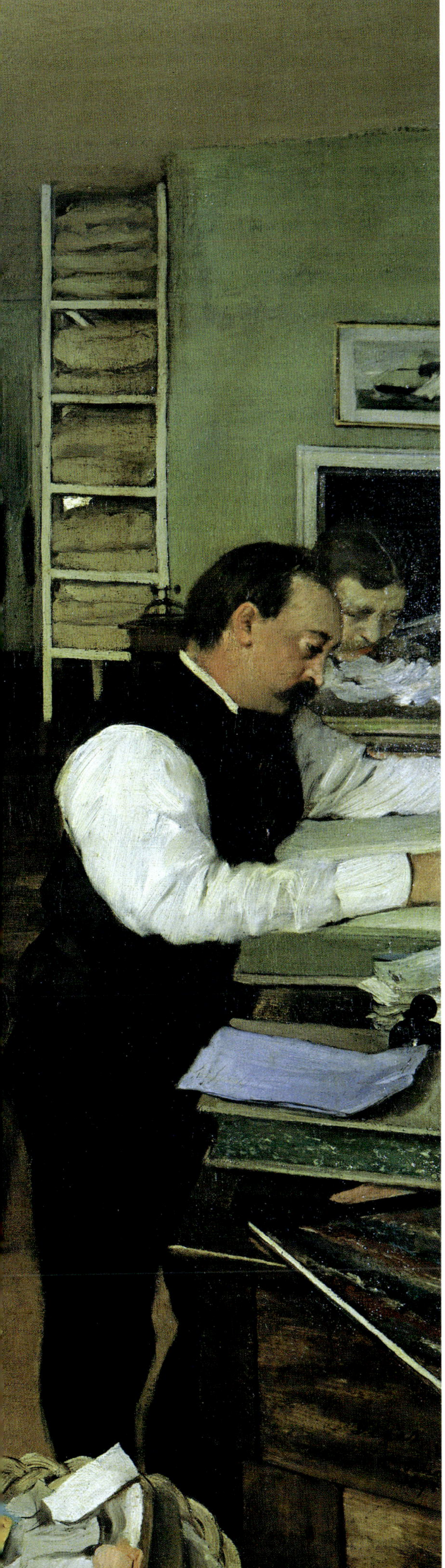

How Edgar Degas Came to Paint the *New Orleans Cotton Exchange*

Guillaume AMBROISE, *Chief Curator at the Musée des Beaux-Arts, Pau, France*

They do nothing here, it's the climate: there's nothing but cotton, people live by and for cotton.

Edgar DEGAS

Painted in 1873, Degas's *New Orleans Cotton Exchange*—the jewel of the Pau museum's collection—could not fail to win the admiration of the Anglo-American colony that came to winter in Pau each year.

"They do nothing here," Degas wrote, "it's the climate: there's nothing but cotton, people live by and for cotton."

It was through a coincidence that in 1878 the art museum in Pau acquired, *primus inter pares*, the Degas canvas titled *New Orleans Cotton Exchange*. The purchase was a particularly astute one in the artistic context of the time, and this picture alone is enough to justify the fame of the museum that houses it.

Degas's career is sufficiently well known and documented for us to focus here on the history of this major work. In 1872, accompanied by his brother René, a resident of New Orleans, Edgar Degas embarked at Liverpool for the Atlantic crossing. Arriving in New York on October 24, they took the train for Louisiana together. On November 4, Degas celebrated a family reunion and immediately set about painting the portraits of his near and dear ones.

Edgar Degas
New Orleans Cotton Exchange, 1873

73 x 92 cm
oil on canvas
Musée des Beaux-Arts, Pau, France

The genesis of the painting

In a letter to James Tissot dated November 19, 1872, Degas mentions his first American painting, with its typically American subject: *Courtyard of a House in New Orleans*, now in the Ordrupgaardsamlingen in Copenhagen. This unfinished canvas is the only one in which we can make out a few characteristics of Louisiana society and the local landscape which Degas describes in his letter to Tissot: "Houses in different styles with columns, painted white, set in gardens of magnolia, orange trees, banana trees..."

Despite the artist's initial response, this tropical exuberance does not appear in Degas's work; his color scheme runs mainly to more or less muted browns, greens, and whites. Having studied under Louis Lamothe at the Ecole des Beaux-Arts in Paris, Degas dutifully puts the emphasis on drawing and, even more so, perspective. The latter is, in fact, given a rough time in *Courtyard of a House in New Orleans*, or, should we say, approached with great inventiveness—the frontal-view background is contradicted by the slanting perspective of the wall in the foreground. In other words, this is a trial run for the composition of the painting now in Pau, except that it is set in the open air.

Another letter to Tissot, dated February 18, 1873, contains vital information on the genesis of the *New Orleans Cotton Exchange*: "After wasting my time trying to turn out family portraits in the worst lighting conditions I've ever come across—or even imagined—I'm tackling quite a good canvas for Agnew which he should be able to find a buyer for in Manchester. If ever a cotton merchant was looking for his ideal painter, then he's found his man. It's called *Intérieur d'un bureau d'acheteurs de coton à La Nouvelle-Orléans, Cotton buyers office*. In it are fifteen or so individuals more or less busy around a table covered with the precious stuff, while two men, the buyer and the agent, are discussing a sample, one leaning over the table and the other half-seated on it. An authentic local picture if ever there was one, and better done than a lot of others."

Mixed reactions

It is interesting to see Degas, after three months in New Orleans, getting away from "family pressures" by opting for a subject whose commercial implications are far from unintentional. The same letter indicates that he was looking forward to a financially rewarding future, and that the current picture would doubtless be sold, via the London dealer Agnew, to "de Cotterel"—in reality William Cottril, a wealth Manchester textile manufacturer. In an openly cynical way then, Degas was speculating on a marriage between the worlds of art and industry. He failed, however, to take account of Cottril's tastes, which were "extremely reasonable" and tended more to rustic views of the English countryside. Nor was Degas aware of the disastrous economic slump that hit most Lancashire textile businesses in 1873.

A little more than a month after writing this letter, Degas was back in Paris, but it was not until 1876, at the second Impressionist exhibition, that the public finally discovered *New Orleans Cotton Exchange*. The critics, for the most part unimpressed by the other works exhibited, were somewhat kinder to Degas. One of them—Arthur Baignères, writing in *L'Echo universel* on April 13, 1876—even went so far as to accord him the status of a "defrocked draftsman." There were also, however, the jibes and outright abuse of Albert Wolf in the *Figaro* of April 3, 1876: "There's no getting Monsieur Degas to understand. You tell him that in art there are certain things that have a name—drawing, color, execution, enthusiasm—and he just laughs in your face and calls you a reactionary." Even Emile Zola failed to do much better in the *Messager de l'Europe* of June 1876: "Here is a painter very much taken with modernity, the inner life and the everyday. The problem is that he spoils everything as soon as he comes to the finishing touches. His best pictures are mere sketches. Those finishing touches make his drawing lamentably vague; pictures like his *New Orleans Cotton Exchange* fall somewhere between seascapes and something from an illustrated newspaper. His capacity for observation is finely honed, but I fear he will never become a creator." It was left to Armand Sylvestre, in *L'Opinion* of April 2, 1876, to speak of "a truly spiritual painting one could spend days looking at."

Despite Zola's reproaches, the drawing in this picture is perfect and so scrupulous that one hesitates to associate the work with the Impressionist movement. Like the picture in Copenhagen, this one surprises with the relative economy of its colors, but here the control of the tonal relationships is of a subtlety rarely equaled. Against a background dominated by browns and dull greens, the black suits stand out vividly, skillfully counterbalanced by the relatively horizontal lines of the cotton, the newspaper, and the accountant's sleeves. The discreetly handled perspective confirms the interest in slanting planes already evident in the Copenhagen picture. The framing, too, is remarkable for the way it "chops off" the bodies and the walls, lending the work an instantaneous character that inevitably makes us think of photography and, more indirectly, the Japanese print.

Returning to the subject of the painting, it is worth mentioning that here we are in the office of a family business and that all those present have been positively identified. Interesting, too, is the fact that Degas's brother René is reading the *Daily Picayune*, a local paper which on February 1, 1873, had announced that this very same business was going into liquidation. Despite the relaxed poses, then, Degas is portraying a firm in deep financial difficulty. Lastly, it should be noted that there exists another version of this scene, now in the Fogg Art Museum in Cambridge, Massachusetts. This work is singularly lacking in boldness and finish and is, doubtless wrongly, considered a preliminary sketch for the Pau canvas.

It is probable that after the Impressionist exhibition, Degas, whose own financial problems were very real and success far from certain, did everything he could to sell *New Orleans Cotton Exchange*—especially as it was a thoroughly finished work.

The Pau acquisition

Degas's chance came in 1878, thanks to two faithful friends—Alphonse Cherfils and probably Paul Lafond, respectively vice-president and secretary of the Pau Art Society—who had already helped him find a place in the society's annual salon in 1876 and 1877. Bearing the number 87 in the catalogue for 1878, *New Orleans Cotton Exchange* had an estimated value of 5000 francs. Charles Le Coeur, honorary president of the Pau Art Society and curator of the Musée des Beaux-Arts, proposed that it should be acquired for 2000 francs. Far from offended by the price offered, Degas hastened to thank Le Coeur in an enthusiastic letter of March 31, 1878: "I cannot hold back. I thank you wholeheartedly for the honor you do me. I must admit that this is the first time a museum has offered me this distinction and that I find this official recognition most flattering."

Why Pau? And how did the offer come to be made? The background to this inspired acquisition lies in the story of a generous patron, Emile Noubilos. A resident of Pau, Noubilos was a descendent of a family whose business interests focused on textiles, linen and cotton in particular. An art lover, Noubilos died in 1875 at the age of forty-two, leaving the Musée des Beaux-Arts an annual legacy of 8000 francs to be used for the acquisition of "pictures of the modern—or what is called the contemporary—school." Degas was the first to benefit from Noubilos's generosity.

Doubtless the purchase of this picture, whose subject was the cotton trade, seemed to the acquisitions jury a sincere tribute to the social origins of the museum's benefactor. So in the end, the painting Degas had originally seen as destined for an English textile manufacturer was acquired, five years later, for the very same reason.

Also noteworthy is the extraordinary receptiveness shown by Pau cultural circles of the time to the liveliest forms of contemporary painting, even if this enthusiasm was tempered by a certain opportunism: a picture painted in the United States and dealing with an American subject could not fail to draw the attention of the large Anglo-American colony that visited Pau—and its museum—every year.

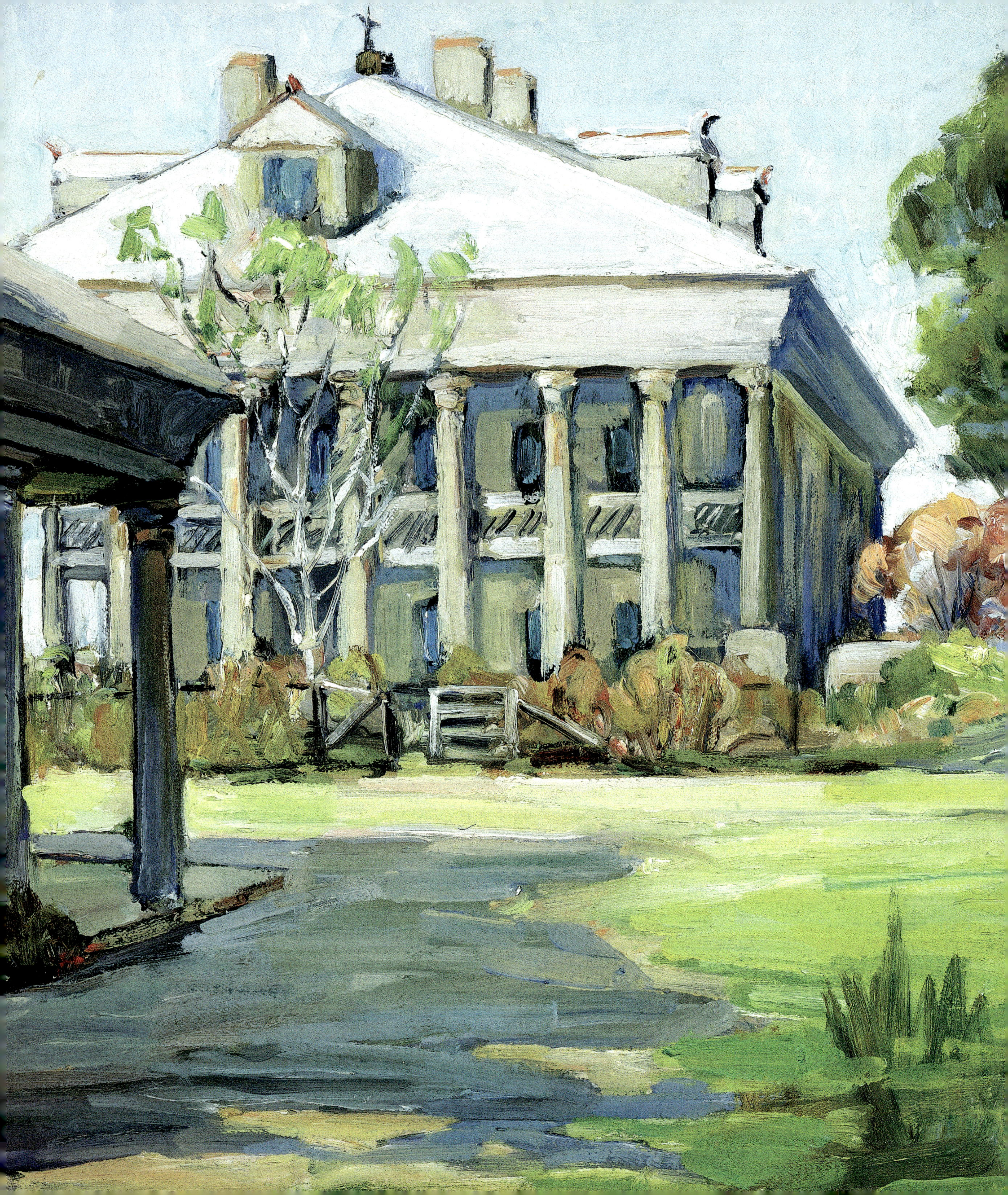

Picturing the Idea of New Orleans: The Visual Arts, 1870-1940

John H. LAWRENCE, *Director of Museum Programs, The Historic New Orleans Collection*

The "idea" of New Orleans that exists today, a combination of both reality and myth, took shape over several decades, albeit unintentionally, through the blended talents of a vibrant arts community: painters, draftsmen, graphic artists, photographers, designers, authors, playwrights, composers, musicians, and performers. In the sense that no official act or sanctioned movement was involved in accomplishing this process, it may be said that New Orleans itself was the principal agent that formed its identity.

The character of the Crescent City resulted from various channels of influence that by the early decades of the twentieth century merged to form a single stream that has identified the city as exotic and unique ever since. The development of the visual arts in New Orleans, which experienced an explosion of growth beginning in the last quarter of the nineteenth century and lasting until the middle of the twentieth century, is a principal element of the city's identity.

The initial flourishing came about from factors both internal and external—an awareness among local artists of the special character of New Orleans; the "discovery" of New Orleans culture by outsiders; general trends in the field of art education and its practical applications; and the phenomenon of international expositions. As a consequence of these events, visual arts both initiated and defined perceptions of New Orleans as a place simultaneously rooted in its "southernness" and unique in the world.

It must be stressed that this essay is an overview, hitting some highlights of the era and leaving much for the reader to discover. The objects chosen for this section are important for different reasons: they are examples of works exploring the character of New Orleans and the surrounding region; of styles influential on subsequent generations of artists; and of subjects representing local attitudes and tastes. They also support the broad range of ideas explored in the other three sections of the exhibition.

During the period under examination, extending roughly from the end of the Civil War to the country's entry into World War II, New Orleans was the largest and most important city in the southern United States, having grown from a population of slightly less than 200,000 in 1870 to nearly 600,000 in 1950. From the standpoint of sheer numbers, New Orleans has been a place to inspire artistic productivity. *The Encyclopaedia of New Orleans Artists, 1718-1918*, published by the Historic New Orleans Collection in 1987, contains entries for over 2,700 artists and art organizations concerned with the principal visual arts of painting, sculpture, ceramics, and drawing. Photographers, architects, and furniture makers are not included. The eighty-six years since 1918 have likely yielded a far greater number of people engaged in the practice of fine arts. Indeed, The Collection's Artists Files contain over 20,000 dossiers on artists, art organizations, museums, and galleries, covering the colonial period to the present. Nonetheless, the artistic community initially gravitated toward relatively small areas of the city—the Vieux Carré and the upriver campuses of Tulane University and Newcomb College. After the mid-twentieth century, advances in communication and mobility and an ever increasing published record of art led to stronger national and international influences on regional art and artists.

The tradition of the visual arts in New Orleans was not much in evidence (at least in surviving examples) before the early nineteenth century, when, by virtue of the Louisiana Purchase (1803), New Orleans became the largest American city between the Appalachian Mountains and the lands west of the Mississippi River. Though this territorial acquisition nominally "Americanized" the city, the art produced following the event was not always inspired by typical American influences. Furthermore, taste for art, architecture, and furnishings from the colonial French and Spanish period dominated certain segments of society for decades afterwards.

For much of its post-1803 existence, New Orleans was neither wholly American nor totally southern or European. It was, and is, a mixture unto itself. The earliest nineteenth-century view of the city, painted by J. L. Boqueta de Woiseri in 1803 and reproduced that same year in an engraving, shows a city struggling to become American—by government if not temperament—but dominated by elements of its colonial past. Featured are the plantation and sawmill belonging to French Creole planter Bernard de Marigny and the towers of the Catholic church of St. Louis.

Before the appearance of landscape painting, there was a tradition of portraiture in New Orleans. From the works of José Salazar (ca. 1750-1802), who created likenesses of leading citizens and government officials during the last decade of Spanish colonial rule, and Christophe Colomb, described by French colonial prefect Pierre Clément Laussat as "a second-rate dauber in paints," to the more sophisticated and accomplished portraits of French-trained Jean-Joseph Vaudechamp (1790-1866) and Jacques Amans (1801-1888), local patronage of portraiture flourished. Portrait artists found clients both among the Creole gentry and the recently arrived and newly wealthy Americans from the eastern part of the country. Concurrent with this trend was a robust trade in high-quality miniatures, which was stemmed but not wholly curtailed by the introduction of the daguerreotype to New Orleans in 1840 by Jules Lion (1810?-1866), a free man of color.

From the beginning of colonization in the early eighteenth century, recording the landscape, natural history, and later the architecture of southern Louisiana was of interest to Europe. Although this interest was motivated more by intellectual and scientific curiosity than artistic concerns, the work is no less interesting. In a watercolor, now housed in the Archives d'Outre-Mer in Aix-en-Provence, Jean Pierre de Lassus gives us perhaps the earliest purely pictorial view of the young city of New Orleans in 1726. Some thirty years later, the illustrations of Louisiana's flora, fauna, and indigenous population in Antoine-Simon Le Page du Pratz's *Histoire de la Louisiane* (published in French and English) both informed and intrigued a multilingual audience.

Even decades after the Louisiana Purchase and the nominal "Americanization" of New Orleans, European depictions of the city

John Antrobus

Plantation Burial, 1860

oil on canvas

The Historic New Orleans Collection 1960.46

Englishman John Antrobus's *Plantation Burial* ranks as one of the most important paintings ever made depicting the life of African American slaves. In scale, conception, and sympathy, the painting has few equals. About 1858, Antrobus planned a series of twelve paintings portraying life in the South. Only two of the paintings are known to have been completed; this work being the only one known to survive. It is presumed that the Civil War interrupted the completion of the series. The setting for the painting is the Tucker plantation in Carroll Parish, Louisiana, near the town of Lake Providence, which can be seen along the riverbank through the clearing in the trees. Focusing on slaves attending the burial of a comrade, Antrobus relegated the white plantation owners and overseer to the right and left edges of the canvas respectively.

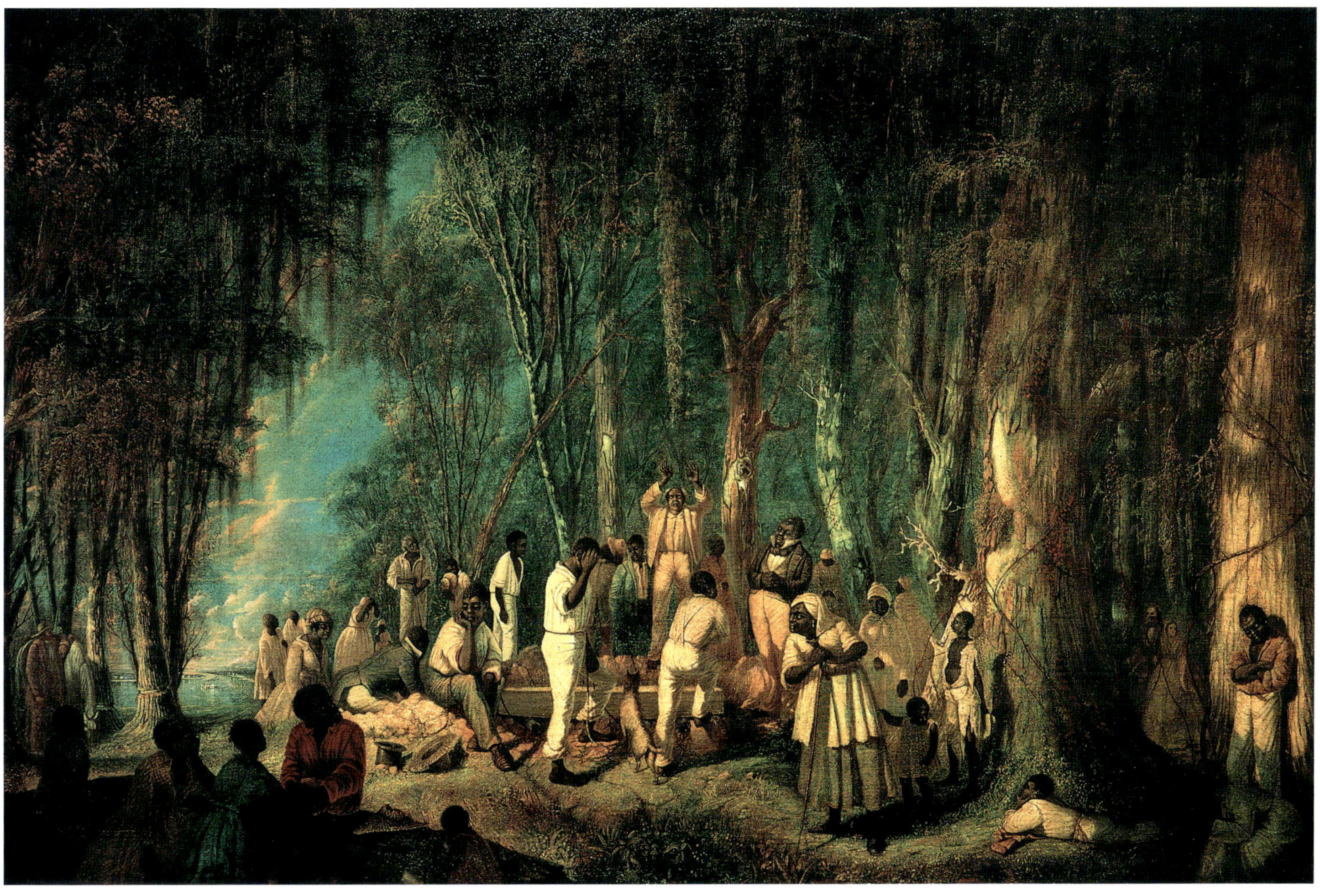

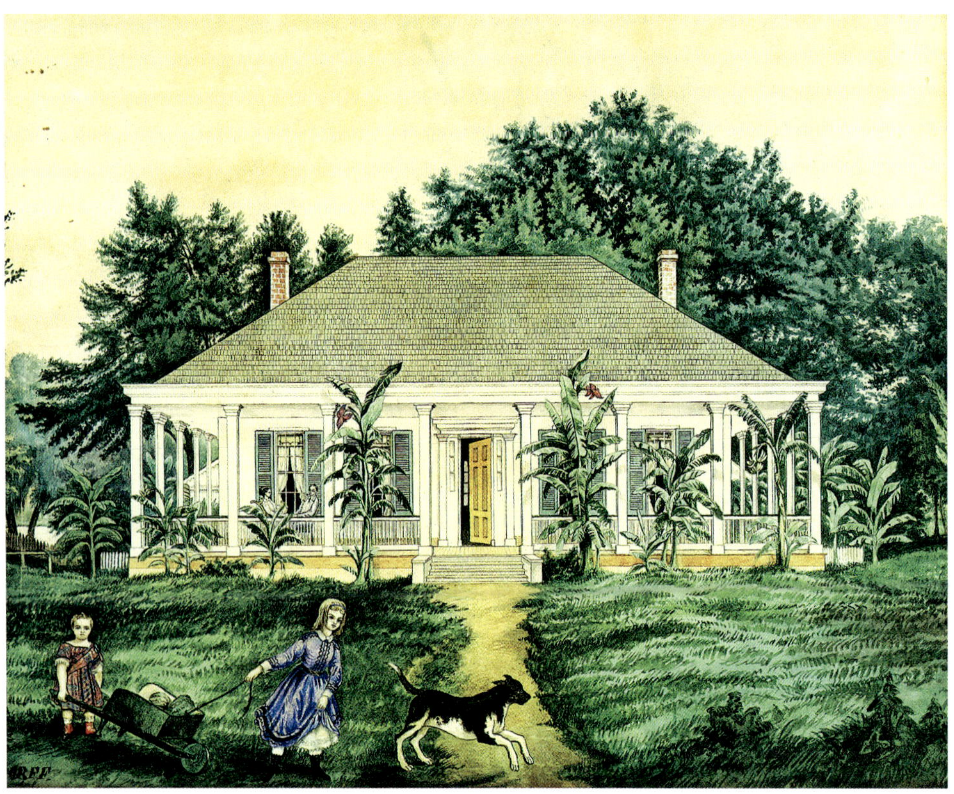

Dorff
Westover Plantation, 1868
ink and watercolor
The Historic New Orleans Collection 1939.3

These two works present the opposite ends of the spectrum in plantation architecture. Built in 1859, Nottoway, designed by Irish-born architect Henry Howard, was one of the largest plantation houses in the lower Mississippi Valley, surrounded by acres of productive sugarcane fields. Westover, a more modest, single-story structure, typified the dozens of small plantation and farming operations that existed throughout Louisiana.

continued to be produced in lithographs, drawings, and paintings by artists such as Edouard de Montulé (1810s), Félix Achille de Beaupoil, marquis de Saint-Aulaire (1820s), Ambroise-Louis Garneray (1830s), Charles-Alexandre Lesueur (1830s), and Henry Lewis (1840s). Over the course of a century, these works of art, sometimes accurate, sometimes not, created an image of south Louisiana and New Orleans as a place unlike any other. The peculiarities of its landscape, people, customs, and environment continued to interest residents as well as those who passed through briefly and recorded a host of visual impressions.

The uniqueness of New Orleans was expressed in different ways—from interpretations of the antebellum plantation culture of the lower Mississippi River valley to the endless attempts to visually define the concept of "Creole." Paintings such as *Plantation Burial* (1860) by John Antrobus (1831-1907), *Westover Plantation* (1868) by Dorff, and *Nottoway Plantation* (ca. 1875) by Cornelia R. Murrell reveal the architecture and daily life of the plantation system in Louisiana. The naive style of these works recalls the insouciance of the days before the war. Louisiana paintings rarely depicted individual slaves or slave life; Antrobus's work was a notable exception. But in the years following the Civil War, William Aiken Walker (1838-1921) devoted most of his career as an artist to portraying the rural life of African Americans in the South. His ubiquitous cabin scenes and individual figure studies, though at times verging on caricature, nonetheless provide a large and useful body of work on the subject. As a group, the paintings and drawings can be used as entryways for the study of other themes ranging from vernacular architecture, to social structures and folkways, to clothing history. Walker's works were disseminated to a larger audience by at least two chromolithographs published by Currier & Ives in the mid-1880s.

Long after the antebellum plantation ceased as a working model for the southern agricultural economy, the historic romance and architecture of the great manor houses continued to interest painters and photographers working in twentieth-century Louisiana. Photographers Walker Evans, Edward Weston, and especially native-born Clarence John Laughlin produced significant bodies of photographs on the subject. Perhaps no twentieth-century artist responded to the plantation idea more strongly than Julian B. Rivet (1923-1985), whose 1968 painting *Constancia, Uncle Sam Plantation* serves as both allegory and documentation for the changing role of the plantation theme in Louisiana art. Illinois artist George Gardner Symons (1861-1930) takes a purely painterly approach in his painting of the same subject. His is the trained visual response of an outsider intrigued by the compositional and chromatic possibilities of the scene before him.

The legacy of images that define a concept of New Orleans and southern Louisiana has been crafted by both natives and visitors; by academically trained artists and those who are self-taught; by men and women; by nineteenth- and twentieth-century practitioners.

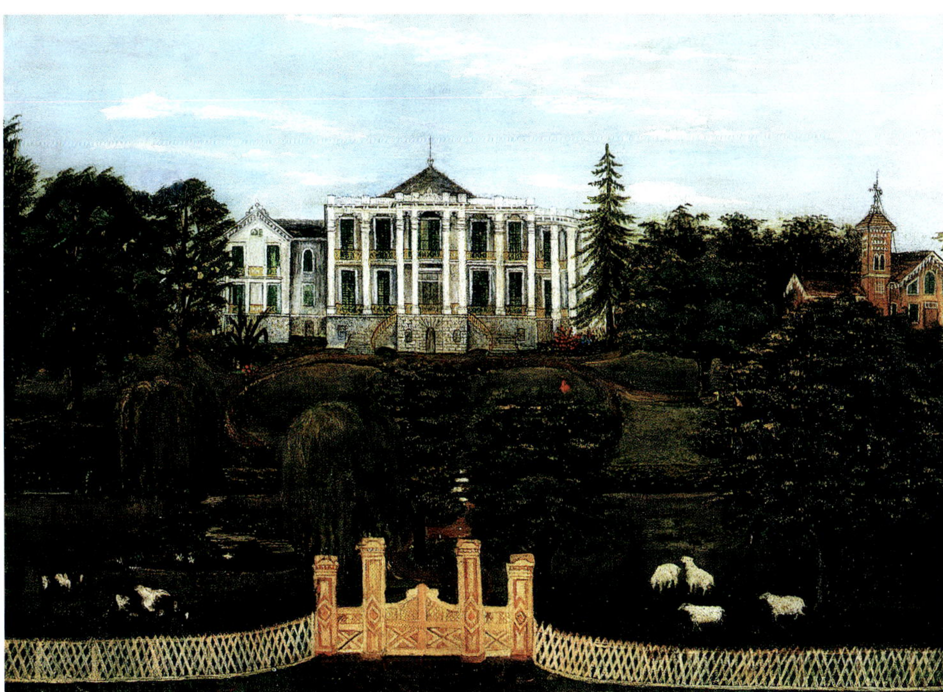

Cornelia R. Murrell
Nottoway Plantation, ca. 1875
oil on canvas
The Historic New Orleans Collection 1958.36

Shortly after the conclusion of the Civil War, a distinct "Louisiana school" of landscape painting emerged. Drawing in spirit on two principal movements in nineteenth-century French painting—the *plein air* tradition of the Barbizon painters and the experiential honesty of the Realists—Louisiana painters began to explore their surroundings with an artistic rather than a documentary response. The specifics of place, the quality of light, and the rendition of atmosphere became important factors in the paintings of these artists. Impressionism, though ultimately influential in Louisiana painting, was years away from having an effect on artists working in the region.

Key among these early landscape artists is Richard Clague (1821-1873). Indeed, he is frequently acknowledged as the father of Louisiana landscape painting. Clague, who, although born in Paris, was the son of New Orleanians, studied at the Ecole des

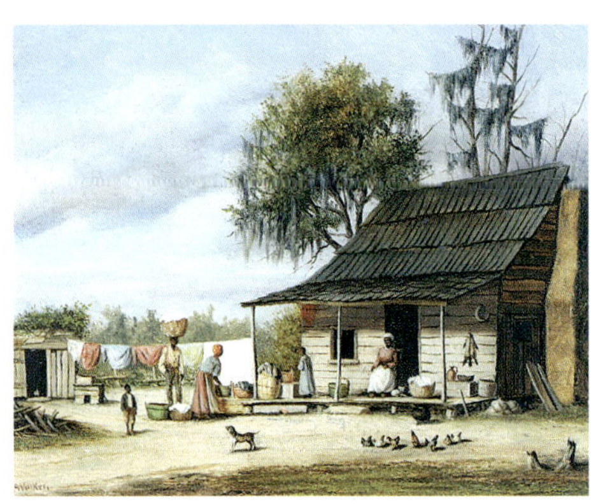

William Aiken Walker
Cabin Scene, between 1878 and 1920
oil on board
The Historic New Orleans Collection 1997.130.14
The Monroe-Green Collection

Other artists have painted scenes depicting the lives and surroundings of southern African Americans, but none so completely focused on the subject or claimed it as their own as William Aiken Walker. Walker traveled for over forty years, from the Carolinas to Florida and westward along the Gulf Coast to Texas. His African American paintings fall into broadly defined themes: field scenes of sugarcane and cotton, individual workers in agricultural settings, figures engaged in activity on the riverfront, and cabin scenes. Walker painted other subjects—including portraits, landscapes, and still lifes—but these subjects are but a small percentage of his work.

Beaux Arts in 1849. His career was spent between New Orleans and Paris until 1857, after which time he remained solely in New Orleans. In the years following the Civil War, Clague taught painting in addition to working as a painter. His *In Old Louisiana*, an uncharacteristically vertical composition, is in other ways typical of his approach to the Louisiana landscape. Following his death, two of Clague's pupils, Marshall J. Smith, Jr. (1854-1923) and William Henry Buck (1840-1888), became well-known exponents of the Louisiana landscape school. Smith and Buck are best known for their studies of the Louisiana swamp and bayou landscapes, populated with animals, the modest dwellings of country folk, and an occasional human figure. Buck's *Fishing Camp on Lake Pontchartrain* (1880) seems initially a setting of pure idyllic tranquility, until one notices the railroad train and tracks bisecting the canvas as a secondary horizon and the activity implied by the boats in the distance. The natural bounty found in Lake Pontchartrain's waters and along its shores served as a commercial resource for trappers and fishermen. The shore forms the northern border of New Orleans and was a popular playground for those in the city seeking a more pleasant summer climate. On the other hand, *Bayou Teche* (1877) by the same artist is totally bucolic. The placid bayou rendered by Buck belies its important role as a route of commerce and transportation in the Acadian parishes of southwest Louisiana. George David Coulon (1822-1904), a versatile painter of this period and a founding member of both the Southern Art Union and the Artists' Association of New Orleans, is associated with the Louisiana Landscape School as well. His *Southern Landscape* (1887), unidentified as to specific location, is one of his most important works.

The World's Industrial and Cotton Centennial Exposition (WICCE) of 1884-85 provided both the impetus for cultural self-examination and a showcase of that culture to the rest of the world. This world's fair was designed to wrench the South from the economic doldrums caused by the Civil War and its aftermath. It lasted for a year and included two principal components devoted to the visual arts. The Art Gallery contained a selection of American and European paintings and sculptures by artists with established reputations, addressing broad international tastes. The Creole Art Gallery, one that focused on the culture of New Orleans and its environs, presented examples of paintings by artists active in the region. Emblematic of the resurrection of the southern economy was John Genin's (1830-1895) *Allegory of Sugar Cane* (1884), one of four

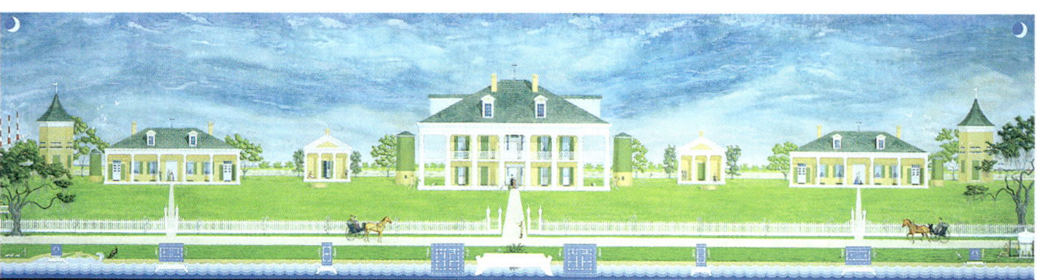

Brother Julian B. Rivet
Constancia, Uncle Sam Plantation, Convent, St. James Parish, Louisiana
between June 1968 and June 1969
oil on Masonite™
The Historic New Orleans Collection 1969.13.1

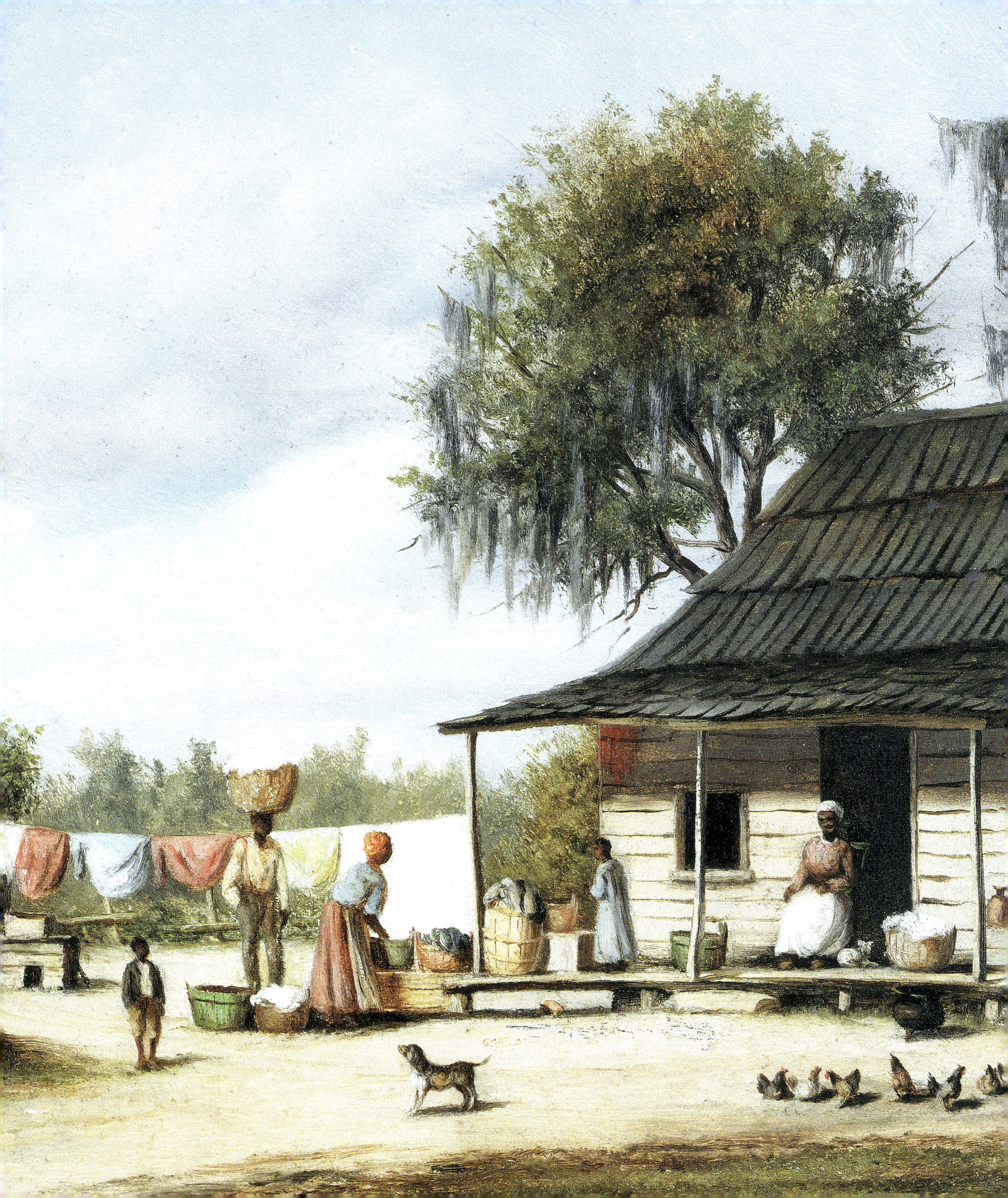

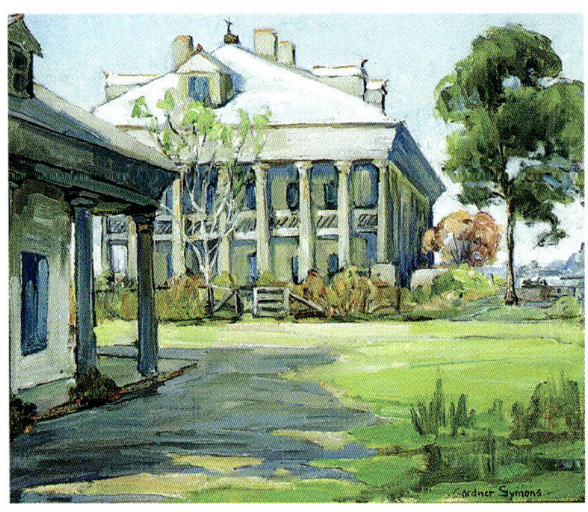

George Gardner Symons

Uncle Sam Plantation, St. James Parish, Louisiana, ca. 1920s

oil on canvas

The Historic New Orleans Collection 1999.44.2

Two artists could have hardly reacted more differently to the same subject—the plantation known as Uncle Sam, located about forty-five miles above New Orleans on the left bank of the Mississippi River. Symons responded to the lush greenery and brilliant play of sunshine on the architecture. Rivet's memories of the site and the history of the building inspired his cleanly rendered version of Uncle Sam and its array of auxiliary buildings (seen on page 62). In an effort to tie the history of the plantation to his own life, Rivet painstakingly wrote the names of family members and former slaves along the fence at the back of the property. Allegorical figures and other symbols, along with representations of Rivet's ancestors relate to the history of the site and its builders. A chemical factory that now occupies the site looms in the distance. In the late 1930s, Uncle Sam had the most complete group of antebellum structures in the South. The Army Corps of Engineers determined that the complex was in danger of being inundated by the encroaching Mississippi River and ordered the buildings demolished so that a new protection levee could be built. Requests to save Uncle Sam from destruction reached officials too late; the demolition of the buildings came about in 1938.

such works he exhibited during the course of the WICCE, each focusing on a different agricultural product. Genin was principally known for his portrait paintings.

Outside of these two main art sections, exhibits produced by nations, territories, and individual states contained other examples of art-and-craft work particular to those places. Immediately preceding the exposition, the formation of arts organizations, schools, and galleries in the city had provided the local audience for these exhibitions exposure to the arts. The Southern Art Union was started in 1880, and in the following year a school operated by the organization opened. In 1883 commercial galleries operated by Frederic Seebold and Theodore Lilienthal presented exhibitions encompassing hundreds of works by painters working in Louisiana and from outside the region. In the wake of the exposition, visual artists formed additional clubs and associations providing forums for discussing

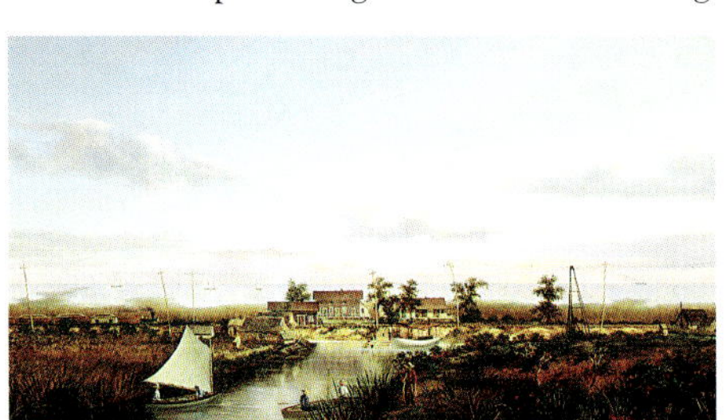

William Henry Buck

Fishing Camp on Lake Pontchartrain, 1880

oil on canvas

The Historic New Orleans Collection 1968.9

William Henry Buck was born in Norway but spent much of his life in New Orleans. A cotton broker by profession, Buck was a student of Richard Clague's. Buck opened his own studio in 1880 and began painting full time. His rural landscapes often include boats, buildings, and figures, giving the paintings a human element. With Clague and contemporaries Marshall J. Smith, George David Coulon, and Charles Giroux, among others, Buck cemented the notion of a "bayou school" of painting in Louisiana.

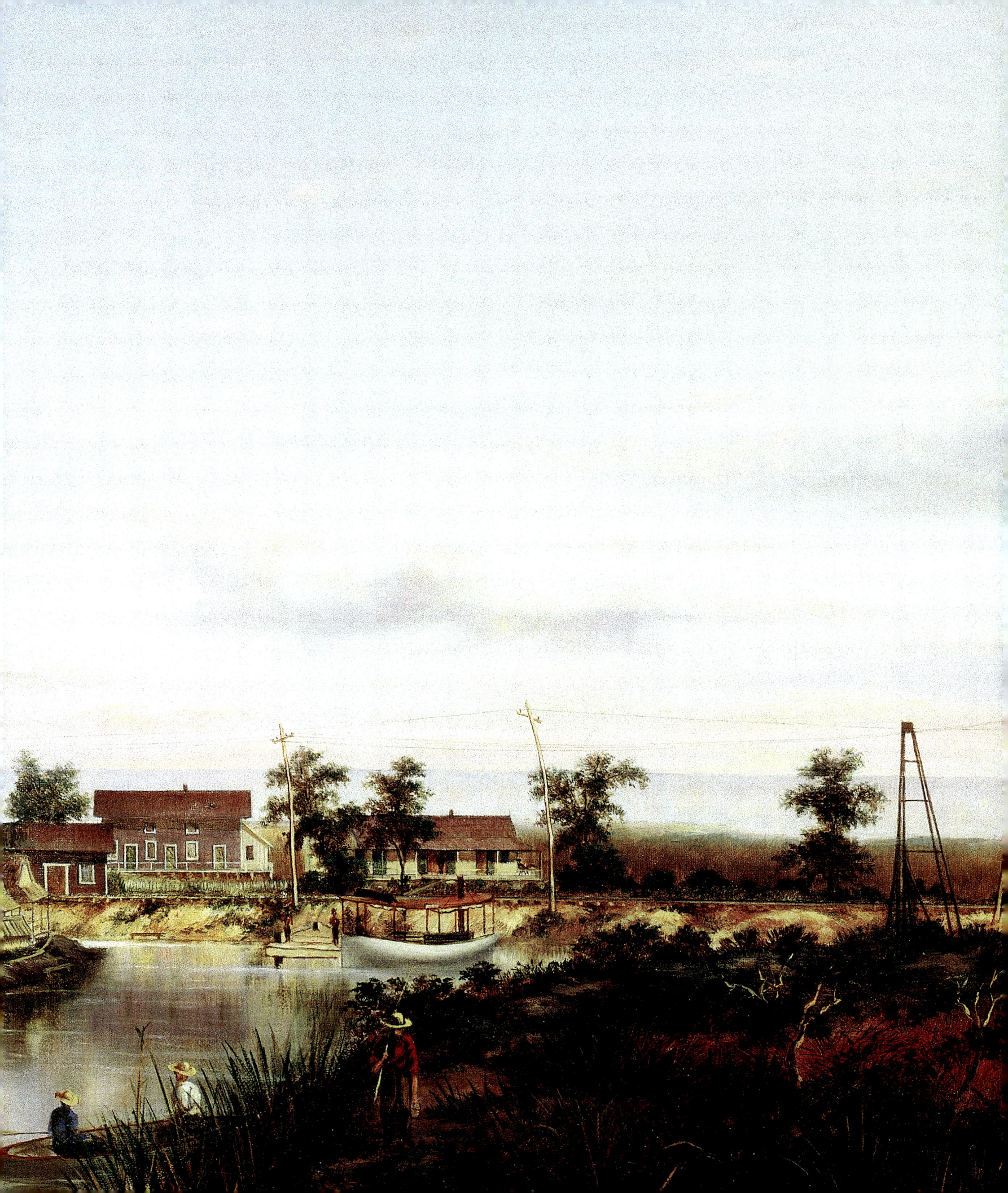

art theory and the promotion of their work. The long-lived Artists' Association of New Orleans was incorporated in 1886 and continued under a new name, the Art Association of New Orleans, until 1959. In 1887 the journal *Art and Letters*, devoted to southern subjects, was first published. In the early twentieth century, the Arts and Crafts Club (1922) and the Isaac Delgado Museum of Art (1911) were the bellwether organizations exhibiting works of Louisiana artists and their national and international contemporaries. As art historian and curator Judith H. Bonner has pointed out in her writings, these efforts, pioneering in their scope and intent in terms of the region, collectively provided a solid grounding for the practice of painting and drawing in the city and for the public appreciation of those arts.

Visual artists engaged in more popular or practical artistic pursuits as well: executing murals and altarpieces for church interiors, producing theater and opera sets, and designing elements of Mardi Gras pageants and parades. Art historian William Gerdts notes that this type of mixed career for nineteenth-century artists, though not atypical of other communities in the United States, was more prevalent in New Orleans than elsewhere.

Writers, too, seized upon the culture, social structure, cuisine, and architecture of the city and published their observations in books and the popular press. Leading this vanguard was journalist and author Lafcadio Hearn (1850-1904) who arrived at the time of the 1884-85 exposition. Hearn's newspaper columns and verbal sketches for the *Daily Item* and *Times-Democrat* are often written equivalents to the painted subjects created by artists of that day. Hearn was a keen observer of his surroundings and the human condition and was fascinated by the quirky encounters of everyday life in New Orleans. An outsider, Hearn held up a mirror to the culture he found in New Orleans and in the process validated the importance of the vernacular as a subject for literature and art. It was an enduring reflection.

Other writers of Hearn's generation—including George Washington Cable (1844-1925), Grace King (1852-1932), and Kate Chopin (1851-1904)—augmented his work in the written celebration of a vivid and unique semitropical culture. National magazines such as *Century* and *Scribner's*, though they had always reported on newsworthy events in New Orleans, spread the word about New Orleans's culture. This dissemination of information (real or exaggerated) helped to establish the unique character of the metropolis among a wide audience. Writers during the first half of the twentieth century, lured by the exoticism and perceived bohemian nature of the city's French Quarter and anxious to experience its undiluted charms before the onset of modernization, continued to add layers of richness to the image of New Orleans.

The years between World Wars I and II not only galvanized the cultural community in New Orleans but saw an influx of influences from visiting writers and visual artists, providing more lenses through which to interpret and view the Crescent City.

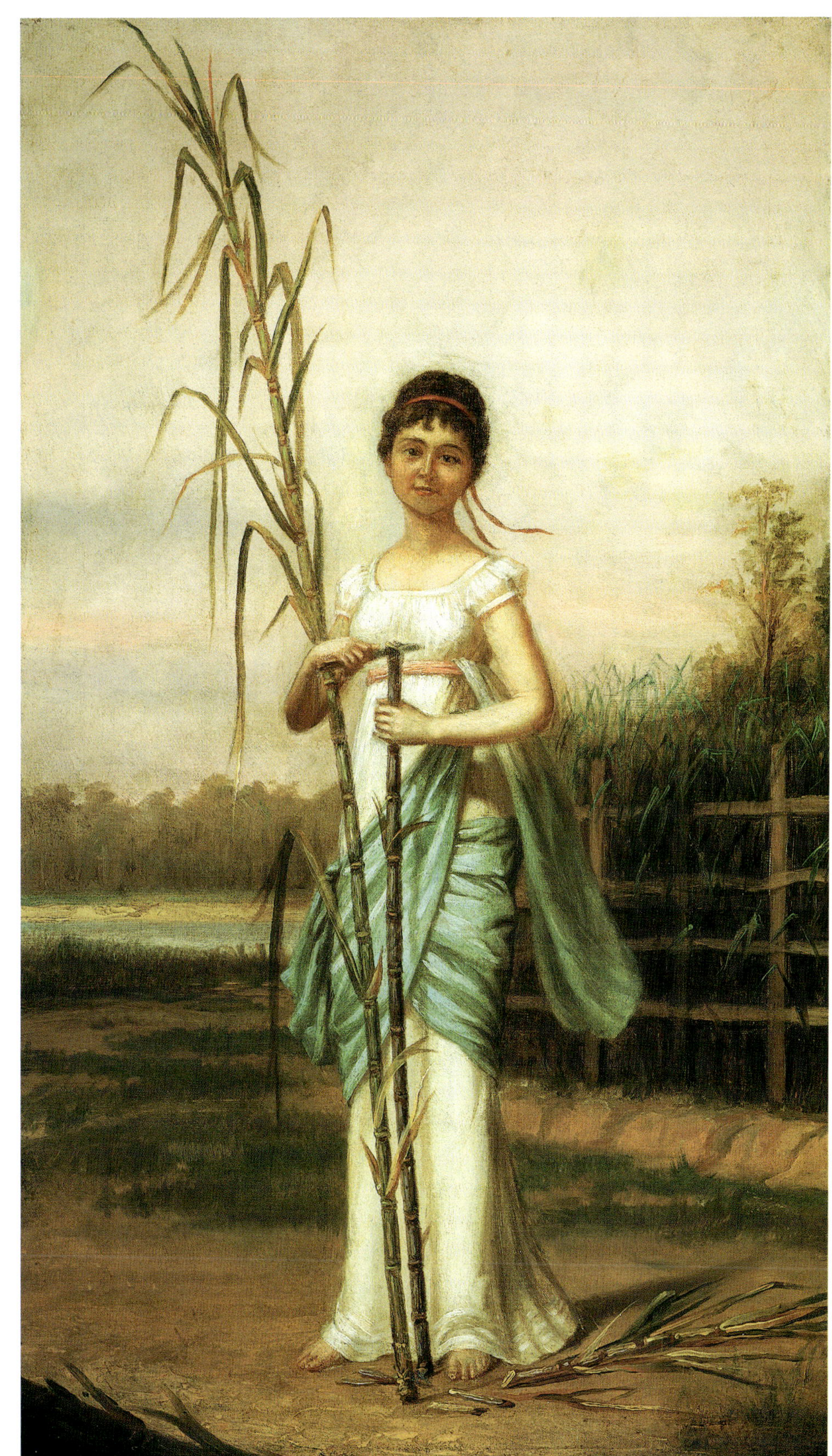

John Genin
Allegory of Sugar Cane, 1884
oil on canvas
The Historic New Orleans Collection 1997.20.1

John Genin was a highly regarded portrait painter in New Orleans, active in the 1870s and '80s. His allegorical figure celebrating sugar production in Louisiana emphasized the importance of the crop to the economy of Louisiana. Louisiana's modern sugarcane industry had begun about ninety years prior to Genin's painting, when Etienne de Boré first achieved commercial-scale granulation of sugar at his plantation on the site of what is now Audubon Park in New Orleans. Ironically, the World's Industrial and Cotton Centennial Exposition, where this painting was exhibited, was held on the site of Boré's sugar plantation.

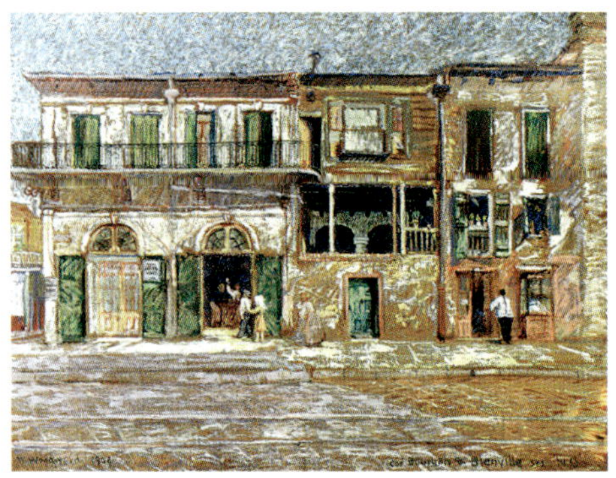

William Woodward

Old Absinthe House, Corner of Bourbon and Bienville Streets, New Orleans, 1904

Rafaelli oil crayon on canvas
The Historic New Orleans Collection 2001.98.1
gift of Laura Simon Nelson

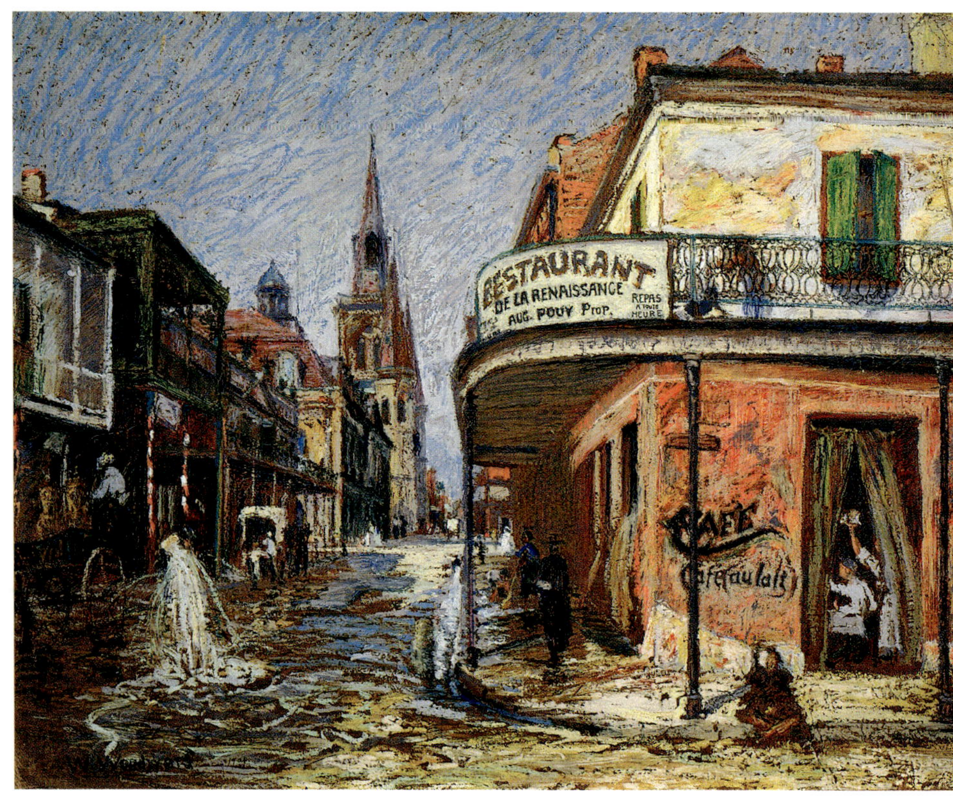

William Woodward

Restaurant de la Renaissance, 1904

Rafaelli oil crayon on board
The Historic New Orleans Collection 1976.181

William Woodward's interest in architecture predates his founding of the Architecture School at Tulane University in 1907. These two works, executed in the medium of oil crayon, suggest his early and continued involvement with the buildings of the Vieux Carré. After coming to New Orleans in 1885 from his native Massachusetts, Woodward made the city his home, though frequent travels provided him opportunities to paint and sketch other locales. In 1921, a fall from scaffolding while working on a mural restricted his dexterity. He ultimately moved to Biloxi, Mississippi, a coastal community some eighty miles east of New Orleans. In addition to large works on canvas and board, Woodward was a prolific draftsman and printmaker. His later graphic works were printed from plates of synthetic plastic, a technique he perfected after his fall because metal plates were too hard for him to work with traditional tools.

The Absinthe House is one of several extant examples of a particular colonial building type. The unusually tall ground floor penetrated by arched openings secured with heavy wooden doors accommodated an "entresol"—a mezzanine-like storage area between the first and second stories that was illuminated by light from the arched windows. Woodward's view of the building and its immediate surroundings captures the flavor of the old city at the turn of the twentieth century. The streetcar tracks are those of the Desire route, immortalized some forty-three years later by Tennessee Williams in *A Streetcar Named Desire*.

Woodward's *Restaurant de la Renaissance* portrays a bustle of activity at the corner of Chartres and Wilkinson Streets: liquid spills from a wagon, an urchin sits in the gutter, and two figures peer from behind the curtained doorway of the restaurant. The Cabildo, the seat of government in Spanish Louisiana, and the towers of St. Louis Cathedral are visible in the distance.

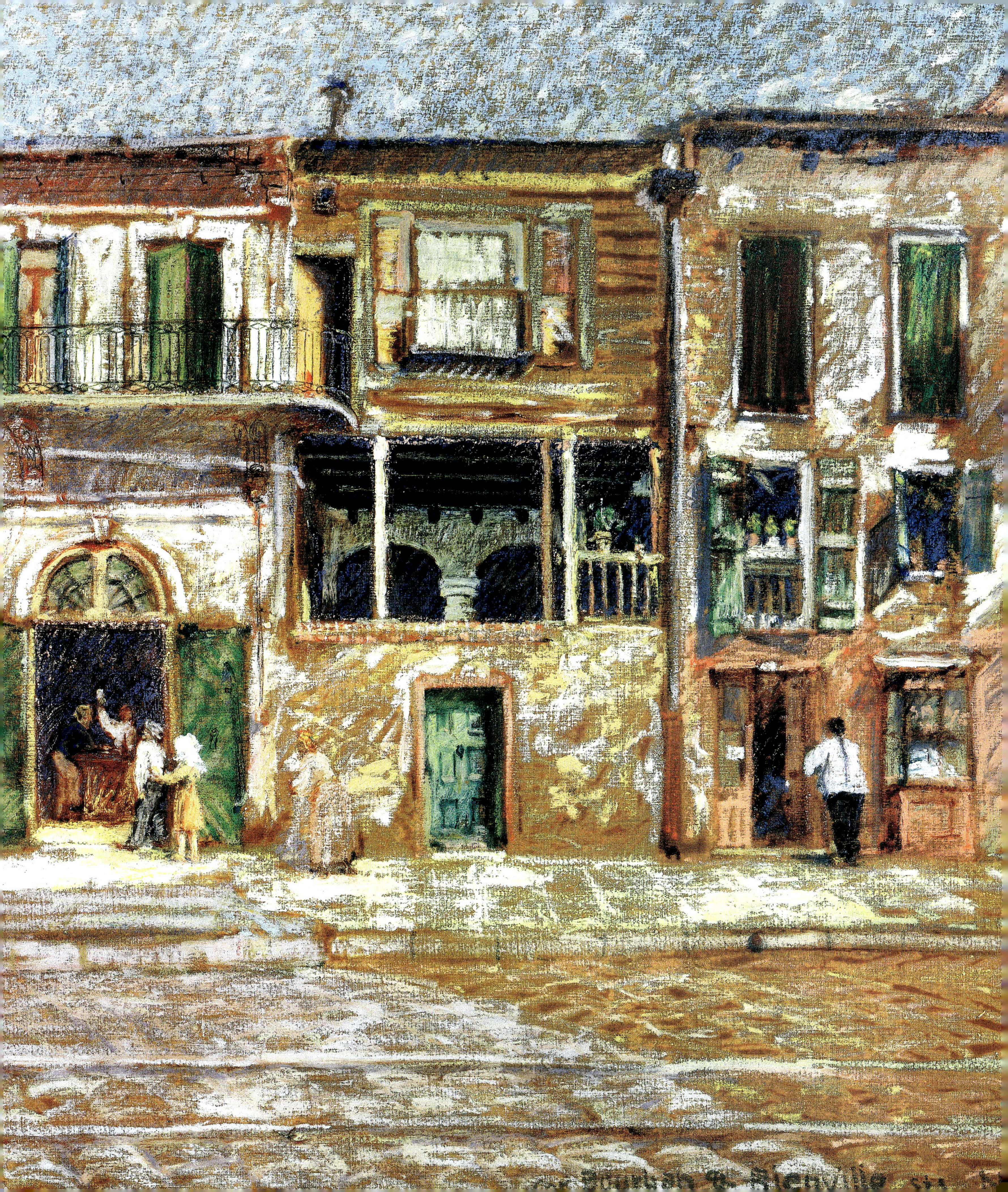

William Faulkner (1897-1962), Sherwood Anderson (1876-1941), and Tennessee Williams (1911-1983) added their literary voices to the chorus of homegrown writers like Roark Bradford (1896-1948), Lyle Saxon (1891-1946), Edward Larocque Tinker (1881-1968), and Stanley Clisby Arthur (ca. 1875-1963) who were honing the perception of New Orleans based on their observations and experiences.

Nearly concurrent with the WICCE was the establishment of the Newcomb College School of Art. Some twenty years after that, the School of Architecture at Tulane University was established. The moving forces behind these enterprises were the Woodward brothers—Ellsworth and William respectively. Natives of Massachusetts, the Woodwards came to the city after having received their artistic education and formative teaching experiences at the Rhode Island School of Design in Providence.

William Woodward (1859-1939) was initially hired to teach drawing and painting at Tulane University in 1884. The following year Ellsworth (1861-1939) arrived to undertake a similar position, and in 1887, became the first professor of art at Newcomb College. In 1907, William established the Tulane University School of Architecture. The influence that the Woodwards had on the visual arts in New Orleans, through the ideas that they promoted and the legions of well-trained students who pursued careers in the visual arts, is impossible to overestimate.

The Woodwards brought new ideas to the region based on their educational experiences in the Northeast and their academic training in Munich and Paris. This mix proved critical. Through the years, other painters with European training had taken pupils privately, but it was the Woodwards' solid training and experience in formal pedagogical methods that made them such a force in the city's art scene. Their talents and energy propelled the arts in New Orleans to a level unknown to that point.

Ellsworth was instrumental in establishing the ceramics program at Newcomb College in 1894, based on the success of the New Orleans Art Pottery Company. Under the leadership of decorator Mary Givens Sheerer (1865-1954), New Orleans became the important center of an international craft movement. According to art historian Jessie Poesch, the design theories of artist Arthur Wesley Dow entered heavily into the decorative schemes of Newcomb pottery during Sheerer's tenure. The work produced at the college became renowned as a unique embodiment of principles espoused by the Arts and Crafts Movement. In 1910, ceramic chemist Paul E. Cox (1879-1968) joined the program, and his ideas dominated the design process, according to Poesch. Cox developed and introduced matte glazes to replace the glossy ones that had prevailed in the Newcomb work prior to his time. Employing local clays in the construction of the ceramics and motifs of native and naturalized plant forms, the decorative program of Newcomb pottery extended the image of the Louisiana landscape into objects of everyday use, such as vases, cups, plates, bowls, and candlesticks.

Attention to the elements of design, craft, and chemistry distinguish the best pieces of Newcomb production.

While some painters, including Alexander J. Drysdale (1870-1934), in addition to those already mentioned, celebrated the watery, moss-draped landscape of the area around New Orleans, others turned their attention to the physical characteristics of the urban environment, especially the architecture of the Vieux Carré. None celebrated this subject more than William Woodward. His hundreds of works representing French Quarter buildings were executed primarily in oil crayon and pastels, the bright colors and soft, crumbly textures of the media echoing the characteristics and colors of the buildings themselves. Woodward sketched and produced etchings of his works as well.

William Woodward's paintings not only embodied the ethos of New Orleans architecture, but helped to establish an appreciation of its character by the public and argued strongly for its preservation. By the mid-1920s, the architectural preservation movement in New Orleans was organized and effective. In the mid-1930s, the Vieux Carré Commission, a preservation agency still in existence, was established with William Woodward as a key member.

Woodward's studies of these buildings are of individual structures, such as *Old Absinthe House*, and of the *toute ensemble*, like *Restaurant de la Renaissance*, both made in 1904. These paintings were not the sole visual legacy of French Quarter architecture in the early twentieth century, but they were the most important and extensive body

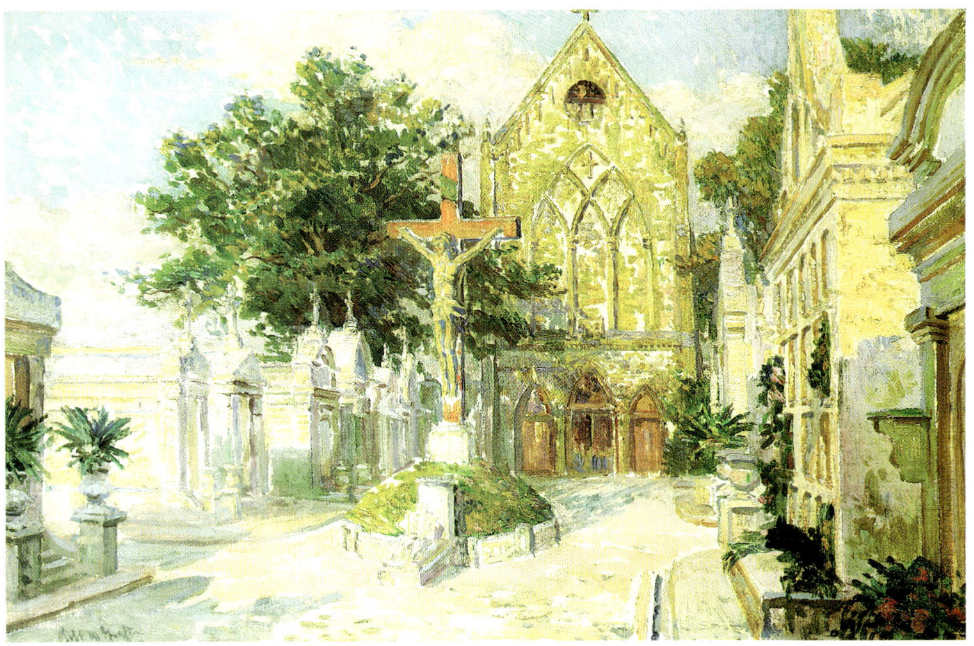

Robert Wadsworth Grafton
St. Roch Cemetery Chapel and Campo Santo, 1917
oil on canvas
The Historic New Orleans Collection 1992.129.7

At the end of the nineteenth century, works of fiction and nonfiction about New Orleans were increasingly published and distributed nationally. Authors like Grace King, George Washington Cable, Lafcadio Hearn, and Kate Chopin intrigued readers nationwide with the character and culture of the city. Well into the twentieth century, many artists and writers, such as Robert Wadsworth Grafton of Illinois, visited the city regularly or took up seasonal residence there.

St. Roch Cemetery and Chapel would have appealed to a visiting artist as particular to New Orleans. Since the early eighteenth century, the dead have been buried in above-ground tombs. St. Roch Cemetery opened in 1874, followed two years later by the construction of the chapel. Built by Father Richard Thevis to fulfill a promise to an answered prayer, the chapel contains a shrine dedicated to St. Roch where even today people leave votive offerings for favors granted.

of work on the subject. Other artists, including Robert Wadsworth Grafton (1876-1936) of Illinois, whose works included *St. Roch Cemetery Chapel and Campo Santo* (1917), Louis Oscar Griffith (1875-1956), and New York photographer Arnold Genthe (1869-1942) were among those who responded visually to the architecture of the city. These artists created a loose community within the Quarter that became part of its charm and allure. William Spratling (1900-1967) and William Faulkner immortalized a number of these French Quarter notables in a playfully satirical book of caricatures, *Sherwood Anderson and Other Famous Creoles* (1926).

During the first quarter of the twentieth century, Ellsworth Woodward's influence on the arts grew beyond his role as a teacher. As a practicing artist, Woodward executed paintings that were exemplars of late American Impressionism. He assumed an active role in both the creation and the administration of the Isaac Delgado Museum of Art (now the New Orleans Museum of Art). According to art historian George E. Jordan, Ellsworth Woodward's influence on artistic taste in the city continued until his death in 1939 through his selection of works to be shown in exhibitions sponsored by the museum. Woodward's masterpiece *Backyard in Covington* (1930s) underscores not only his longtime dedication to Impressionism, but also a vitality that remained in his work throughout his career. Indeed, Jordan credits the Woodwards, especially Ellsworth, with spreading the message of Impressionism throughout the Gulf South, from the late nineteenth century forward.

The influence of the Newcomb art program continued beyond the lifetime of the Woodward brothers. The school attracted nationally influential artists like Will Henry Stevens (1881-1949) who joined the faculty in 1921 and continued teaching until 1948. Stevens, an early southern proponent of nonobjective and abstract art, championed those approaches to painting alongside the more traditional styles taught at the school. He painted directly from nature as his *Landscape with Factory* (ca. 1940) shows. The Newcomb legacy continues today with a strong program in the arts, though the school's renowned pottery production had ceased by the early 1950s.

During the last quarter of the twentieth century, scholarly efforts have been made to address southern art and to place New Orleans and Louisiana art of the nineteenth and early twentieth centuries into that larger regional context. The fit is not always, or not even often, a perfect one. The influences that formed the character of artwork produced in New Orleans were set against a background of traditions and heritage that few other places in the South, let alone the United States, shared. The varied colonial heritage, the influences of so many currents of change that occur in an international port city, and the particular geography of the place influenced the art that developed. But it is difficult to single out one factor as having played a role dominant to any other. External forces always assist in sculpting the character of art. But in the end, it is the artist, reacting individually to the setting, who has the final word.

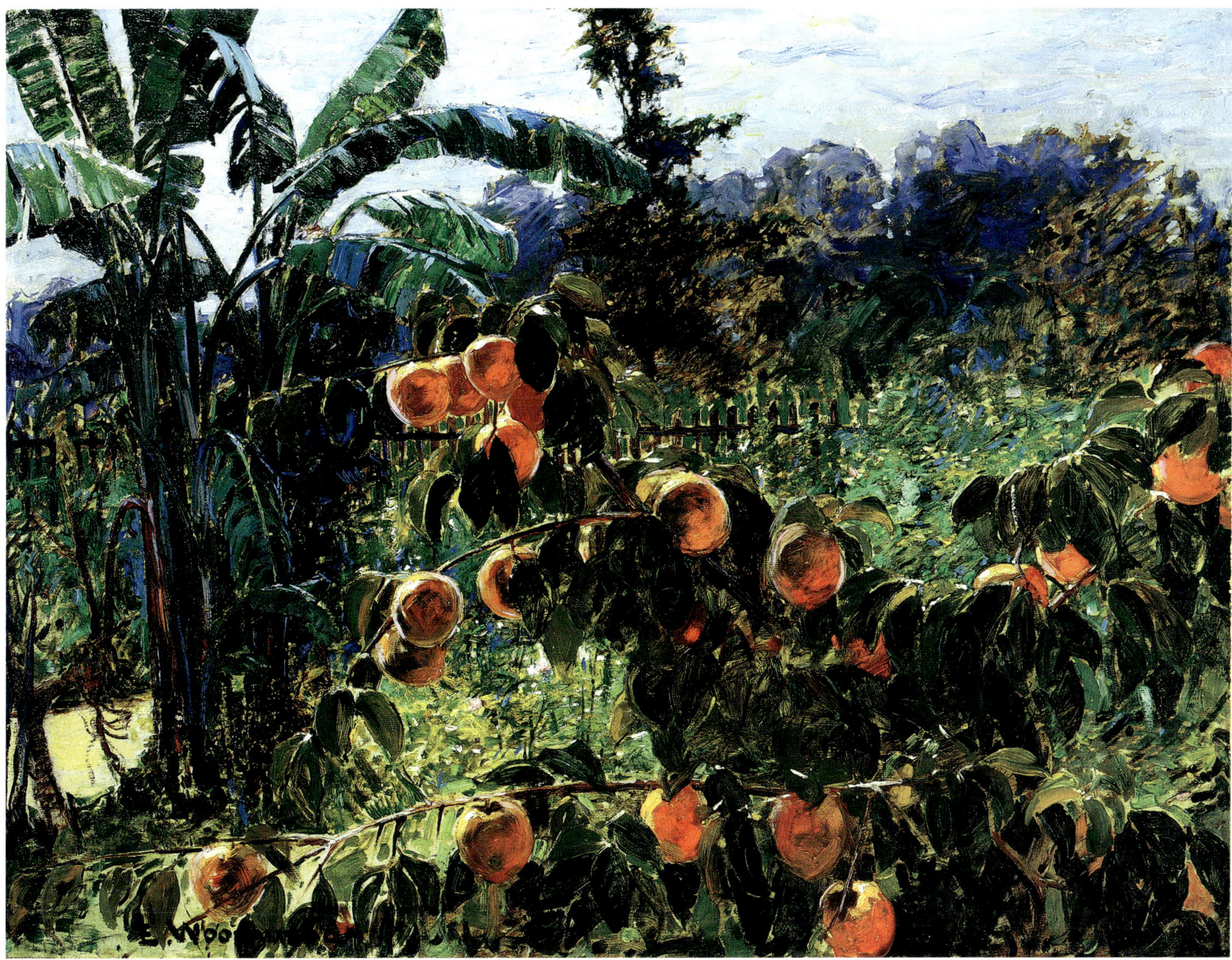

Ellsworth Woodward

Backyard in Covington, between 1930 and 1939

oil on canvas

The Historic New Orleans Collection 1995.103.3

gift of Laura Simon Nelson

Ellsworth Woodward painted primarily in watercolor, but his oil painting *Backyard in Covington* is considered his masterpiece. Woodward moved to Covington, Louisiana, after a long teaching career at Newcomb College. The small community situated north of Lake Pontchartrain was a popular vacation destination for New Orleanians. In the solitude of the large pine forests of St. Tammany Parish (a motif that appears in Woodward's paintings and on Newcomb pottery), Woodward executed the painting of a persimmon tree heavy with ripe fruit, set against a background of lush flowers and other vegetation. Woodward's mastery of Impressionism is evident both in the selection of the subject and its pictorial and painterly treatment. From 1890 until his retirement in 1931, Ellsworth Woodward served as head of the Newcomb College art department. In addition to introducing the highly successful pottery program to the college, he saw that embroidery, metalwork, and bookbinding were added to the curriculum. Tulane University awarded him an honorary doctor of laws degree in 1933. The following year, President Franklin D. Roosevelt appointed him the director of the Gulf States Public Works of Art Project.

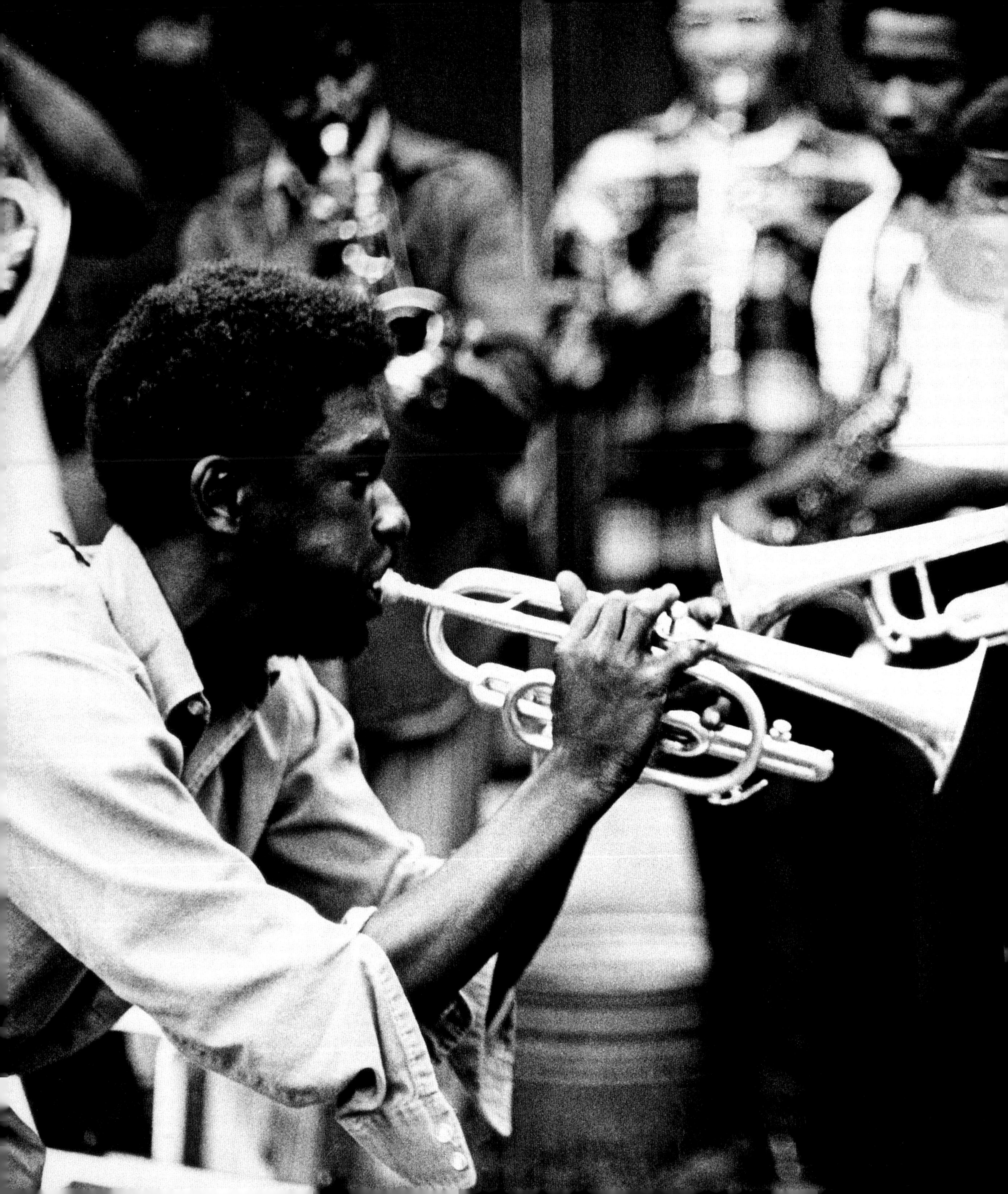

New Orleans: The Cradle of Jazz

Jason WIESE, *Special Collections/Projects Librarian, The Historic New Orleans Collection*

The word "jazz"—initially spelled "jass" or "jasz"—didn't surface in the American popular culture lexicon until about 1914, three years before the first jazz records were made by the Original Dixieland Jass Band. Some historians believe that this slang term referred originally to sex, and originated in New Orleans, where prostitutes favored jasmine perfume, and loose women were called "jezebels." It may also derive in part from the French verb *jaser*, meaning "to chatter" or "to gossip." When applied to music, jazz denoted a distinctive polyrhythmic, syncopated, improvisational sound that was entirely new to its listeners. Jazz was, and still is, a creative fusion of diverse musical traditions and techniques. Historians differ on the question of when and how this fusion began, but the general consensus is that it happened in New Orleans sometime between 1895 and 1914.

New Orleans already had developed a vibrant and diverse musical culture by the mid-nineteenth century. Opera was well established in the city by this time, and dancing was a favored entertainment. In numerous public ballrooms, professional white and Creole orchestras gratified dancers with European waltzes, polkas, schottisches, quadrilles, and Spanish contredanses imported from Cuba. Brass bands performed music at holiday parades, picnics, steamboat arrivals and departures, funerals, and other civic and private occasions. In many respects, music was the glue that held New Orleans's many diverse elements together and preserved the peace between them. Slaves were given permission to gather on Sundays in Congo Square, where they danced and performed music many of them still remembered from West Africa. Curious whites often gathered to witness the fantastic spectacle of hundreds of black slaves singing and dancing to complex African polyrhythms; one such witness was composer Louis Moreau Gottschalk (1829-1869), who based three early compositions on these African American dances and songs, the most famous of which was titled *Bamboula (Danse des Nègres)*. Other composers followed with tunes derived from African American plantation work songs and spirituals. Traveling minstrel shows featured white performers in "blackface," singing so-called "coon songs" often inspired by authentic African American sources. While these performances certainly advanced ugly racial stereotypes, their popularity promoted the music and dance of an oppressed minority and entwined it with other strains of American music.

After the Civil War and Reconstruction, the popularity of brass bands soared throughout the United States, especially in New Orleans. By the 1880s there were many such bands working in the city, and as the nineteenth century drew to a close, a curious fusion began to occur. The polyrhyth-

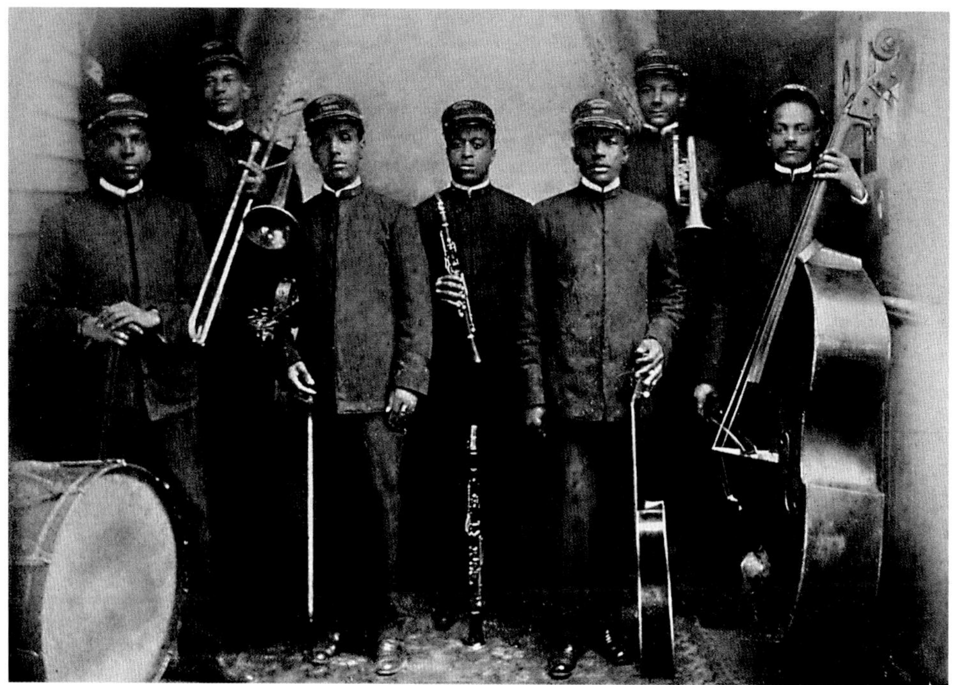

Unidentified Uniformed Black Orchestra
ca. 1900

black-and-white photoprint
The Historic New Orleans Collection 92-48-L
(Mss 520, f. 2312)
William Russell Jazz Collection
Clarisse Claiborne Grima Fund Purchase

Bands such as the Peerless Orchestra, the Superior Orchestra, and the Olympia Band performed at picnics, building dedications, open-air concerts and dances at parks and resorts, funerals, and numerous parades that wound their way around the city. Black or white, these bands wore uniforms when marching in parades and suits for indoor concerts, as the situation required. They played polkas, rags, mazurkas, spirituals, schottisches, or blues—whatever their audiences wanted to hear. There were many of these seminal bands, and they often shared personnel.
Most early players understood and helped to refine the basic premise of jazz music: collective improvisation.

mic sensibility inherited from the earlier Congo Square slave dances began to blend with the popular brass band marches, waltzes, and polkas of the time, even as New Orleans bands absorbed new musical influences such as "rags." Ragtime, a musical style made popular by composer Scott Joplin, offered lively, syncopated dance songs that drew on a variety of musical sources, including minstrel tunes, marches, spirituals, and folk songs. "Ragging" a song meant rearranging its rhythm and melody to make it more danceable, and New Orleans musicians did so at every opportunity, whether in parades or dance halls. Finally, the arrival in New Orleans of thousands of unemployed cotton and sugarcane workers brought the final ingredients needed to form jazz music and imbue it with a soul: black Baptist church hymns and their popular counterpart, the blues.

The music of early African American spiritualist churches was quite different from the familiar Latin Catholic masses then common in New Orleans. It featured call-and-response singing, hand clapping and foot stomping, expressive chants and body language, and dramatic oratory that could transport its listeners. The blues shared many similarities in emotion and expression, but were intended to amuse and entertain, often with profane lyrics. No one knows when or where the blues were born; some musicians believe that they have always existed. Musically, black Baptist hymns and blues songs were somewhat interchangeable, marked by identical cries and moans. Jazz clarinetist Sidney Bechet would later recall that "both of them, the spirituals and the blues, they was a prayer."

New Orleans musicians were the first to blend European instrumentation and melody with "ragging," African polyrhythms, and African American blues and church music. Their horns were the first to echo the moans of the congregation and to reproduce the joyful call-and-response between the preacher and his flock. Their drums and pianos were the first to mimic the cross-rhythms of clapping hands and stomping feet. And they were the first to inflect their music with blue notes and to recall the three-chord, twelve-bar arrangements that would allow for infinite variations and collective improvisation. In short, they were the first to play the music that would eventually be called "jazz."

Bands in New Orleans—black, Creole, and white—were expected to play music for any occasion. White bandleader "Papa" Jack Laine had so many musicians working for him that, in addition to his own Reliance Marching Band, he could supply several other bands simultaneously. The Olympia Brass Band existed on and off from 1900 to 1915, led by cornetist Freddie Keppard, with Joe Oliver playing second cornet and Alphonse Picou, Sidney Bechet, and Lorenzo Tio on clarinets. Oscar "Papa" Celestin formed the Original Tuxedo Orchestra in 1910. There were countless occasions demanding live music, particularly dances. One of the more popular venues for dances was Economy Hall in the historically black Tremé neighborhood, but there were many others, such as Lincoln Park, the Masonic (or Odd Fellows) Hall, Perseverance Hall, San Jacinto Hall, and the Union Sons Hall, better known as "Funky Butt Hall." This last venue was made famous by the legendary cornetist Charles "Buddy" Bolden (1877-1931).

Bolden may have been the first jazz innovator, at a time when jazz was in its infancy. Years after his death, musicians continued to trade stories about the loudness and majesty of his tone. Relatively little is known about Bolden. He was never recorded and appears in only one photograph. All that remains are the stories. His band started playing around 1895 in honky-tonks, parades, and dances and eventually rose to become one of the most popular bands in the city. It was said that when Bolden appeared, people would flock to the sound of his horn. Musicians of the time remembered him as one of the finest cornet players they had ever heard. He apparently favored the blues and played them with such soul and originality that it brought tears to his listeners' eyes. "Bolden got most of his tunes from the 'Holy Roller Church,' the Baptist church on Jackson Avenue and Franklin," claimed trombonist Edward "Kid" Ory in a later interview. "He went there to get ideas on music." By 1906, no black musician in New Orleans

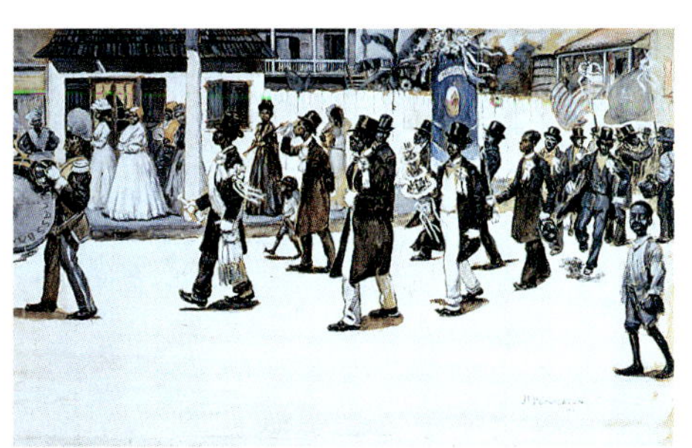

Sons of Hope

color poster print, ca. 1970s
reproduction from original painting by John Peter Pemberton, between 1890 and 1914
The Historic New Orleans Collection 1978.82

The early history of jazz funerals is uncertain, but funeral processions by military bands have existed for centuries. In New Orleans, a unique combination of cultural traditions gradually turned solemn funeral processions to lively, joyful parades probably beginning in the nineteenth century when the city was beset by devastating epidemics of yellow fever. Funeral processions at this time were often sponsored by benevolent societies or Masonic lodges that were racially divided. Over time, black burial societies such as Les Jeunes Amis invested the traditional military funeral march with elements of African ritual dance traditions, especially the use of joyful, up-tempo music and "cutting loose" as the procession left the cemetery after the body's interment.
By contrast, white burial societies ceased to sponsor "funerals with music" in about 1905, perhaps in reaction against a tradition largely shaped by black people.

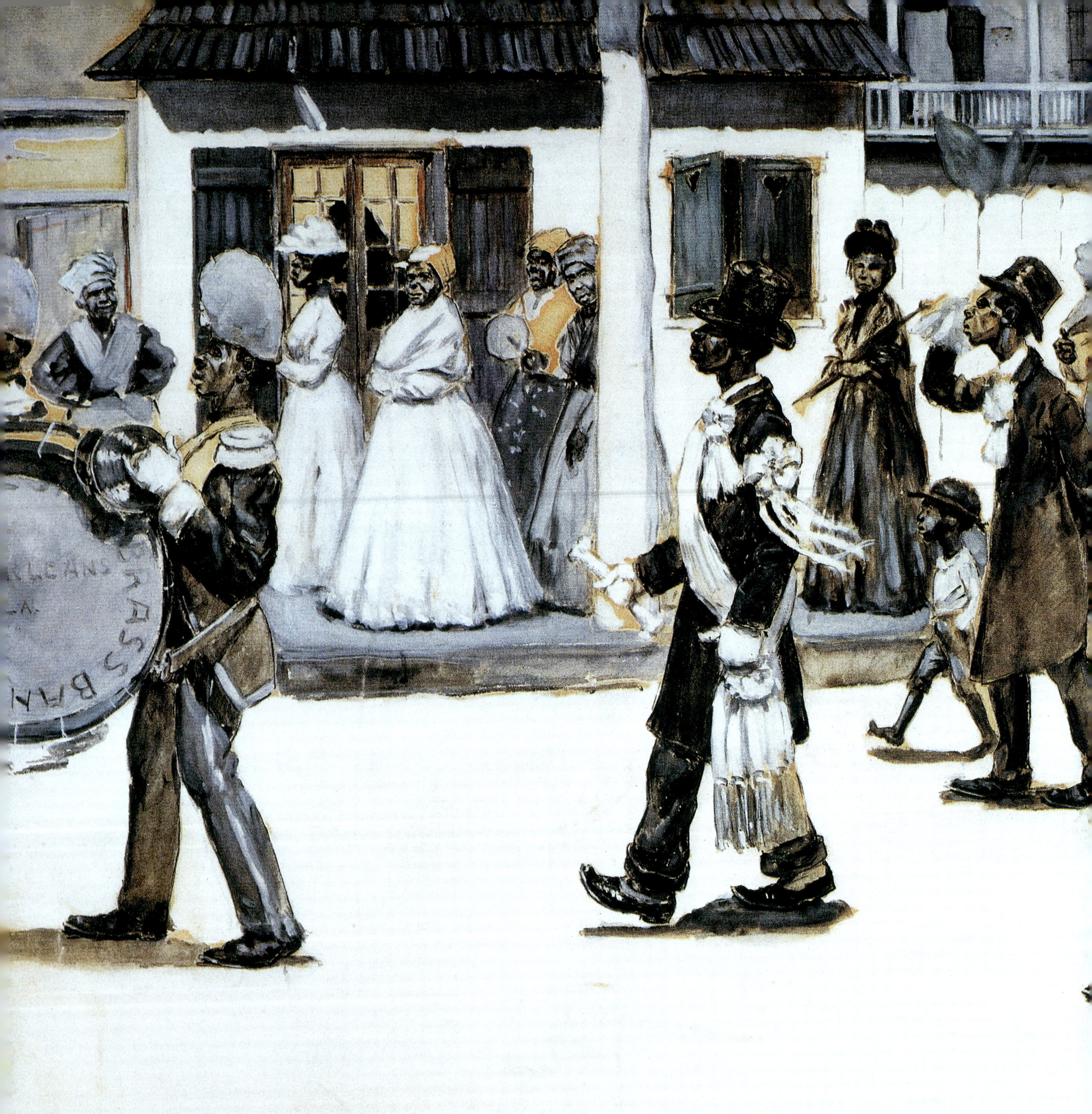
BRASS

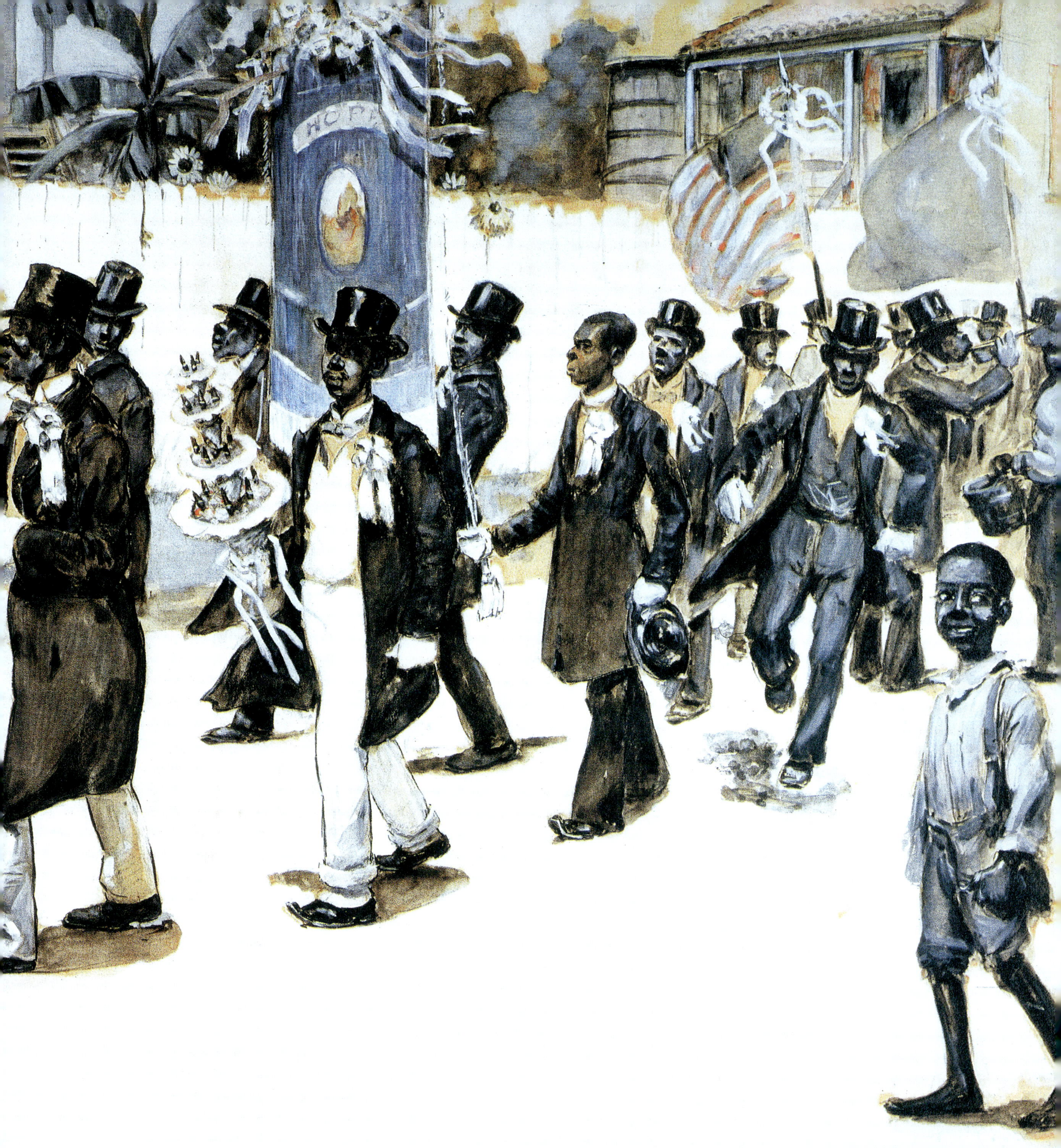
HOPE
J.P. PEMBERTON

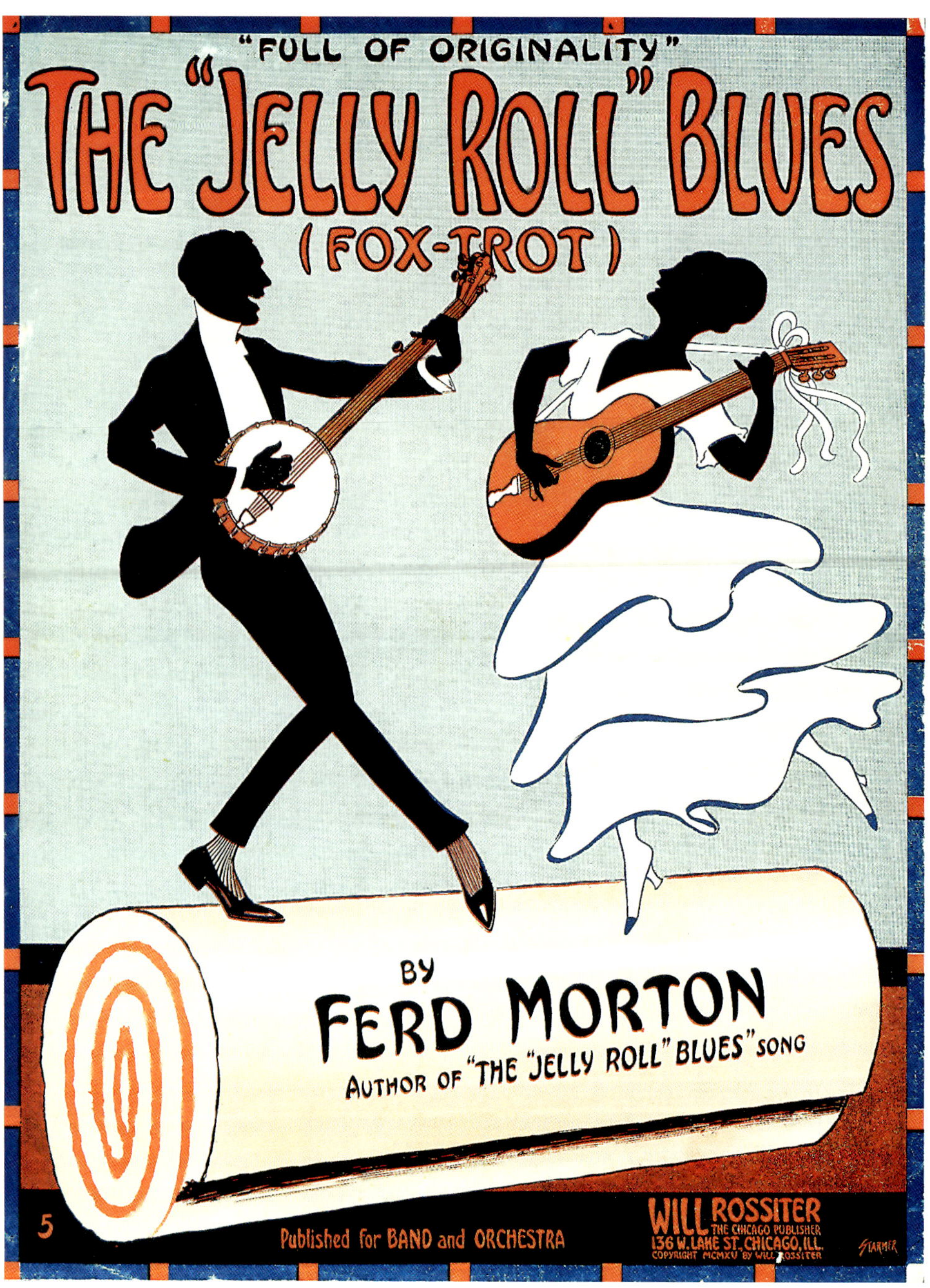

The Jelly Roll Blues
by Ferd Morton (composer)

sheet music for piano by Will Rossiter,
Chicago, Ill., 1915

The Historic New Orleans Collection 92-48-L
(Mss 526, f. 109A)
William Russell Jazz Collection
Clarisse Claiborne Grima Fund Purchase

Jelly Roll Morton's first big hit was a tune called "Wolverine Blues," made famous by a white band, the New Orleans Rhythm Kings. Morton composed a host of classic jazz songs, such as "Jelly Roll Blues," "The King Porter Stomp," "Dead Man Blues," "Black Bottom Stomp," and "The Pearls." Many were published by Melrose Music Company in Chicago. Though Morton was prodigiously talented as a musician, his skills as a businessman were less sharp, and he neglected to secure copyright to his compositions. By the 1930s, when his fame had been overshadowed by a younger generation of musicians, Jelly Roll fell on hard times and was reduced to writing letters in an ultimately futile attempt to recover unpaid royalties from Melrose.

was more famous than "King" Bolden, but his fame was not to last. The popular story is that he broke his own heart with the beauty of his playing, but the more prosaic reality is that he began to suffer headaches and episodes of dementia. Finally, during a Labor Day parade in 1907, Bolden broke down and walked away, never to play his horn in public again. Eventually committed to the state insane asylum, Buddy Bolden spent the last twenty-five years of his life there, tormented and oblivious to the music that he had helped to define.

Jazz coalesced in the streets and neighborhoods throughout New Orleans, but it came to be associated with a particular part of the city. Storyville, also known as "The District," was the legendary "red light" section of New Orleans that operated legally between 1897 and 1917. Named after a city alderman who had proposed that vice be restricted to a single district of the city, Storyville boasted numerous lavishly decorated saloons, gambling dens, and brothels. Prostitution was Storyville's primary business, but music and entertainment were profitable sidelines. While jazz was not born there, the district did expose the new music to a wider audience. Smaller brothels featured piano "professors," while most jazz musicians in the district were employed in dance bands in clubs and restaurants such as Pete Lala's, the 101 Ranch, the Tuxedo Dance Hall, and the Big 25. Some of the city's most popular musicians, including Bolden's protégé Freddie Keppard, cornetist Joe "King" Oliver, and his bandmate Kid Ory, would play respectable venues in the evening—society dances at Tulane University, for example—and then come down to Storyville to play "hot" music until dawn for the gamblers and whores. A high premium was placed on musicianship, and it was not unusual for bands and individual musicians to compete in "cutting" or "bucking" contests, trying to outdo one another with difficult tunes and masterful playing. King Oliver won his crown from Freddie Keppard and was so protective of his own improvisations and techniques that he would occasionally cover his hand with a handkerchief so that other cornet players could not see how he fingered his valves.

Another prominent musician who honed his skills in Storyville was Ferdinand "Jelly Roll" Morton (1890-1941). Jelly Roll Morton was famous in the "sporting houses" for the racy, impromptu songs he played on the piano for the amusement of the customers. Morton would go on to become one of jazz's great performers and composers. A born showman who sported flashy clothes and a haughty demeanor, the light-skinned Creole Morton was a seasoned performer who had gained valuable experience on the vaudeville circuit, sometimes appearing in blackface with comedian Sammy Russell and singer Rosa Brown. Morton left New Orleans for the West Coast and eventually ended up in Chicago, where he made several groundbreaking jazz recordings on the Victor Records label with his Red Hot Peppers—a band consisting of the very best handpicked New Orleans musicians, including clarinetist Johnny Dodds, his brother, drummer Warren "Baby" Dodds, trombonist Kid Ory, and Johnny St. Cyr on banjo and guitar. Other musicians came and went during these historic sessions. Though Morton's Red Hot Peppers apparently excelled at New Orleans-style collective improvisation, every song was in fact carefully arranged by Morton and repeatedly rehearsed. Nevertheless, they sound relaxed, exuberant, and swinging, and are, in the words of critic Tom Piazza, "full aesthetic statements made within the three-minute limit of the standard 10-inch 78-rpm records of the time."

As jazz music grew in popularity, some musicians sought to enhance their marketability by claiming to have invented it. In truth, no one person or band could take the credit for something made and refined by scores of musicians, but that didn't matter. Predictably, Jelly Roll Morton was one such claimant. By the early 1920s Morton made a point of insisting, even on his business cards, that he himself had originated jazz. Not everyone believed him. According to jazz guitarist Danny Barker, Morton was "his own press agent," and many jazz musicians and aficionados were put off by his penchant for self-promotion. Yet Morton certainly was among the earliest performers of jazz and was its first serious composer and theorist. The songs he wrote, beginning in 1905, incorporated elements of both blues and ragtime—as well as romantic French, Italian, and Spanish songs. Morton tried to emulate on a piano the joyful polyphony of the New Orleans marching bands he had known. Morton's virtuosity at the keyboard brought his compositions to life and set them apart as something genuinely new.

Another credible claim came from the Original Dixieland 'Jass' Band, a five-piece white ensemble from New Orleans that included veterans of Papa Jack Laine's marching bands. After successful shows in Chicago and New York, this group became the first jazz band to be recorded, by Columbia Records in January of 1917. A subsequent recording session at Victor Records propelled the Original Dixieland Jass Band—and jazz music—into the hearts and homes of millions of Americans. These records created a huge sensation, even back in New Orleans, where established black and white bands cut their rosters to duplicate the five-man lineup of the ODJB. Midway through 1917, the Original Dixieland Jazz Band corrected the spelling of their name, and Victor Records catalogs and publicity described them as the "creators of jazz." Young Louis Armstrong bought some of the ODJB's records and taught himself to duplicate the intricate clarinet solos with his cornet. Other musicians, like Sidney Bechet, dismissed both the ODJB and its claim to have invented jazz. "Those were all numbers they had learned from playing opposite us back in New Orleans," Bechet later wrote.

Whatever the music's origins, the phenomenal popularity of the Original Dixieland Jazz Band led dancehalls and clubs in Chicago and other northern cities to seek out and hire other musicians who could play "New Orleans-style" music to satisfy the lucrative new demand for it. Thus began the exodus of New Orleans musicians up the Mississippi River. Legendary Storyville jazzmen King Oliver and Kid Ory headed north in search of wider fame and fortune. Riverboat jazz orchestras plied the river from New Orleans to St. Paul, Minnesota, and also to towns on the Mississippi's tributaries, such as Kansas City and Omaha on the Missouri River and towns on the Ohio River as far as Pittsburgh. Music publishers issued torrents of sheet music for jazz tunes like "Ballin' the Jack," "Ramblin' Blues," and "New Orleans Hop Scop Blues." However, not everyone in America was happy about the spread of this new music. Some musicians and music critics dismissed it as noise, a "Bolshevistic

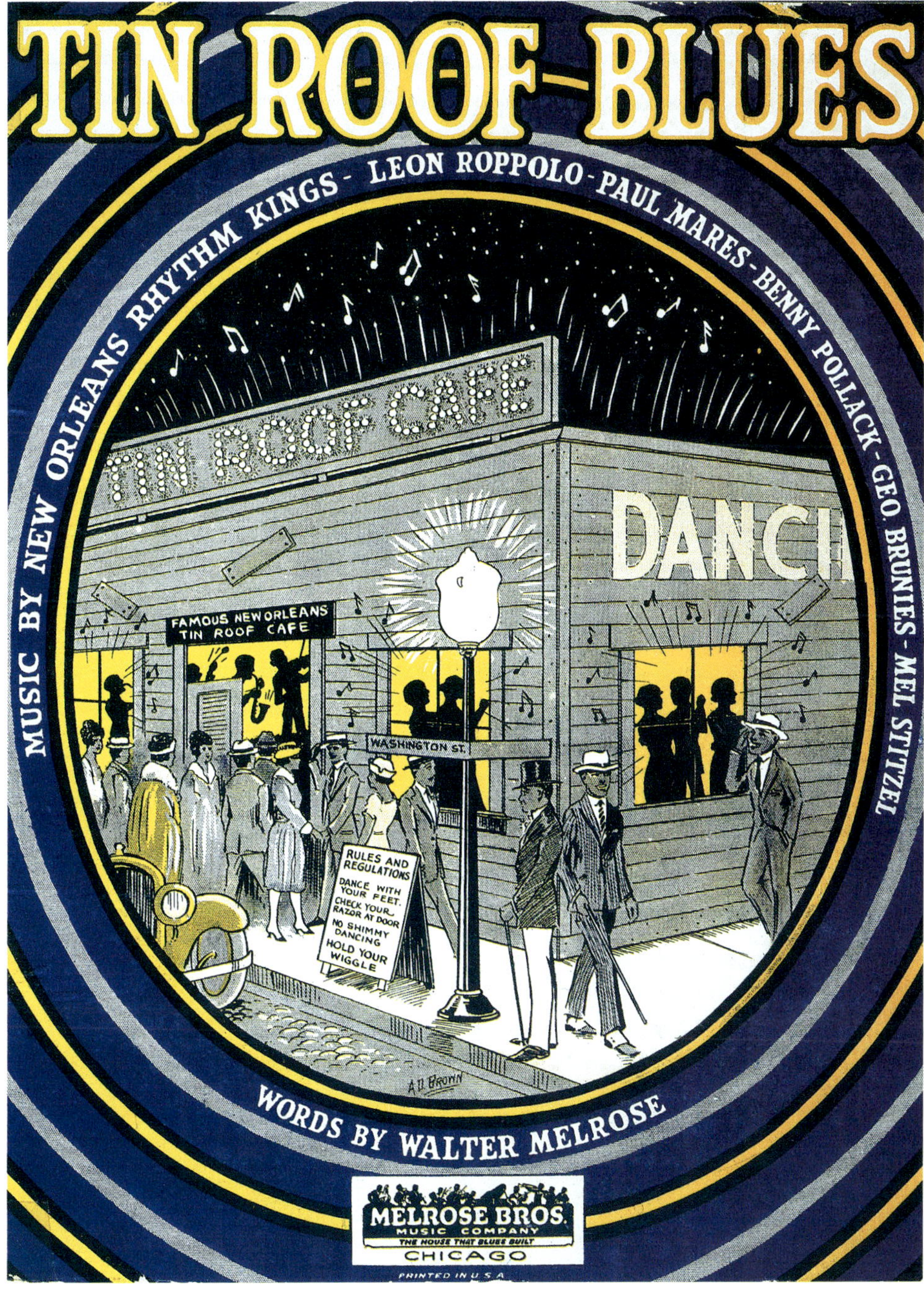

Tin Roof Blues
by New Orleans Rhythm Kings (composers)

sheet music by Melrose Brothers Music Company, Chicago, Ill., 1923
The Historic New Orleans Collection 92-48-L
(Mss 526, f. 940)
William Russell Jazz Collection
Clarisse Claiborne Grima Fund Purchase

In the days before radio, printed sheet music was a primary means of broadcasting new songs. From 1917 through the 1920s, publishers issued music for countless jazz tunes, some of them destined to become standards. Sheet-music covers of this period, generally adorned with colorful, decorative scenes, are highly prized by collectors today. Songs were typically published in "short score"—with the accompaniment reduced to a piano part and often to chord symbols or tablature for use with guitar or banjo—though full orchestrations were published as well. The New Orleans Rhythm Kings were heavily influenced by King Oliver's Creole Jazz Band and became the first group to put out a "racially mixed" jazz record in 1923 with "Sobbin' Blues" featuring Jelly Roll Morton.

smashing of the rules and tenets of decorous music." Others believed that jazz—and the dancing it encouraged—did irreparable harm to the nation's moral character. Aside from its comparatively fast pace, jazz's African American origins upset some older white Americans, who believed that this music "from the Negro brothels of the South" would stimulate the young in unwholesome ways and lead them to moral disaster. Some even associated it with voodoo and claimed that it excited "brutality and sensuality" in its listeners. Yet these denunciations did little to stem the flow of jazz, which even penetrated small-town dances in the Midwest.

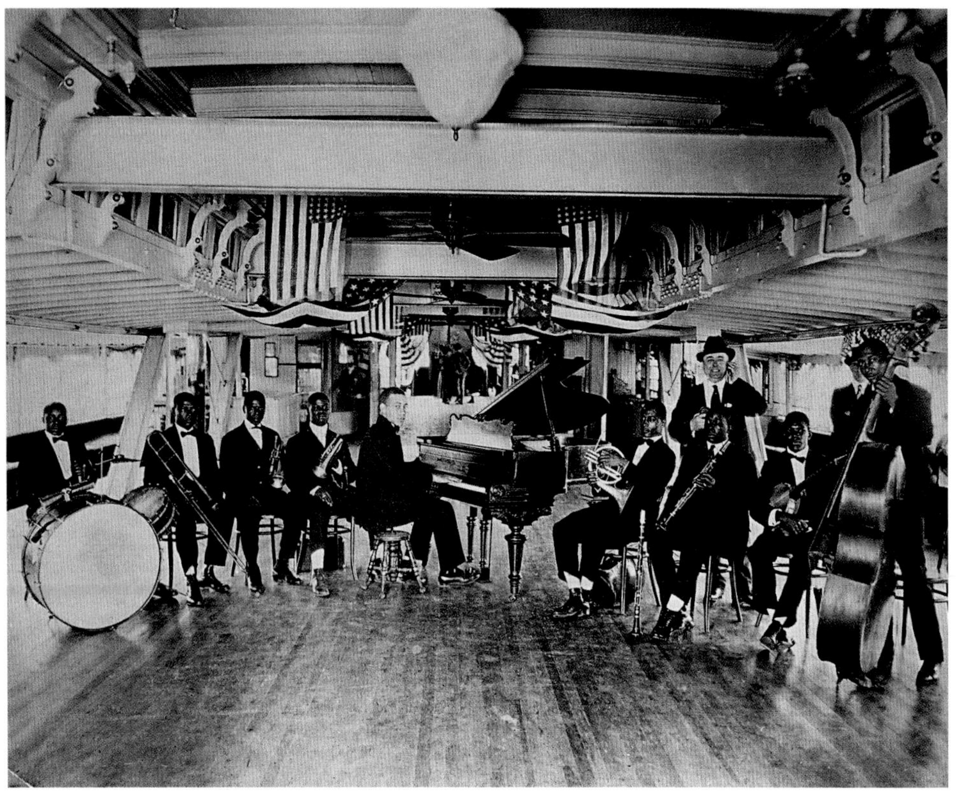

Fate Marable's S. S. Sidney Band
ca. 1918

black-and-white photoprint
The Historic New Orleans Collection 92-48-L
(Mss 532, f. 79)
William Russell Jazz Collection
Clarisse Claiborne Grima Fund Purchase

Fate Marable led what many early musicians called "The Conservatory." His bands on the Strekfus Mississippi riverboat line served as a training academy for many of the great jazz musicians of the 1920s. Marable, who insisted that his musicians learn to read music, played piano and riverboat steam calliopes.

The keys of the steam calliope sometimes grew so hot that Marable had to wear gloves to play it. The musicians shown here are, from left to right, Warren "Baby" Dodds, Bebé Ridgely, Joe Howard, Louis Armstrong, Fate Marable, David Jones, Johnny Dodds, Johnny St. Cyr, and George "Pops" Foster. Riverboat orchestras like this one did a great deal to spread New Orleans jazz to other river cities in America.

As the 1920s dawned, recording company executives recognized that, along with their white customers, African Americans constituted a significant audience for recorded jazz music, so long as it was recorded by black musicians. Soon a thriving trade in so-called "race records" began, led by a division of the General Phonograph Corporation called Okeh. These records, which featured black artists, were initially intended for black buyers, as it was generally believed that white listeners preferred music by white musicians. Such was the social climate in America at the time. Soon enough it became clear that certain songs and musicians transcended race and could be in demand by everybody. The first major crossover success from Okeh Records was a young cornet player from New Orleans named Louis Armstrong.

Born in 1901 in a rough New Orleans neighborhood of brothels and gambling dens, Louis Armstrong had every reason to die young, penniless, and unknown. Few would have guessed that "Little Louis," as he was then known, would grow up to be the most famous jazz musician in the world and a twentieth-century American icon. The turning point came in the Colored Waifs Home, where Armstrong had been sent as a juvenile delinquent. The home had a band, and Armstrong, already devoted to New Orleans's street music, seized the chance to join it as a cornet player. He may have picked the cornet because of his admiration for Willie "Bunk" Johnson, who played with Louis's favorite, the Eagle Band, named after the Eagle Saloon at the corner

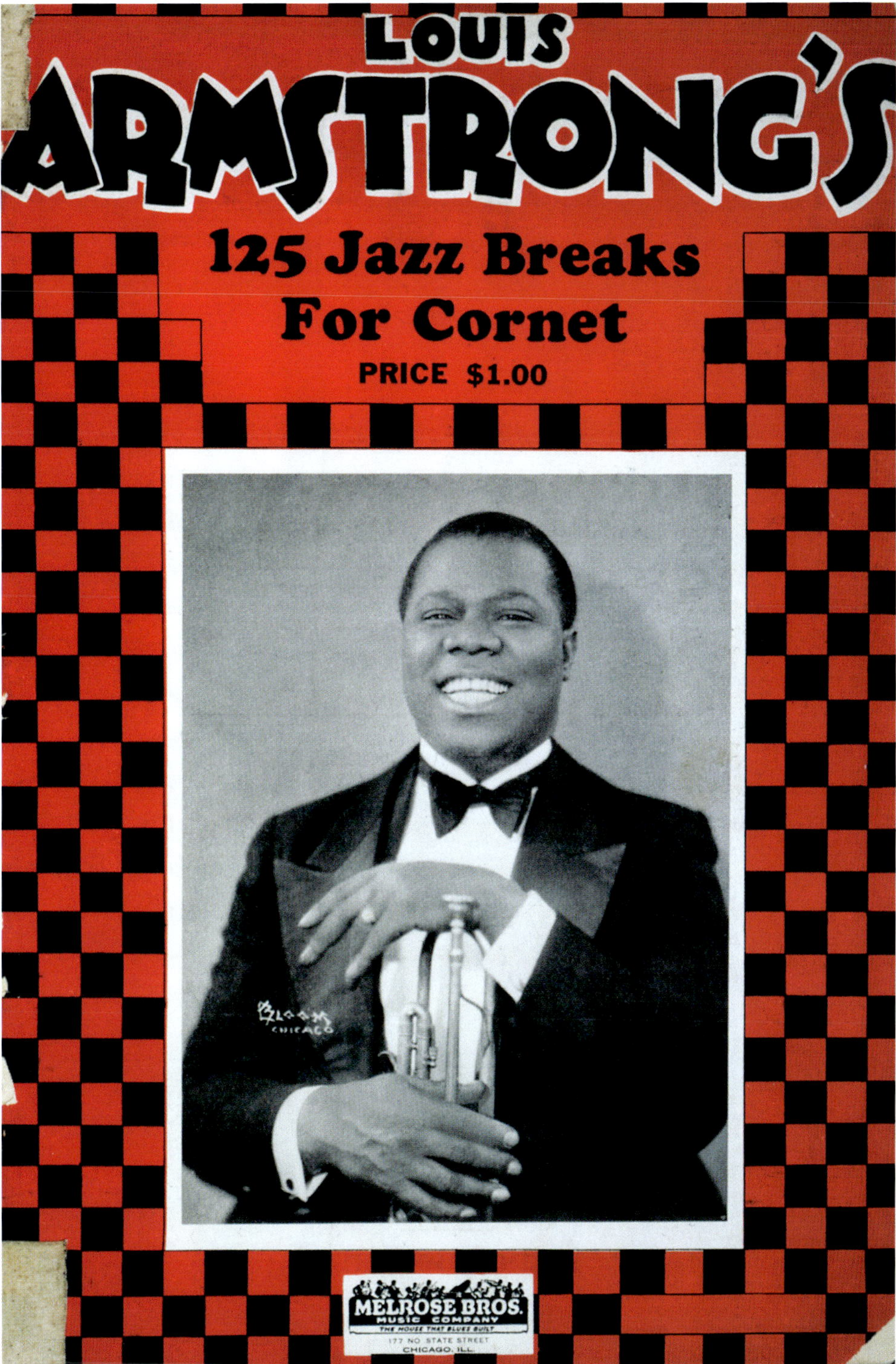

Louis Armstrong's 125 Jazz Breaks for Cornet

sheet music by Melrose Bros. Music Company, Chicago, 1927
The Historic New Orleans Collection 92-48-L
(Mss 536, Armstrong, f. 320)
William Russell Jazz Collection
Clarisse Claiborne Grima Fund Purchase

"Breaks" in jazz are short solos played by one musician while the rest of the band pauses. Louis Armstrong's recorded solos and live performances set a new standard for cornet players, who would endlessly replay his records and practice his solos note-for-note. The opening cadenza of "West End Blues" was particularly difficult, and few, if any, mastered it. The Melrose Brothers Music Company in Chicago approached Armstrong in 1927 with the idea of transcribing his cornet breaks for publication. Armstrong agreed and played 125 selections into a Dictaphone. The recordings were subsequently lost, but the transcribed breaks were published. Armstrong bought himself a new car with the proceeds and left Chicago for even greater fame in New York City.

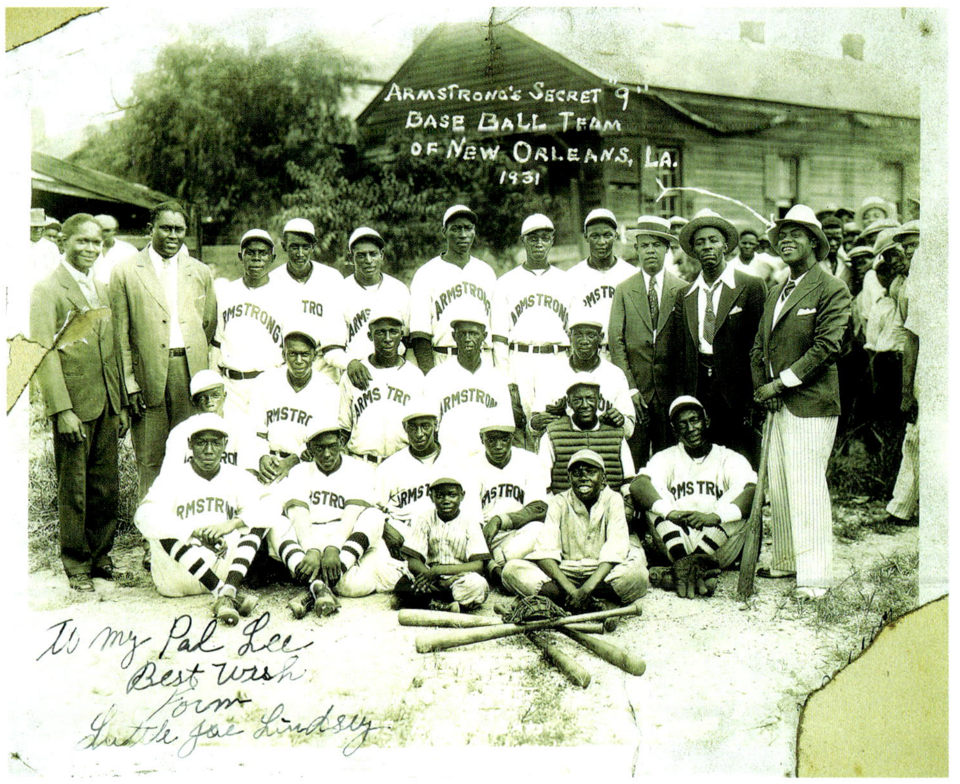

Armstrong's "Secret 9" Baseball Team of New Orleans, La., 1931

black-and-white photoprint
The Historic New Orleans Collection 92-48-L
(Mss 536, Armstrong, f. 329)
William Russell Jazz Collection
Clarisse Claiborne Grima Fund Purchase

It is impossible to overstate the magnitude of Armstrong's celebrity when he made a triumphant return to his hometown in June 1931. Surrounded by crowds of adoring black fans—who were proud that "one of their own" had achieved such fame in the wider world—Armstrong toured his old neighborhood, visited the Colored Waifs Home where he'd lived as a boy, and played a series of successful concerts. He also sponsored the baseball team shown here, drawn mostly from the membership of the Zulu Social Aid and Pleasure Club. Armstrong, standing at far right, would serve in 1949 as the monarch of Zulu's Mardi Gras parade. The print is inscribed by "Little Joe" Lindsey, a musician who had played with Armstrong in 1917.

of South Rampart and Perdido Streets. After leaving the Waifs Home at the age of fourteen, Armstrong spent a few years working odd jobs around the city and occasionally playing music with other young musicians, including Sidney Bechet. In 1917, Armstrong met and fell under the musical influence of the great King Oliver. When Oliver went north, the young Armstrong took over his place as cornet player in Kid Ory's Brown Skinned Babies Band. Further training came courtesy of a stint with Fate Marable, who led bands on Mississippi riverboats. Yet Louis was not ready to stray far from the Crescent City. After two seasons with Marable, Armstrong returned to New Orleans and played for a time with his friend Zutty Singleton's band in Storyville. Aside from building his amazing skill and endurance as a cornet player, Armstrong composed a number of tunes during this period, including a local hit called "I Wish I Could Shimmy Like My Sister Kate." His stage presence and masterful playing spread his reputation far beyond Rampart Street, and it wasn't long until Louis received a telegram from King Oliver in Chicago, whose Creole Jazz Band was the talk of the town.

In the summer of 1922, Armstrong took Oliver up on his offer and finally left his beloved hometown for a musical career in the North. Joining Oliver's band was, as Armstrong would later write, his boyhood dream come true. For almost two years, Armstrong and Oliver thrilled thousands of listeners—including many professional and aspiring musicians—at their live performances at the Lincoln Gardens Dance Hall. Their fabled duet breaks showed that the young Armstrong was already a master of his instrument, and in time, it became apparent that the young man would soon outshine the great King himself. Encouraged by Lil Hardin, who played piano for Oliver's band, Armstrong struck out on his own in June 1924. His reputation in Chicago had earned him an invitation to join the great Fletcher Henderson's Orchestra in New York, and he seized the opportunity. Soon, New York was dazzled as well. Henderson's orchestra, which had been crisp and professional, was blown away by Armstrong's searing, bluesy originality. Audiences flocked around the bandstand, refusing to let him leave and insisting that he play and replay choruses. "He made the men really swing-conscious with that New Orleans style of his," Henderson would later note. Armstrong's first stay in New York would be rounded out by some memorable recordings with well-known blues singers such as Ma Rainey and Bessie Smith.

Armstrong returned in triumph to Chicago in November 1925, where he thrilled audiences at the famous Dreamland and Vendome clubs. He also organized his famous Hot Five group for recording sessions with Okeh Records—the first recordings to be made under his name. Armstrong lured trombonist Kid Ory up from New Orleans and drafted clarinetist Johnny Dodds and

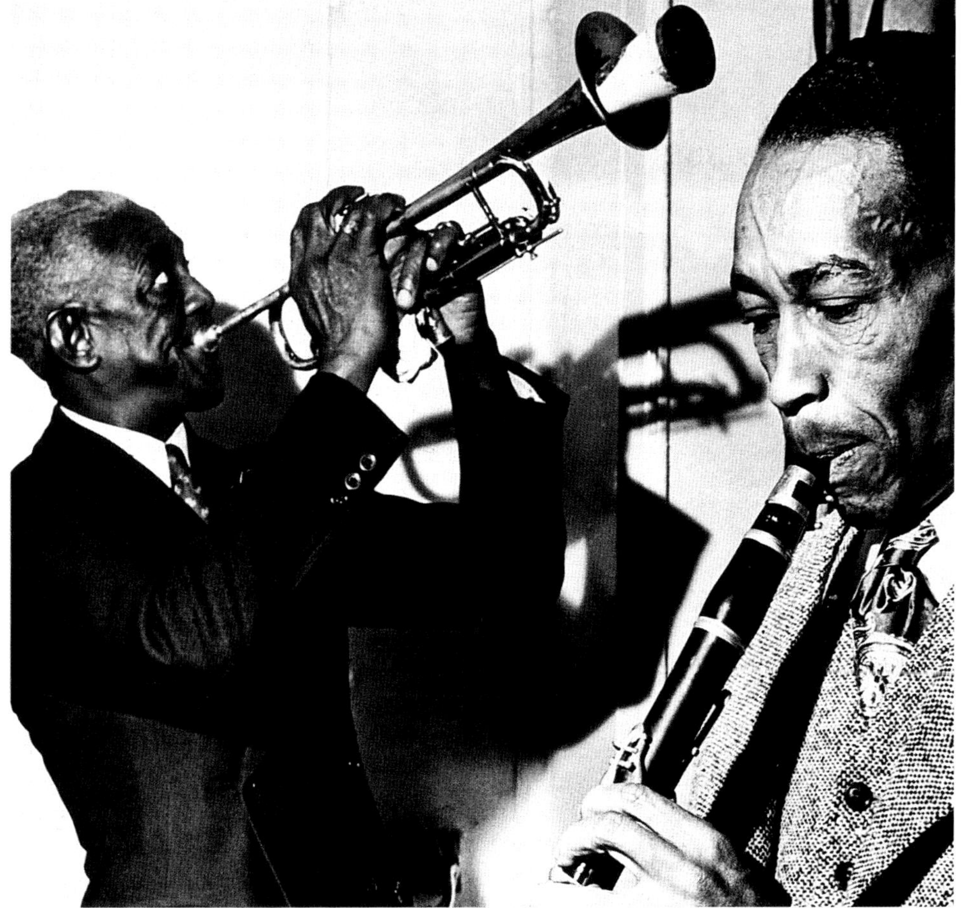

Bunk Johnson and George Lewis at Rehearsal
ca. 1940s

black-and-white photoprint
The Historic New Orleans Collection 92-48-L
(Mss 516, f. 1049)
William Russell Jazz Collection
Clarisse Claiborne Grima Fund Purchase

Bunk Johnson claimed to have played with the famous Buddy Bolden at the turn of the century but in fact was probably too young to have done so. He did play with the Eagle Band and other groups, traveling widely until he retired from music in 1934. Rediscovered six years later, Bunk embarked on a second musical career, leading his own bands in New Orleans and elsewhere in the United States. He played a number of concerts in New York City, including a brief engagement with Sidney Bechet. Clarinetist George Lewis went on to play with the world-famous Preservation Hall Jazz Band in the 1960s.

banjo player Johnny St. Cyr from King Oliver's band. Lil Hardin Armstrong, now Louis's wife, rounded out the original five. They met in informal sessions that yielded what many critics consider to be the finest recordings in jazz history. Armstrong's Hot Five—and later his Hot Seven—made over sixty recordings that recalled the collective polyphony of New Orleans traditions and transcended them through the sheer power and imagination of Armstrong's playing. "Cornet Chop Suey," recorded in 1926, relies entirely on Armstrong's mastery of his instrument and drove legions of would-be musicians to memorize his thrilling stop-time solo and final cadenza. Another tune from this time, "Heebie Jeebies," featured Armstrong's "scat" singing—an inspired chorus of nonsense syllables that brilliantly mimicked an instrumental solo. Armstrong had learned scat singing in New Orleans, but his exuberance and rhythmic drive elevated it to the realm of art. One need only compare the solos from earlier jazz recordings to Armstrong's solos on these records to hear the magnitude of difference. In short, the genius and confidence that Armstrong demonstrated in these epic recordings single-handedly turned jazz from an ensemblist's art to a soloist's art. Armstrong would soon trade his cornet for a trumpet, and while jazz would continue to evolve in the decades that followed, countless jazz musicians would idolize Armstrong for having led the way, and would also struggle to emerge from beneath his long shadow.

As brilliant as Louis Armstrong was, he certainly wasn't the only soloist from New Orleans to delight and amaze his listeners. By 1925, Sidney Bechet had already established a reputation for thrilling and complex runs on his clarinet. His career spanned more than four decades, from his early days in New Orleans to his later fame as an expatriate jazzman in France. Though he was among the greatest New Orleans clarinetists, he is better known for his unsurpassed mastery of the soprano saxophone. He exerted a considerable influence on later soprano sax players, including John Coltrane. Bechet's sound on soprano was, in the words of jazz critic Tom Piazza, "wide, full of vibrato, and bursting with emotion." Like Armstrong, Bechet could simultaneously play with and shine through an ensemble, projecting his musical personality and giving the bands in which he played a verve they would have lacked without him.

Though they had exported many of their preeminent players, the Crescent City's brass bands continued to perform their traditional roles in parades, funerals, and dance halls, though their music—which had entranced young Louis Armstrong—now sounded quaint and old-fashioned to younger musicians. Jazz in this period had moved away from New Orleans-style group improvisation and turned increasingly through the 1930s toward individual soloists and larger swing bands. Kid Ory moved to California to raise chickens, and Johnny Dodds drove a taxi in Chicago. Even the great Jelly Roll Morton had grown out of style and was reduced to waiting tables in Washington, D.C. The older musicians who had played with Buddy

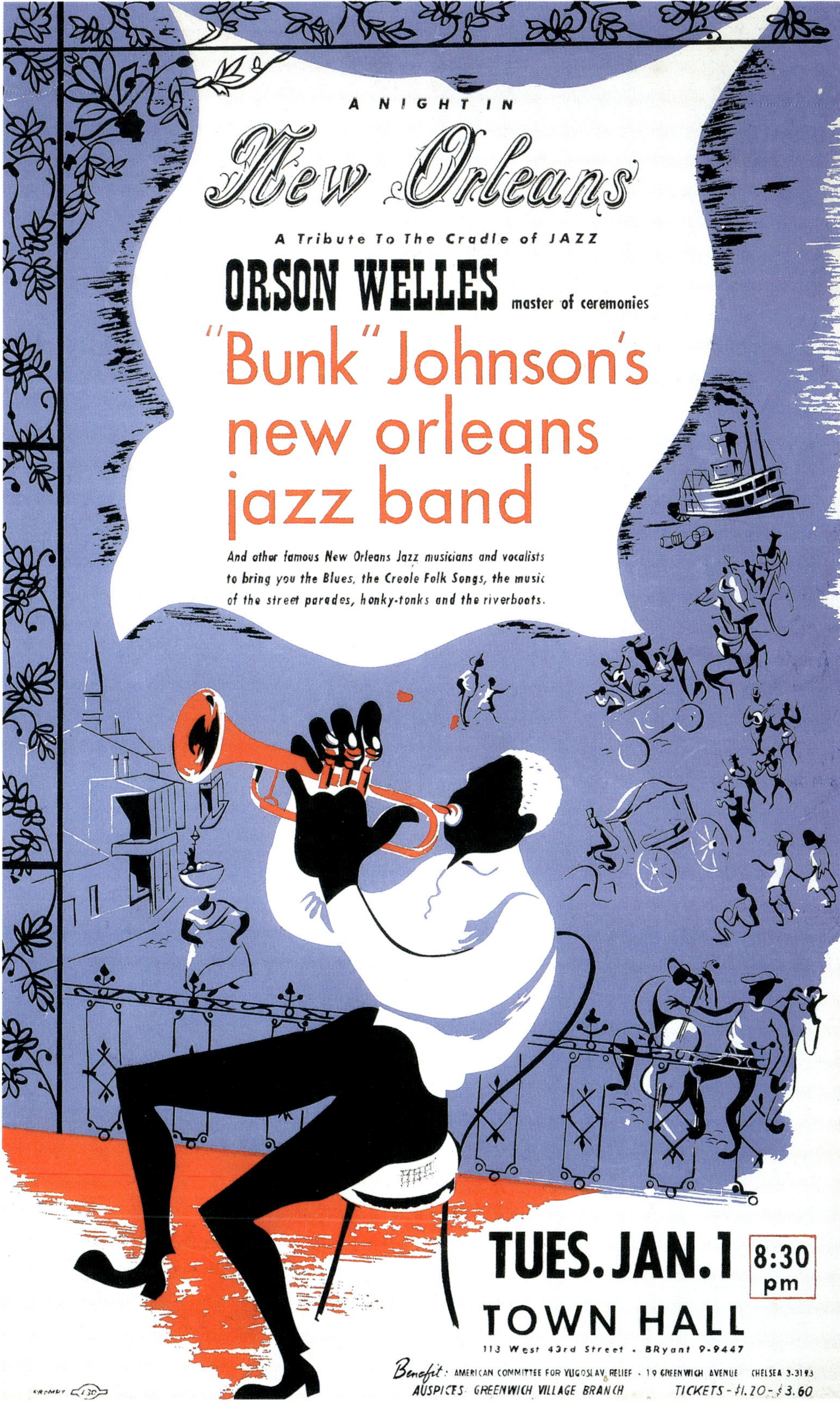

A Night in New Orleans: A Tribute to the Cradle of Jazz, 1946

color printed poster
The Historic New Orleans Collection 92-48-L (Mss 510, f. 964)
William Russell Jazz Collection
Clarisse Claiborne Grima Fund Purchase

New York City's Town Hall featured many landmark jazz concerts, including "jam sessions" organized by Eddie Condon, Louis Armstrong's first appearance with a racially integrated orchestra, an electrifying series of concerts by Sidney Bechet, and Dizzy Gillespie's famous All Stars with Charlie Parker. Bunk Johnson's 1946 concert, hosted by Orson Welles, was part of the revival of New Orleans-style jazz inspired in part by some musicians' aversion to newer jazz forms, like "bebop." Johnson's credentials as a jazzman went back to jazz's earliest days, when he played "gut-bucket blues" with various New Orleans bands. Backed by other old-time musicians like Muggsy Spanier and Albert Nicholas, Bunk took his listeners back to the "cradle of jazz"—New Orleans.

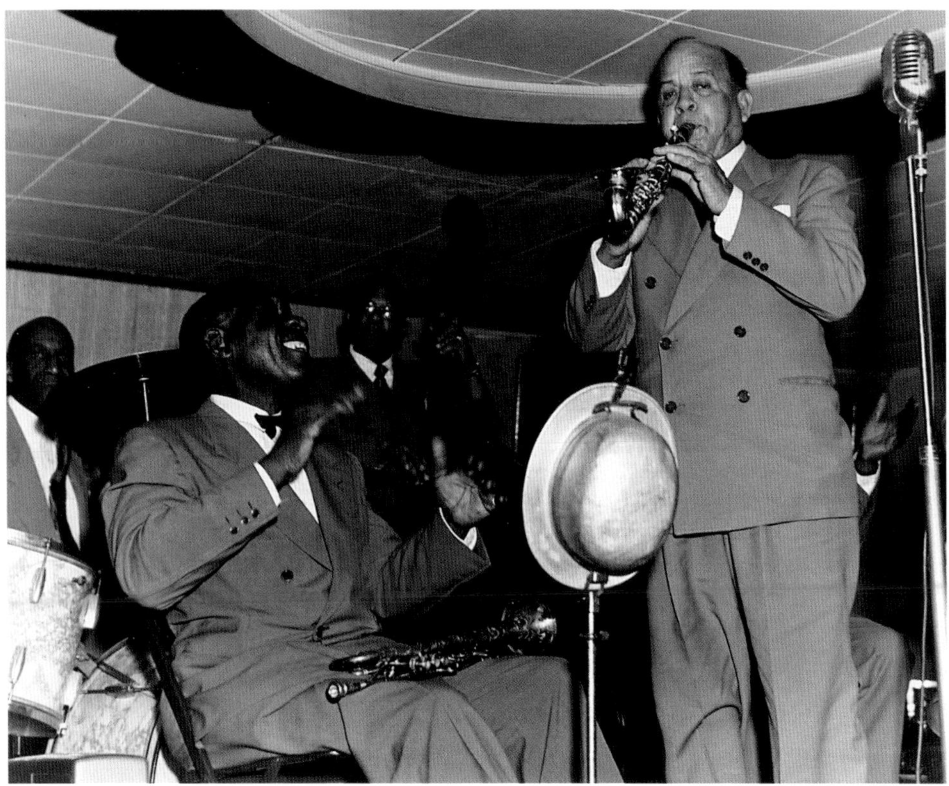

Alphonse Picou Playing on Bandstand with Arthur "Papa" Celestin, ca. 1949

black-and-white photoprint
The Historic New Orleans Collection 92-48-L
(Mss 536, Picou, Alphonse, f. 37)
William Russell Jazz Collection
Clarisse Claiborne Grima Fund Purchase

Creole Alphonse Picou, born in 1878, was one of the earliest jazz clarinetists. He played in the Excelsior Brass Band and Freddie Keppard's Olympia Orchestra, as well as the Tuxedo Brass Band. Picou left the music business in 1932 and worked as a tinsmith until the Dixieland Revival of the 1940s, when he played and made records with cornetist "Papa" Celestin and trumpeter Henry "Kid" Rena. He favored a curious Albert system clarinet with a silver bell, shown here. Picou led his own small group in New Orleans in the 1950s and appeared with the Eureka Band. When he died in 1961, thousands of jazz fans and fellow musicians attended his elaborate jazz funeral.

Bolden were beginning to pass away, and it seemed that early jazz might fade away with them. However, there were some jazz musicians and music enthusiasts who had come to believe that early New Orleans-style music was jazz in its purest form, and their enthusiasm launched what might be termed a Dixieland Revival. One of the key persons involved in this resurrection was William "Bill" Russell.

William Russell, born Russell William Wagner (1905-1992), was a composer, jazz historian, and collector who focused on traditional jazz and its origins in New Orleans. Mr. Russell conducted extensive research into jazz and the cultural milieu from which it arose. Further, he was a friend of many of the musicians he researched, including Louis Armstrong, Bunk Johnson, Manuel "Fess" Manetta, George Lewis,

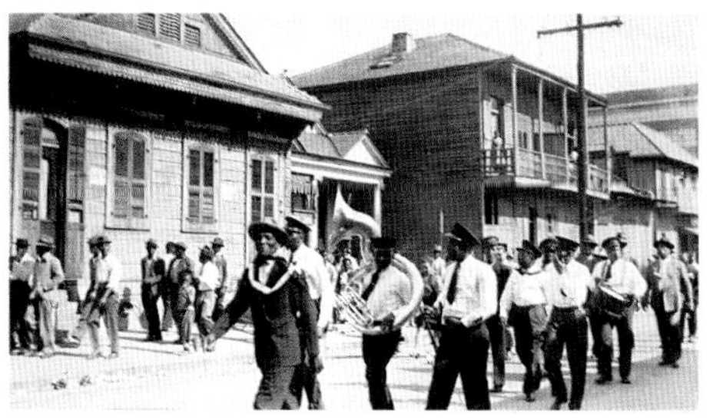

William Russell
Brass Band Funeral March, Dumaine Street, New Orleans, 1946

black-and-white photoprint
The Historic New Orleans Collection 92-48-L
(MSS 520, f. 376)
William Russell Jazz Collection
Clarisse Claiborne Grima Fund Purchase

In March 1946, jazz collector and historian Bill Russell made a series of photographs to document a jazz funeral procession in the historically black Tremé neighborhood. This image shows Kid Howard's brass band—featuring Jim Robinson, Louis Dumaine, and George Lewis—on its way to a funeral home, from which the deceased and mourners would have been accompanied through the streets to one of the local cemeteries. Until the deceased reached his final resting place, the band would have played slow, mournful spirituals, swaying as they walked, and gathering a steadily growing crowd as they moved along. Russell noted that this procession was sponsored by the Square Deal Boys, probably a club or benevolent society based in Tremé. Unfortunately, jazz funerals in recent years have devolved into crowded media spectacles.

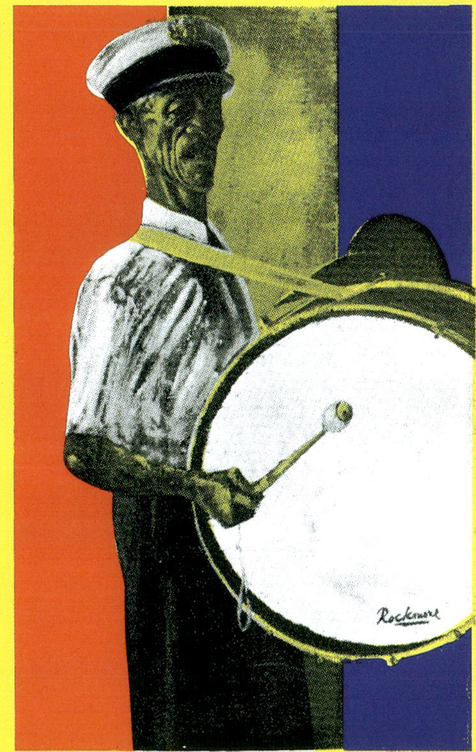

New Orleans Jazz & Heritage Festival, 1970

color silkscreen poster print by Noel Rockmore
The Historic New Orleans Collection 1987.79

In 2003, the New Orleans Jazz and Heritage Festival marked its thirty-fourth year. This poster is from the festival's first year, 1970, when the event was held in historic Congo Square (now Armstrong Park). That year, three hundred musicians entertained an audience of fewer than two hundred. Over the years, the festival has featured performances by the greatest names in jazz, including Louis Armstrong, Duke Ellington, Sonny Rollins, Dizzy Gillespie, and Miles Davis, as well as newer stars such as Wynton Marsalis, Irvin Mayfield, Nicholas Payton, and Diana Krall. Now held at the New Orleans Fairgrounds near Bayou St. John, Jazz Fest spans eleven music-filled days and attracts half-a-million visitors each year.

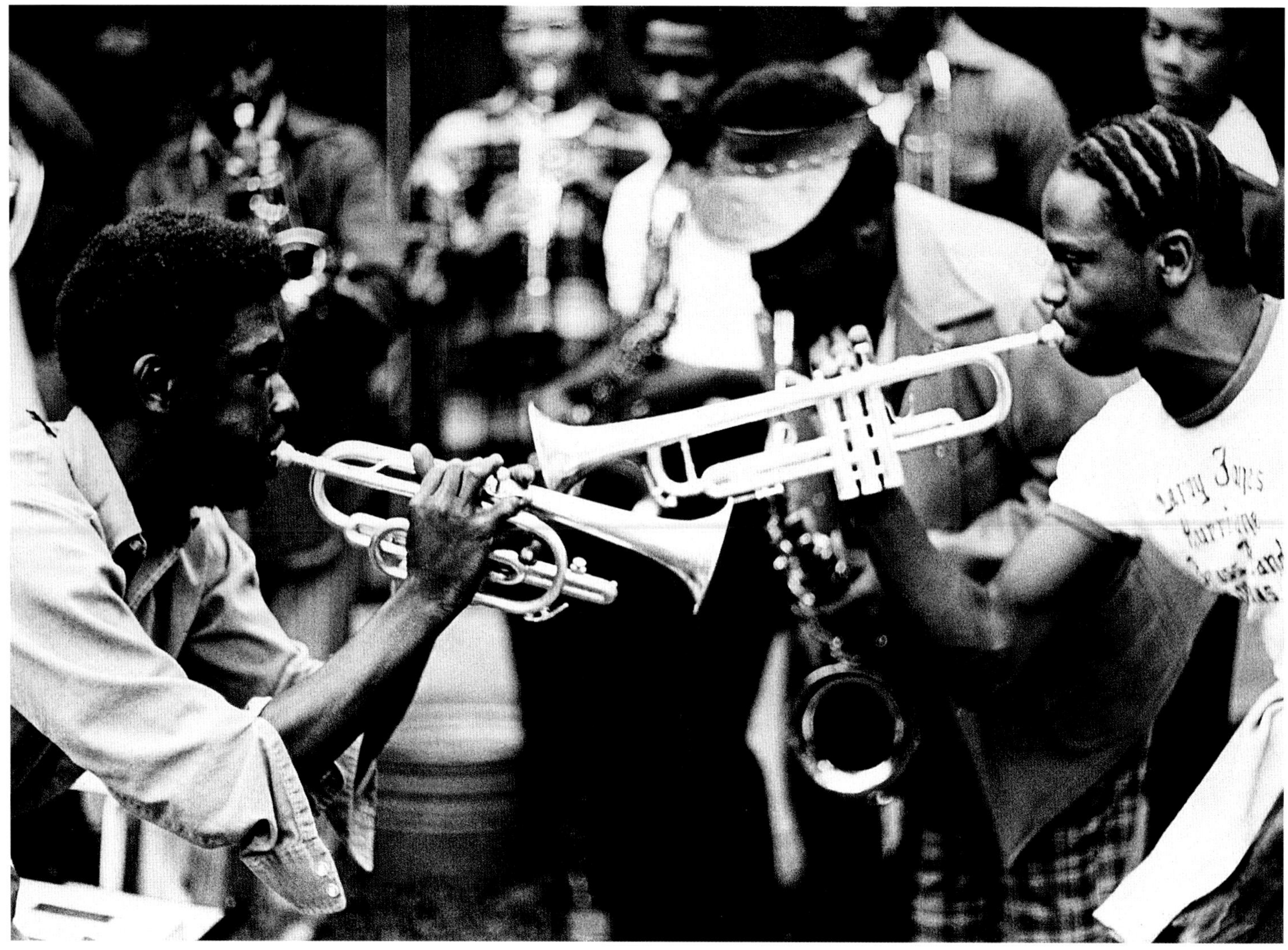

Jules Cahn
Greg Stafford and Leroy Jones of the Hurricane Brass Band, 1975
black-and-white photoprint
The Historic New Orleans Collection 2000.78.8.1
Jules Cahn Collection

This view shows two young trumpet players from the Hurricane Brass Band: Greg Stafford on the left and Leroy Jones on the right. Other unidentified band members can be seen in the background. The Hurricane Brass Band was organized in the 1970s as an outgrowth of the Fairview Baptist Church Band. Most of the teenagers in the band later became professional musicians. In recent years, many young people have joined brass bands, creating a vital new fusion between traditional New Orleans jazz and contemporary urban funk and "hip hop" beats. Groups like the Dirty Dozen, Rebirth, and Little Rascals brass bands have attracted a new generation of listeners to jazz.

Alphonse Picou, and Baby Dodds. On the advice of Armstrong, Russell and two friends—Charles Edward Smith and Frederic Ramsey, Jr.—sought out Bunk Johnson and eventually launched a revival of his career as a musician, after Johnson had lapsed into obscurity as an agricultural laborer in rural Louisiana. Finding, interviewing, and recording early jazz musicians was problematic in many ways, not least because in segregated New Orleans these white men needed police permission to enter the homes and businesses of black people. Russell prevailed through these difficulties and even established his own recording company, American Music Records, to document traditional New Orleans jazz and its surviving practitioners. The recordings of Bunk Johnson and clarinetist George Lewis in particular constitute a priceless record of early New Orleans-style jazz as it would have sounded in the beginning, when Johnson played with the celebrated Eagle Band. Russell's great love for early music extended also to ragtime and gospel, and for a time he managed the career of the great New Orleans gospel singer Mahalia Jackson.

The Crescent City has played a continuing role in the evolution of jazz. In the late 1960s and through the 1970s, jazz music in America was eclipsed by other forms of popular music and went into decline—though it continued to attract listeners abroad, particularly in western Europe and Japan. Then, in the 1980s, a new generation of musicians emerged to simultaneously explore the roots of this American music and take it in new directions. Trumpeter Wynton Marsalis stood at the vanguard of this movement, along with other "young lions" from New Orleans: saxophonists Branford Marsalis and Donald Harrison, Jr., and trumpeters Terrence Blanchard and Nicholas Payton. These young musicians, and others from around the country, continue to pick up the threads of music and history first laid down a century ago by musicians like Buddy Bolden, Kid Ory, and Joe Oliver and scores of others, some famous, some forgotten, yet all alive in the music.

Christopher Porché-West

Second Line Parade under the Claiborne Avenue/I-10 Overpass, New Orleans, 1981

black-and-white photoprint

The Historic New Orleans Collection 1981.115
gift of Stanton M. Frazar

An integral part of the brass-band parade and jazz funeral traditions in New Orleans is the so-called "second line." The term refers to the people following behind the band or spontaneously joining the parade to dance. Second-line parades date back to the nineteenth century and are a testament to the natural inclination of New Orleanians to respond joyfully and actively to music.
There are numerous second-line clubs of long standing, many of which originated in the Tremé neighborhood. Members of these clubs routinely parade with brass bands on major holidays and often wear colorful and color-coordinated outfits, with hats, fans, and umbrellas to shield them from the sun.
These clubs, with names like the Money Wasters Social Aid and Pleasure Club, Avenue Steppers, and New Orleans Buck Jumpers, function in part as benevolent societies that provide residents of black neighborhoods with basic insurance, paid from membership dues to those in need.

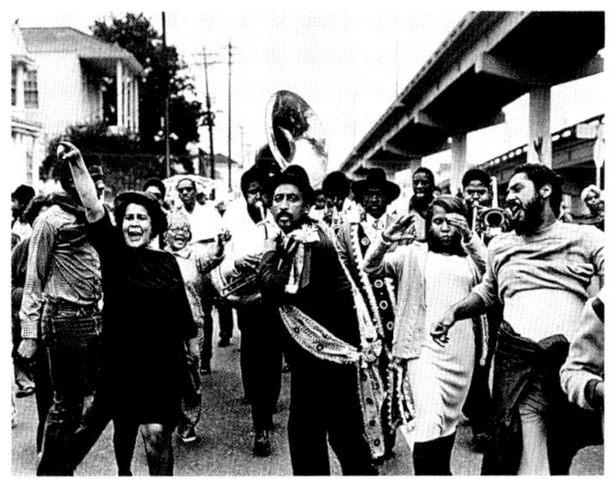

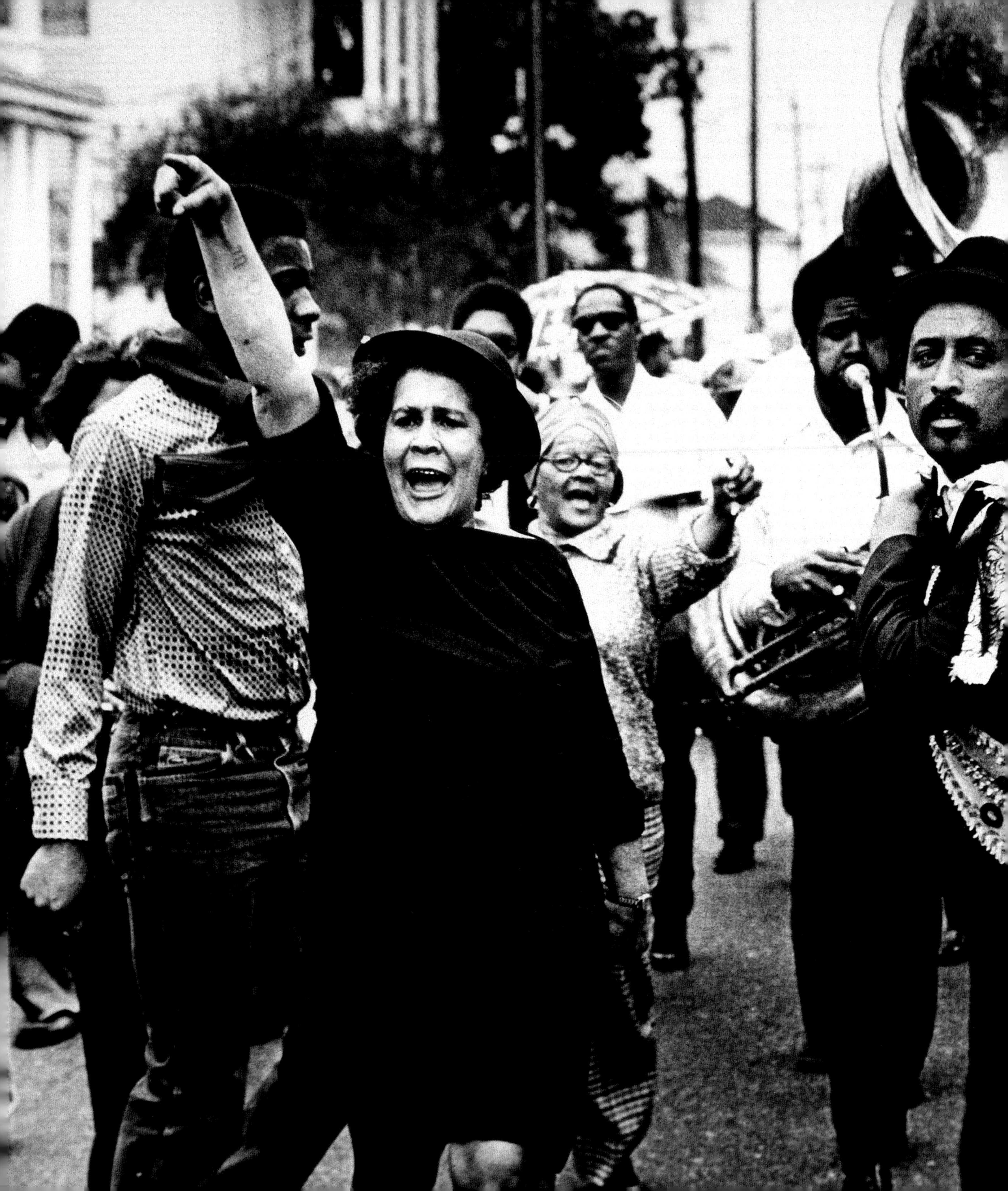

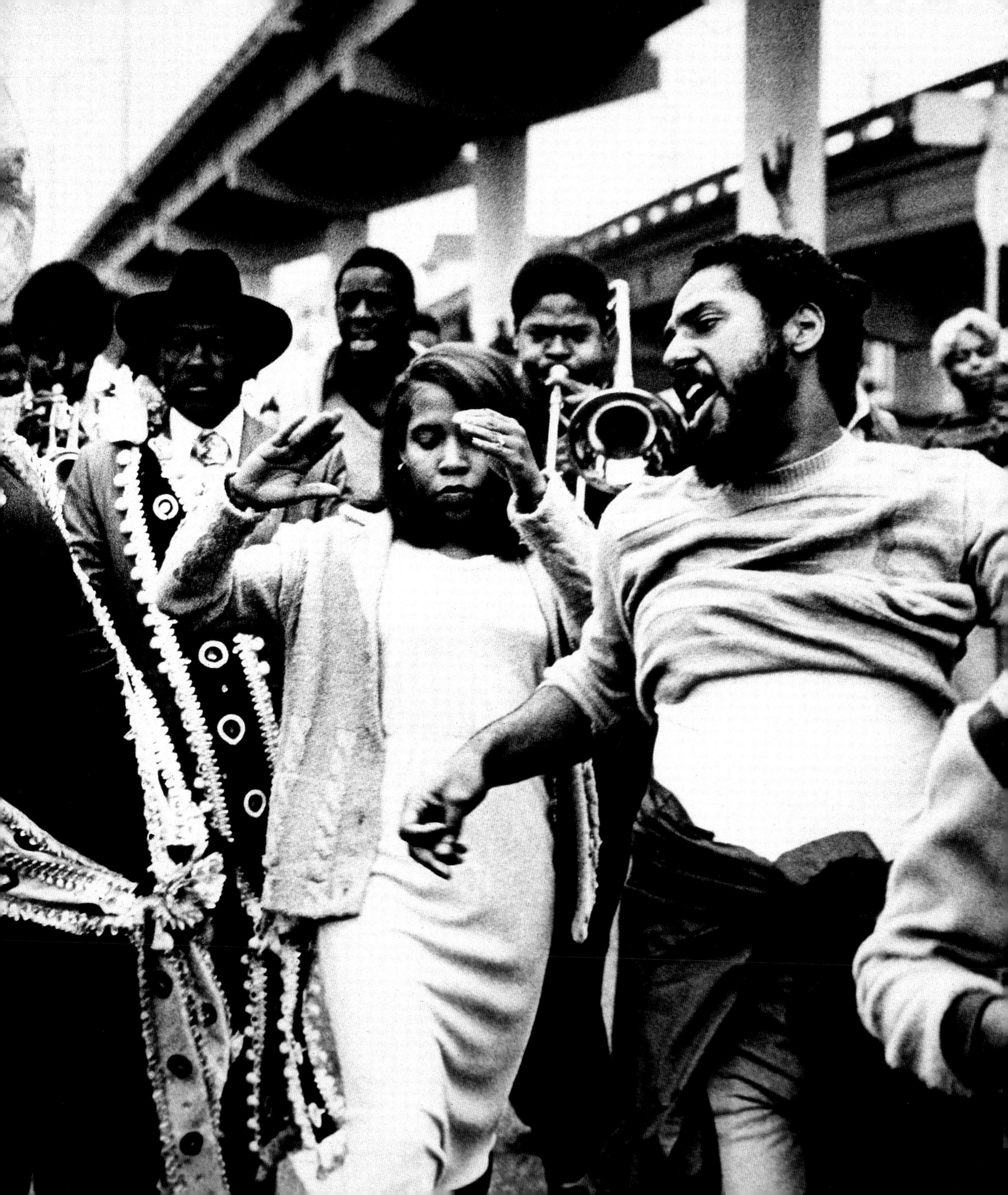

The Authors

Alfred E. Lemmon received a Ph.D. in Latin American studies from Tulane University. An authority on French and Spanish colonial cultural history, his writings have been published in numerous books, encyclopedias, and scholarly journals in the United States, Europe, and Latin America. Dr. Lemmon's expertise also extends into the fields of Louisiana and archival history. He is director of the Williams Research Center at The Historic New Orleans Collection and curator of manuscripts.

Gilles-Antoine Langlois holds two doctorates—one in history from the Sorbonne and one from the Institute of Town Planning at the University of Paris XII, where he is a lecturer. His work focuses on the history of gardens, architecture, and approaches to urbanization, with a special focus on the history of Paris and cities of French origin in Louisiana. Dr. Langlois also acts as a consultant in the field of contemporary town-planning operations. In 2003 he was appointed by the French ministry of culture to oversee the bilingual website www.louisiane.culture.fr.

John Magill is curator/head of research services at The Historic New Orleans Collection. He holds a master's degree in history from the University of New Orleans and has written and lectured extensively on the urban development, neighborhood growth, infrastructure, and architecture of New Orleans. He has contributed to several books including *Marie Adrien Persac: Louisiana Artist*, *Classic New Orleans*, and *Charting Louisiana: Five Hundred Years of Maps*, for which he also served as an editor.

Guillaume Ambroise is the curator of collections at the Musée des Beaux-Arts and the Musée Bernadotte in Pau. A graduate of l'Ecole du Louvre and a former student of l'Ecole du Patrimoine, his particular interest is in European figurative painting from the first half of the twentieth century. He is vice-president of the association of museum curators of the Aquitaine region and is also a member of the commission in charge of museum acquisitions for the Midi-Pyrenées region.

John H. Lawrence is director of museum programs at The Historic New Orleans Collection, where he is responsible for planning and implementing museum exhibitions, lectures, seminars, and related activities. Mr. Lawrence holds degrees in literature and art history from Vassar College and a certificate from the Getty Foundation's Museum Management Institute. He has written and lectured widely about aspects of contemporary and historic photography and the administration and preservation of pictorial collections. His recent publications include chapters in *Marie Adrien Persac: Louisiana Artist* and *Haunter of Ruins: The Photography of Clarence John Laughlin*, for which he also served as co-editor.

Jason Wiese, a jazz enthusiast, holds advanced degrees from Iowa State University and Louisiana State University. He is the special collections/projects librarian at The Historic New Orleans Collection and previously served as a reference librarian at Tulane University's Latin American Library. He was contributing editor of *Charting Louisiana: Five Hundred Years of Maps*. In addition to writing essays for various journals and magazines, Mr. Wiese writes short fiction; his story "The Dive" appeared in an anthology titled *French Quarter Fiction: The Best New Stories from America's Oldest Bohemia*.

Historical Documents Featured in the Paris Exhibition

MINISTÈRE DES AFFAIRES ÉTRANGÈRES
DIRECTION DES ARCHIVES

Acte de cession de la Louisiane par le roi de France au roi d'Espagne (Fontainebleau)
November 3, 1762
Traités, Espagne, 1762 0005-1

Instrument de ratification du traité conclu à Saint-Ildephonse le 1er octobre 1800 pour l'agrandissement des États de Parme et la cession de la Louisiane à la France (San Lorenzo)
October 31, 1800
Traités, Espagne, 1800 0005

Instrument de ratification de l'acte de cession de la Louisiane aux États-Unis et des deux conventions financières par le président Jefferson
October 21, 1803
Traités, États-Unis 1803 0010-11

Procès-verbal de prise de possession de la Louisiane (La Nouvelle-Orléans)
December 20, 1803
Traités, États-Unis 1803 0010-16

CENTRE DES ARCHIVES DIPLOMATIQUES DE NANTES

Lettre d'Alcée Fortier invitant le gouvernement français à la célébration du centenaire de la vente de la Louisiane
December 20, 1902
Consulat de la Nouvelle-Orléans, A417

CENTRE DES ARCHIVES D'OUTRE-MER, AIX-EN-PROVENCE

Procès-verbal de la prise de possession de la Louisiane par Cavelier de La Salle, au nom de Louis XIV
April 9, 1682
C13c3

Projet d'arrêt réunissant les Illinois à la province de la Louisiane
September 27, 1717
C13a5

La Nouvelle-Orléans: vue générale depuis la rive opposée du fleuve, Jean-Pierre Lassus
1726
DFC, Louisiane, 71

Réflexions détaillées sur la révolution arrivée à la Louisiane et du discours que M. Aubry a tenu au Conseil
December 14, 1768
C13a48

MINISTÈRE DE LA DÉFENSE
SERVICE HISTORIQUE DE LA MARINE

Carte manuscrite du cours du Missisipi avec vignettes, anonymous hand-drawn map of the Mississippi prepared from the sketches by Joseph Warin for the published account of General Collot's journey
1797-1805
Recueil 66, pièce 7

Carte d'une partie du cours du Mississippi, Nicholas de Finiels
1797-98
Recueil 69, pièce 64

THE HISTORIC NEW ORLEANS COLLECTION

Code noir ou Recueil d'édits, déclarations et arrêts concernant les esclaves nègres de l'Amérique
Paris, 1743
*K (1743) 80-6540RL

Plan de la ville La Nouvelle-Orléans, Capitale de la Province de la Louisiane, Thierry
1755
1939.8

Estado Veridico de la Luisiana, Santiago Disdier
ca. 1762
81-36-L (MSS 178)

Diario de las occurrencias en la expedición para la provincia de la Luisiana, Ciudad de Nueva Orleans y Río Missisipi
ca. 1770
97-30-L

La Louisiane, Attacapa. Terre de Louis Bonain, François Gonsoulin
1801
EL11.1984 (G58)
gift of The Historic New Orleans Collection to the State of Louisiana

Plano figurative de la posesion dado al Soguero Elias Winters de un terreno de 100 pies defrente con 600 pies de profunidad
Vicente Pintado, after Carlos Trudeau, 1791
November 3, 1819
1979.243
gift of Samuel Wilson, Jr.

Plan del local de las tierras que rodean la Ciudad de Nueva Orleans, Carlos Trudeau
1803
1940.2

Plan de l'habitation de Feu Jn. Bte. De Marigny pour servir au partage des héritiers, Barthélémy Lafon
September 15, 1806
1980.96

M. EDOUARD DE LAMAZE

Model of La Dauphine
2003
Jean-Charles de Pradel, son of Jacques de Pradel, sieur de Lamaze, departed France for Louisiana on *La Dauphine* in April 1715.

Selected Bibliography

Works in English

Aiton, Arthur S., "The Diplomacy of the Louisiana Cession," *American Historical Review* 39 (July 1931): 701-20.

Barker, Danny, *Buddy Bolden and the Last Days of Storyville*, London, Cassell, 1998.

Bechet, Sidney, *Treat It Gentle: An Autobiography*, Cambridge, Mass., Da Capo Press, 2002.

Berry, Jason, "Churches: The Missing Link in Jazz History," *Louisiana Cultural Vistas* 9 (fall 1998).

Berry, Jason, "Good Grief: New Orleans Jazz Funerals," *Louisiana Cultural Vistas* 12 (winter 2001-2002).

Conrad, Glenn R., "The Faces of French Louisiana," in *Cross, Crozier, and Crucible*, edited by Glenn R. Conrad, Lafayette, Center for Louisiana Studies, 1993.

Delehanty, Randolph, *Art in the American South: Works from the Ogden Collection*, Baton Rouge, Louisiana State University Press, 1996.

Dufour, Charles L., *Ten Flags in the Wind: The Story of Louisiana*, New York, Harper & Row, 1967.

Ekberg, Carl J., *French Roots in the Illinois Country: The Mississippi Frontier in Colonial Times*, Urbana, University of Chicago Press, 1998.

Encyclopaedia of New Orleans Artists, 1718-1918, edited by Patricia Brady Schmit, John A. Mahé II, and Rosanne McCaffrey, New Orleans, The Historic New Orleans Collection, 1987.

Federal Writers' Project, *American Guide Series: New Orleans City Guide*, Boston, Houghton Mifflin Co., 1938.

Fossier, Albert A., *New Orleans: The Glamour Period, 1800-1840*, New Orleans, Pelican Publishing Co., 1957.

Genthe, Arnold, *Impressions of Old New Orleans*, New York, George H. Doran Co., [1926].

Gerdts, William H., George E. Jordan, and Judith H. Bonner, *Complementary Visions of Louisiana Art: The Laura Simon Nelson Collection at The Historic New Orleans Collection*, New Orleans, The Historic New Orleans Collection, 1996.

Green, Nancy E., and Jessie J. Poesch, *Arthur Wesley Dow and American Arts and Crafts*, New York, Harry N. Abrams, 2000.

Hardy, D. Clive, *The World's Industrial and Cotton Centennial Exposition*, New Orleans, The Historic New Orleans Collection, 1978.

Hazeldine, Mike, ed., *Bill Russell's American Music*, New Orleans, Jazzology Press, 2002.

Hirsch, Arnold R., and Joseph Logsdon, eds., *Creole New Orleans: Race and Americanization*, Baton Rouge, Louisiana State University Press, 1992.

Kemp, John R., *New Orleans: An Illustrated History*, Sun Valley, Calif., American Historical Press, 1997.

Kernfeld, Barry, *The New Grove Dictionary of Jazz*, London, Macmillan Press, 1991.

Kukla, Jon, et al, *Jazz Scrapbook: Bill Russell and Some Highly Musical Friends*, New Orleans, The Historic New Orleans Collection, 1998.

Laussat, Pierre Clément de, *Memoirs of My Life*, translated and introduction by Agnes-Josephine Pastwa, O.P., edited with a foreword by Robert D. Bush, Baton Rouge, Louisiana State University Press, 1977.

Lawrence, John, and Patricia Brady, eds., *Haunter of Ruins: The Photography of Clarence John Laughlin*, Boston, Bulfinch, 1997.

Lemmon, Alfred E., John Magill, and Jason Wiese, eds., *Charting Louisiana: Five Hundred Years of Maps*, New Orleans, The Historic New Orleans Collection, 2003.

Newton, M. B., Jr., *Louisiana: A Geographical Portrait*, Baton Rouge, Geoforensics, 1991.

Pennington, Estill Curtis, *Down River: Currents of Style in Louisiana Painting, 1800-1950*, Gretna, La., Pelican Publishing Co., 1990.

Piazza, Tom, *The Guide to Classic Jazz*, Iowa City, University of Iowa Press, 1995.

Poesch, Jessie J., *The Art of the Old South: Painting, Sculpture, Architecture & the Products of Craftsmen, 1560-1860*, New York, Knopf, 1983.

Rigai, Amiram, "Louis Moreau Gottschalk, 1829-1869," liner notes in *Louis Moreau Gottschalk: American Piano Music played by Amiram Rigai*, Smithsonian/Folkways CD SF 2\40803, released 1999.

Rose, Al, and Edmond Souchon, *New Orleans Jazz: A Family Album*, Baton Rouge, Louisiana State University Press, 1967.

Russell, William, "Louis Armstrong," in *Jazzmen*, edited by Frederick Ramsey, Jr., and Charles Edward Smith, New York, Harcourt, Brace, 1939.

Schindler, Henri, *Mardi Gras New Orleans*, Paris, Flammarion, 1997.

Stewart, Jack, "Cuban Influences on New Orleans Music," liner notes in *The Cuban Danzón: Before There Was Jazz, 1906 to1929*, Arhoolie Records CD 7032, released 1999.

Taylor, Joe Gray, *Louisiana: A History*, New York, Norton, 1976.

Ward, Geoffrey C., and Ken Burns, *Jazz: A History of America's Music*, New York, Alfred Knopf, 2000.

Weddle, Robert S., *The French Thorn: Rival Explorers in the Spanish Sea, 1682-1762*, College Station, Texas A&M, 1991.

Whitaker, Arthur P., "The Retrocession of Louisiana in Spanish Policy," in *The Spanish Presence in Louisiana, 1763-1803*, edited by Gilbert Din, Lafayette, Center for Louisiana Studies, 1996.

Wilson, Samuel, Jr., *The Vieux Carré New Orleans: Its Plan, Its Growth, Its Architecture*, New Orleans, Bureau of Governmental Research, 1968.

Wilson, Samuel, Jr., Patricia Brady, and Lynn Adams, eds., *Queen of the South: New Orleans, 1853-1862, The Journal of Thomas K. Wharton*, New Orleans, The Historic New Orleans Collection, 1999.

Recent works in French

Augé, Jean-Louis, et Romanens, Marie-Paule (dir.), *La France et la conquête de l'Amérique*, Musée Goya, Castres, et L'Albaron, Thonon-les-Bains, 1992.

Catala, Michel (éd.), *Histoires d'Europe et d'Amérique, le monde atlantique contemporain, Mélanges offerts à Yves-Henri Nouailhat*, Ouest-Éditions, Nantes, 1999.

Collectif, *La Louisiane francophone autour d'une famille : les Pecquet du Bellet de Verton*, Musée national de la Coopération franco-américaine et musée du Nouveau Monde, La Rochelle, Réunion des musées nationaux, Paris, et Musées d'Art et d'Histoire de La Rochelle, 1987.

Collectif, *Présence française en Louisiane au XIXe siècle*, Ministère des Affaires étrangères, Centre des archives diplomatiques de Nantes, Médiathèque de la ville de Nantes éditeur, Nantes, 1992.

Creagh, Ronald, *Nos cousins d'Amérique, histoire des Français aux États-Unis*, Paris, Payot, 1988.

Creagh, Ronald, et Clark, John P. (dir.), *Les Français des États-Unis, d'hier à aujourd'hui*, Éditions Espaces 34, Université Montpellier III, Montpellier, 1994.

Crété, Liliane, *La Vie quotidienne en Louisiane, 1815-1830*, Paris, Hachette, 1978.

Dawson, Nelson Martin, *L'Atelier Delisle : l'Amérique du Nord sur la table à dessin*, Sillery (Québec), Les éditions du Septentrion, 2000.

Giraud, Marcel, *Histoire de la Louisiane française (1698-1723)*, 4 t., Paris, Presses universitaires de France, 1953-1974.

Hamel, Réginald, *La Louisiane créole littéraire, politique et sociale, 1762-1900*, 2 t., Ottawa, Léméac, 1984.

Haudrère, Ph., *La Compagnie française des Indes au XVIIIe siècle*, Paris, 1989.

Heffer, Jean, et Weil, François (dir.), *Chantiers d'histoire américaine*, Paris, Belin, 1994.

Jacquin, Philippe, *Français et Indiens en Amérique du Nord, XVIe- XVIIIe siècles*, Paris, Payot, 1987.

Krebs, Albert (dir.), *Naissance de la Louisiane, tricentenaire des découvertes de Cavelier de La Salle*, Délégation aux célébrations nationales, Paris, Délégation à l'action artistique de la ville de Paris et Fondation Macdonald Stewart, Montréal, 1982.

Langlois, Gilles-Antoine, « L'aventure urbaine de la Louisiane », *in* Laurent Vidal et Émilie d'Orgeix (éd.), *Les Villes françaises du Nouveau Monde : des premiers fondateurs aux ingénieurs du roi (XVIe-XVIIIe siècles)*, Paris, Somogy, 1999.

Langlois, Gilles-Antoine, *Des villes pour la Louisiane française, théorie et pratique de l'urbanistique coloniale au XVIIIe siècle*, L'Harmattan, « Villes et Entreprises », Paris, 2003.

Lefrançois, Thierry (dir.), *La Traite de la fourrure, les Français et la découverte de l'Amérique du Nord*, La Rochelle, Musée du Nouveau Monde, et Thonon-les-Bains, L'Albaron, 1992.

Le Ménestrel, Sarah, *La Voie des Cadiens, tourisme et identité en Louisiane*, Paris, Belin, 1999.

Marienstras, Élise, et Rossignol, Marie-Jeanne (dir.), *Mémoire privée, mémoire collective dans l'Amérique préindustrielle*, Paris, Berg international, 1994.

Orgeix, Émilie d', et Vidal, Laurent, *Les Villes françaises du Nouveau Monde, des premiers fondateurs aux ingénieurs du roi (XVIe-XVIIIe siècles)*, Paris, Somogy éditions d'art, 1999.

Oury, Dom Guy-Marie, *La Croix et le Nouveau Monde, histoire religieuse des Français d'Amérique du Nord*, Chambray-lès-Tours, CLD, et Montréal, CMD, 1987.

Parent, Alain (dir.), *Une autre Amérique*, La Rochelle, Musée du Nouveau Monde, 1982.

Saussol, Alain, et Zitomersky, Joseph (dir.), *Colonies, territoires, sociétés, l'enjeu français*, Paris et Montréal, L'Harmattan, 1996.

Schindler, Henri, *Mardi Gras New Orleans*, Paris, Flammarion, 1997.

Smith-Thibodeaux, John, *Les Francophones de Louisiane*, Paris, Entente, 1977.

Vissière, Isabelle, et Jean-Louis (éd.), *Peaux-Rouges et robes noires, Lettres édifiantes et curieuses des Jésuites français en Amérique au XVIIIe siècle*, Paris, La Différence, 1993.

1493-1971: Important Dates in Louisiana History

1493, 1494 — Papal Bulls of Alexander VI and Treaty of Tordesillas declare that present-day North America is Spanish territory

1539 — Ill-fated exploration of the region by Hernando de Soto

1682 — René Robert Cavelier, sieur de La Salle claims Louisiana for Louis XIV of France, April 9

1697 — Treaty of Rijswijk upholds La Salle's claim

1697-98 — Iberville prepares a prospectus for Louis XIV detailing the advantages of colonizing Louisiana

1700 — Carlos II, last Hapsburg ruler of Spain, dies; Spanish Empire left to duc d'Anjou, grandson of Louis XIV; duc d'Anjou governs Spain as Felipe V

1717 — John Law's Company of the West (later the Company of the Indies) established

1718 — Bienville establishes New Orleans

1719 — First African slaves brought to Louisiana; Code Noir specifying rights and proper treatment of slaves promulgated in 1724

1762 — Treaty of Fontainebleau transfers Louisiana from France to Spain

1763 — Treaty of Paris ends Seven Years' War and upholds French cession of Louisiana to Spain

1763 — Immigration of Acadian exiles begins

1768 — Revolt of French colonists in New Orleans against Spanish rule

1769 — Spanish governor Alejandro O'Reilly arrives and silences all dissidents

1776-82 — American Revolutionary War

1778 — Immigration of the Canary Islanders begins

1788 & 1794 — Fires destroy much of New Orleans

1791 — Slave revolt in Saint-Domingue results in immigration of French planters to New Orleans

1795 — Pinckney's Treaty gives Americans access to Mississippi River and port of New Orleans

1800 — Treaty of San Ildefonso retrocedes Louisiana from Spain to France

1803 — United States agrees to buy Louisiana from France, April 13

1803 — Treaty of Paris signed, April 30

1803 — Louisiana transferred from Spain to France, November 30

1803 — Louisiana transferred to United States, December 20

1812 — Louisiana admitted as a state, April 30

1812 — First steamboat reaches New Orleans

1815 — Battle of New Orleans

1840 — Population of New Orleans reaches 102,000, making it the fourth largest city in the United States

1845 — Louisiana legislature votes to move state capital from New Orleans to Baton Rouge

1861-65 American Civil War

1862 New Orleans falls to Union forces led by Navy commodore David Farragut

1877 Reconstruction ends

1879 Eads's jetties relieve problem at mouth of Mississippi River

1884-85 World's Industrial and Cotton Centennial Exposition held in New Orleans

1885 Jelly Roll Morton born, October 20

1890s Ragtime and blues compositions by Scott Joplin and W. C. Handy become hugely popular

1896 Legality of "Separate but Equal" facilities for blacks and whites upheld by U.S. Supreme Court's decision regarding *Plessy v. Ferguson*

1901 Louis Armstrong born, August 4

1907 Jazz cornetist Buddy Bolden suffers breakdown, is committed to asylum

1917 First jazz recording, "Livery Stable Blues" by the Original Dixieland Jass Band, released by Victor Records; sells 250,000 copies

1917 Storyville, the famous "Red Light" district, shut down by federal authorities

1917-18 American participation in World War I

1920s African Americans migrate to northern cities in search of better opportunities

1920-33 Prohibition era; jazz music thrives in "speakeasies"

1925-28 Louis Armstrong's Hot Five and later Hot Seven bands make their seminal recordings including "Cornet Chop Suey" and "West End Blues"

1929-35 Stock market crashes, world economic depression ensues; rise of big swing bands and Hollywood motion-picture industry

1936 Vieux Carré Commission established to protect New Orleans's French Quarter

1939-45 American involvement in World War II; big bands become too expensive; jazz returns to small combos

1941 Jelly Roll Morton dies, July 10

1944 William Russell establishes American Music Records to document and record early jazz musicians; New Orleans-style jazz enjoys a renaissance

1954 "Separate but Equal" doctrine ends with U.S. Supreme Court decision *Brown v. Board of Education*; American Civil Rights movement galvanized

1960 Desegregation of New Orleans public schools ordered

1961 Preservation Hall established by Allan and Sandra Jaffe

1965 Hurricane Betsy causes extensive flooding and damage in New Orleans

1970 First New Orleans Jazz and Heritage Festival

1971 Louis Armstrong dies, July 6

Photographic credits

All photographs courtesy of:

The Historic New Orleans Collection, New Orleans, Louisiana,
Jan White Brantley, photographer, with the exception of:

pp. 52, 53, Musée des Beaux-Arts de Pau, J.-C. Poumeyrol, photographer
pp. 28, 29, 30, 32, 33, Service historique de la Marine, Fort de Vincennes

THE HISTORIC NEW ORLEANS COLLECTION
EXHIBITION DESIGN AND REGISTRATION STAFF:

Larry Falgoust

Maclyn Hickey

Scott Ratterree

Jude Solomon

Steve Sweet

Terry Weldon

Warren Woods

Color separation by Labogravure (Bordeaux)

Printed by Re.Bus (Italy) in March 2004